C0-APY-259

A

STAR IN THE WEST;

A

STAR IN THE WEST;

OR,

A HUMBLE ATTEMPT TO DISCOVER

THE LONG LOST

TEN TRIBES OF ISRAEL,

PREPARATORY TO THEIR RETURN TO THEIR BELOVED CITY,

JERUSALEM.

BY ELIAS BOUDINOT

Who is wise, and he shall understand these things? Prudent, and he shall know them? For all the ways of the Lord are right, and the just shall walk in them; but the transgressors shall fall therein.—Hosea.

And the Lord answered me and said, write the vision, and make it plain, upon a (writing) table, that he may run who readeth it: for the vision is yet for an appointed time, but at the end it shall speak and not lie; though it tarry, wait for it, because it will surely come. It will not tarry.—Habbak.

BOOKS FOR LIBRARIES PRESS
FREEPORT, NEW YORK

First Published 1816
Reprinted 1970

STANDARD BOOK NUMBER:
8369-5457-2

LIBRARY OF CONGRESS CATALOG CARD NUMBER:
79-121499

PRINTED IN THE UNITED STATES OF AMERICA

CONTENTS.

THE PREFACE.

A VERY bright and portentous Star having arisen in the East, making glad the hearts of God's people and urging the friends of Zion to unusual and almost miraculous exertions in spreading the glad tidings of salvation among the distant nations of the earth; the compiler of the following sheets, animated by this blessed eastern prospect, can no longer withhold the small discovery that has been made of a rising Star in the West, from the knowledge of those who are zealous and anxious to behold the returning Messiah coming "in his own glory and the glory of the Father," attended by all the saints; which star may in the issue, turn out to be *the star of Jacob,* and become a guide to the long suffering and despised descendants of that eminent patriarch, to find the once humble babe of Bethlehem; as the wise men of the east were of old directed in their distant course, to discover in the stable and the manger, the great object of their adoration, joy and hope, even him who "*was born king of the Jews.*"

For more than two centuries, have the aborigines of America engaged the avarice and contempt of those who are commonly called the enlightened nations of the old world. These natives of this wilderness have been always considered by them as savages and barbarians, and therefore have given

B

them little concern, further than to defraud them of their lands, drive them from the fertile countries on the sea shores, engage them in their wars, and indeed destroy them by thousands with ardent spirits and fatal disorders unknown to them before. But these enlightened nations have seldom troubled themselves to enquire into their origin, their real circumstances or their future hopes. Great pains have been taken by traders and others to promote among them every European vice, which has been enforced both by precept and example.

Some exertions indeed, have been made of late years by private societies and individuals, to counteract these unchristian practices, by endeavouring to teach them the things that belong to their everlasting peace; but this was not attempted till they were disgusted and soured with the general character and conduct of white men, by which they concluded, that no one bearing their name or appearance, could be actuated by any other principles, than those of misleading, deceiving and betraying them, for the sake of their lands and peltry.

Wherever honest and upright intentions have prevailed to convince their judgments and engage their confidence, though these have, comparatively, been few and feeble, they have generally succeeded, notwithstanding the opposition they often met with from those, who from the worst motives, have thought themselves greatly benefited by their ignorance, humiliation and misery, and who feared that by their reformation, these opposers might be despoiled of their unjust gain.

Blessed be God, that there is yet hope that the day of their visitation is near—that the day-star from on high, begins to appear, giving joyful hopes that the sun of righteousness will soon arise upon them, with healing under his wings.—There is a possibility, that these unhappy children of misfortune, may yet be proved to be the descendants of Jacob and the long lost tribes of Israel. And if so, that though cast off for their heinous transgressions, they have not been altogether forsaken; and will hereafter appear to have been, in all their dispersions and wanderings, the subjects of God's divine protection and gracious care.

The following pages are an humble attempt to investigate this important subject, which has been the object of the writer's attention for a long time. If he has cast but a mite into the common treasury, he hopes it will not be despised. If it shall lead abler hands and wiser heads to engage as labourers in the master's vineyard, though it should be at the eleventh hour, he will rejoice, so that God alone may at last receive all the glory.—He claims no merit in this labour, but that of integrity, attention and industry, in searching after the truth, and preserving the facts which have come to his knowledge, that others may have all the aid he can afford them in the further pursuit of this interesting investigation.

Yet though he is not entitled to any credit, but as a register of facts, yet he has been much gratified since the completion of this work, to find that he is not alone in his sentiments on this unpopular subject.

The following publication taken out of the Analectic Magazine for February last, is written so much in the style and on the same principles of the following compilation, that the writer of it could not withstand the advantage that might be derived from inserting a copy of the publication in this little tract.*—He was rejoiced to know that such despised sufferers, however degraded, had found compassion in other breasts besides his own. Had these unfortunate out-casts from society, been favoured from the first discovery of their country by Europeans, with inquisitive, learned and disinterested historians, who would have represented them and their cause fully and fairly to posterity, they would have been considered in a very different point of light, from that in which they now appear. That some of their established customs and especially their manner of carrying on war, must appear exceedingly barbarous, and even brutal at the present day, to civilized people, the writer cannot doubt, yet if compared with the conduct of the civilized nations of Europe, Asia and Africa, in ten thousand instances, the balance would be greatly in their favour.† Indeed it is an extraordinary fact, that in all the wars in this country between the English and French—Spaniards and Americans, every one in their turn, have uniformly exerted every nerve to engage the Indians to take part with them, and to fight in their own way, on their side. And those who make the greatest cry against their barbari-

* This is done by express permission of the editor of that work, who very politely consented thereto.

† Plutarch in his Morals, 1 vol. 96, says that the Lacedemonians murdered their children who were deformed or had a bad constitution.

The Romans were allowed by Romulus to destroy all their female children, except the eldest. Human sacrifices were offered up in almost all the eastern countries.

Children were burnt alive by their own parents, and offered to Baal, Moloch, and other pretended deities. Mr. Hume says in his Essay on Political Science; "the most illustrious period of the Roman history considered, in a political view, is that between the beginning of the first and the end of the last punic war; yet at this very time, the horrid practice of poisoning was so common, that during part of a season, a prætor punished capitally, for this crime, above three thousand persons in a part of (enlightened) Italy, and found informations of this nature still multiplying.

ty and inhumanity in carrying on war, are the most forward to furnish them with tomahawks, scalping knives, muskets, powder and ball, to increase their detestable mode of warfare. Nay, they have employed every mean in their power, by rum, feasts, harangues, and every provocative, to rouse their unbridled passions, increase their thirst for blood, and force them on to the destruction of their fellow men. They have forgotten the conclusive adage, "*qui facit per alium facit per se.*"* Must not such people be answerable to the great judge of all the earth for this conduct.

I shall not further detain the reader, but give him the publication in the writer's own words.

TRAITS OF INDIAN CHARACTER.

"In the present times, when popular feeling is gradually becoming hardened by war, and selfish by the frequent jeopardy of life or property, it is certainly an inauspicious moment to speak in behalf of a race of beings, whose very existence has been pronounced detrimental to public security. But it is good at all times to raise the voice of truth, however feeble; to endeavor if possible to mitigate the fury of passion and prejudice, and to turn aside the bloody hand of violence. Little interest, however, can probably be awakened at present, in favor of the misguided tribes of Indians that have been drawn into the present war. The rights of the savage have seldom been deeply appreciated by the white man—in peace he is the dupe of mercenary rapacity; in war he is regarded as a ferocious animal, whose death is a question of mere precaution and convenience. Man is cruelly wasteful of life when

* He who does a thing by another, does it by himself.

his own safety is endangered and he is sheltered by impunity —and little mercy is to be expected from him who feels the sting of the reptile, and is conscious of the power to destroy.

"It has been the lot of the unfortunate aborigines of this country, to be doubly wronged by the white men—first, driven from their native soil by the sword of the invader, and then darkly slandered by the pen of the historian. The former has treated them like beasts of the forest; the latter has written volumes to justify him in his outrages. The former found it easier to exterminate than to civilize; the latter to abuse than to discriminate. The hideous appellations of savage and pagan, were sufficient to sanction the deadly hostilities of both; and the poor wanderers of the forest were persecuted and dishonored, not because they were guilty, but because they were ignorant.

"The same prejudices seem to exist, in common circulation, at the present day. We form our opinions of the Indian character from the miserable hordes that infest our frontiers. These, however, are degenerate beings, enfeebled by the vices of society, without being benefited by its arts of living. The independence of thought and action, that formed the main pillar of their character, has been completely prostrated, and the whole moral fabric lies in ruins. Their spirits are debased by conscious inferiority, and their native courage completely daunted by the superior knowledge and power of their enlightened neighbours. Society has advanced upon them like a many-headed monster, breathing every variety of misery. Before it, went forth pestilence, famine and the sword; and in its train came the slow, but exterminating curse of trade. What the former did not sweep away, the latter has gradually blighted. It has increased their wants, without increasing the means of gratification. It has enervated their strength, multiplied their diseases, blasted the powers of their minds, and superinduced on their original barbarity the low vices of civilization. Poverty, repining and hopeless poverty—a canker of the mind unknown to sylvan life—corrodes their very hearts.—They loiter like vagrants through the settlements, among spacious habitations replete with artificial comforts, which only render them sensible of the comparative wretchedness of their own condition. Luxury spreads its ample board before their eyes, but they are expelled from the banquet. The forest which once furnished them with ample means of subsistence has been levelled to the ground—waving fields of grain have sprung up in its place; but they have no participation in the harvest; plenty revels around them, but they are starving amidst its stores; the whole wilderness blossoms like a garden, but they feel like the reptiles that infest it.

" How different was their case while yet the undisputed lords of the soil. Their wants were few, and the means of gratifying them within their reach. They saw every one around them sharing the same lot, enduring the same hardships, living in the same cabins, feeding on the same aliments, arrayed in the same rude garments. No roof then rose, but what was open to the houseless stranger; no smoke curled among the trees, but he was welcome to sit down by its fire, and join the hunter in his repast. "For," says an old historian of New-England, "their life is so void of care, and they are so loving also, that they make use of those things they enjoy as common goods, and are therein so compassionate that rather than one should starve through want, they would starve all: thus do they pass their time merrily, not regarding our pomp, but are better content with their own, which some men esteem so meanly of." Such were the Indians while in the pride and energy of primitive simplicity: they resemble those wild plants that thrive best in the shades of the forest, but which shrink from the hand of cultivation, and perish beneath the influence of the sun.

"In the general mode of estimating the savage character, we may perceive a vast degree of vulgar prejudice, and passionate exaggeration, without any of the temperate discussion of true philosophy. No allowance is made for the difference of circumstances, and the operations of principles under which they have been educated. Virtue and vice, *though radically the same*, yet differ widely in their influence on human conduct, according to the habits and maxims of the society in which the individual is reared. No being acts more rigidly from rule than the Indian. His whole conduct is regulated according to some general maxims early *implanted in his mind*. The moral laws that govern him, to be sure, are but few, but then he conforms to them all. The white man abounds in laws of religion, morals, and manners; but how many does he violate?

"A common cause of accusation against the Indians is, the faithlessness of their friendships, and their sudden provocations to hostility. But we do not make allowance for their peculiar modes of thinking and feeling, and the principles by which they are governed. Besides, the friendship of the whites towards the poor Indians, was ever cold, distrustful, oppressive, and insulting. In the intercourse with our frontiers they are seldom treated with confidence, and are frequently subject to injury and encroachment. The solitary savage feels silently but acutely; his sensibilities are not diffused over so wide a surface as those of the white man, but they run in steadier and deeper channels. His pride, his affections, his superstitions, are all directed towards fewer objects, but the wounds inflicted on them are proportionably severe, and furnish motives of hostility which we cannot sufficiently appreciate. Where a community is also limited in number, and forms, as in an Indian tribe, one great patriarchal family, the injury of the individual is the injury of the whole; and as their body politic is small, the sentiment of vengeance is almost instantaneously diffused. One council fire is sufficient to decide the measure. Eloquence and superstition combine to inflame their minds. The orator awakens all their martial ardour, and they are wrought up to a kind of religious desperation, by the visions of the prophet and the dreamer.

"An instance of one of these sudden exasperations, arising from a motive peculiar to the Indian character, is extant in an old record of the early settlement of Massachusetts. The planters of Plymouth had defaced the monuments of the dead at Passonagessit, and had plundered the grave of the sachem's mother of some skins with which it had been piously decorated. Every one knows the hallowed reverence which the Indians entertain for the sepulchres of their kindred. Even now, tribes that have passed generations, exiled from the abodes of their ancestors, when by chance they have been travelling, on some mission, to our seat of government, have been known to turn aside from the highway for many miles distance, and guided by wonderful accurate tradition, have sought some tumulus, buried perhaps in woods, where the bones of their tribe were anciently deposited; and there have passed some time in silent lamentation over the ashes of their forefathers. Influenced by this sublime and holy feeling, the sachem, whose mother's tomb had been violated, in the moment of indignation, gathered his men together, and addressed them in the following beautifully simple and pathetic harangue—an harangue which has remained unquoted for nearly two hundred years—a pure specimen of Indian eloquence, and an affecting monument of filial piety in a savage.

"When last the glorious light of all the sky was underneath this globe, and birds grew silent, I began to settle, as my custom is, to take repose. Before mine eyes were fast closed, methought I saw a vision, at which my spirit was much troubled, and, trembling at that doleful sight, a spirit cried aloud—behold my son, whom I have cherished; see the breasts that gave thee suck, the hands that lapped thee warm and fed thee oft! canst thou forget to take revenge of those wild people, who have defaced my monument in a despiteful manner, disdaining our antiquities and honorable customs. See now, the sachem's grave lies like the common people, defaced by an ignoble race. Thy mother doth complain, and implores thy aid against this thievish people, who have newly intruded in our land. If this be suffered I shall not rest quiet in my everlasting habitation.—This said, the spirit vanished, and I, all in a sweat, not able scarce to speak, began to get some strength and recollect my spirits that were fled, and determined to demand your counsel, and solicit your assistance."

"Another cause of violent outcry against the Indians, is their inhumanity to the vanquished. This originally arose partly from political and partly from superstitious motives. Where hostile tribes are scanty in their numbers, the death of several warriors completely paralyzes their power; and many an instance occurs in Indian history, where a hostile tribe, that had long been formidable to its neighbour, has been broken up and driven away, by the capture and massacre of its principal fighting men. This is a strong temptation to the victor to be merciless, not so much to gratify any cruelty of revenge, as to provide for future security. But they had other motives, originating in a superstitious idea, common to barbarous nations, and even prevalent among the Greeks and Romans— that the manes of their deceased friends, slain in battle, were soothed by the blood of the captives. But those that are not thus sacrificed are adopted into their families, and treated with the confidence and affection of relatives and friends; nay, so hospitable and tender is their entertainment, that they will often prefer to remain with their adopted brethren, rather than return to the home and the friends of their youth.

"The inhumanity of the Indians towards their prisoners has been heightened since the intrusion of the whites. We have exasperated what was formerly a compliance with policy and superstition into a gratification of vengeance. They cannot but be sensible that we are the usurpers of their ancient dominion, the cause of their degradation, and the gradual destroyers of their race. They go forth to battle, smarting with injuries and indignities which they have individually suffered from the injustice and the arrogance of white men, and they are driven to madness and despair, by the wide-spreading desolation and the overwhelming ruin of our warfare. We set them an example of violence, by burning their villages and laying waste their slender means of subsistence; and then wonder that savages will not show moderation and magnanimity towards men, who have left them nothing but mere existence and wretchedness.

"It is a common thing to exclaim against new forms of cruelty, while, reconciled by custom, we wink at long established atrocities. What right does the generosity of our conduct give us to rail exclusively at Indian warfare. With all the doctrines of christianity, and the advantages of cultivated morals, to govern and direct us, what horrid crimes disgrace the victories of christian armies. Towns laid in ashes; cities given up to the sword; enormities perpetrated, at which manhood blushes, and history drops the pen. Well may we exclaim at the outrages of the scalping knife; but where, in the records of Indian barbarity, can we point to a violated female?

"We stigmatize the Indians also as cowardly and treacherous, because they use stratagem in warfare, in preference to open force; but in this they are fully authorized by their rude code of honor. They are early taught that stratagem is praiseworthy; the bravest warrior thinks it no disgrace to lurk in silence and take every advantage of his foe. He triumphs in the superior craft and sagacity by which he has been enabled to surprise and massacre an enemy. Indeed, man is naturally more prone to subtlety than open valor, owing to his physical weakness in comparison with other animals. They are endowed with natural weapons of defence; with horns, with tusks, with hoofs and talons; but man has to depend on his superior sagacity. In all his encounters, therefore, with these, his proper enemies, he has to resort to stratagem; and when he perversely turns his hostility against his fellow man, he continues the same subtle mode of warfare.

"The natural principle of war is to do the most harm to our enemy, with the least harm to ourselves; and this of course is to be effected by cunning. That chivalric kind of courage which teaches us to despise the suggestions of prudence, and to rush in the face of certain danger, is the offspring of society, and produced by education. It is honorable, because in fact it is the triumph of lofty sentiment over an instinctive repugnance to pain, and over those selfish yearnings after personal ease and security which society has condemned as ignoble. It is an emotion kept up by pride, and the fear of shame; and thus the dread of real evils is overcome by the superior dread of an evil that exists but in the mind. This may be instanced in the case of a young British officer of great pride, but delicate nerves, who was going for the first time into battle. Being agitated by the novelty and awful peril of the scene, he was accosted by another officer of a rough and boisterous character—"What, sir," cried he, "do you tremble?" "Yes sir," replied the other, "and if you were half as much afraid as I am you would run away." This young officer signalized himself on many occasions by his gallantry, though, had he been brought up in savage life, or even in a humbler and less responsible situation, it is more than probable he could never have ventured into open action.

"Besides we must consider how much the quality of open and desperate courage is cherished and stimulated by society. It has been the theme of many a spirit-stirring song, and chivalric story. The minstrel has sung of it to the loftiest strain of his lyre—the poet has delighted to shed around it all the splendours of fiction—and even the historian has forgotten the sober gravity of narration, and burst forth into enthusiasm and rhapsody in its praise. Triumphs and gorgeous pageants have been its reward—monuments, where art has exhausted its skill, and opulence its treasures, have been erected to perpetuate a nation's gratitude and admiration. Thus artificially excited, courage has arisen to an extraordinary and factitious degree of heroism; and, arrayed in all the glorious "pomp and circumstance" of war, this turbulent quality has even been able to eclipse many of those quiet, but invaluable virtues, which silently ennoble the human character, and swell the tide of human happiness.

"But if courage intrinsically consist in the defiance of danger and pain, the life of the Indian is a continual exhibition of it. He lives in a perpetual state of hostility and risk.—Peril and adventure are congenial to his nature, or, rather, seem necessary to arouse his faculties and give an interest to existence. Surrounded by hostile tribes, he is always equipped for fight, with his weapons in his hands. He traverses vast wildernesses, exposed to the hazards of lonely sickness, of lurking enemies, or pining famine. Stormy lakes present no obstacle to his wanderings; in his light canoe of bark, he sports like a feather on their waves, and darts with the swiftness of an arrow down the roaring rapids of the rivers.—Trackless wastes of snow, rugged mountains, the glooms of swamps and morasses, where poisonous reptiles curl among the rank vegetation, are fearlessly encountered by this wanderer of the wilderness. He gains his food by the hardships and dangers of the chase; he wraps himself in the spoils of the bear, the panther, and the buffalo, and sleeps among the thunders of the cataract.

"No hero of ancient or modern days can surpass the Indian in his lofty contempt of death, and the fortitude with which he sustains all the varied torments with which it is frequently inflicted. Indeed we here behold him rising superior to the white man, merely in consequence of his peculiar education. The latter rushes to glorious death at the cannon's mouth; the former coolly contemplates its approach, and triumphantly endures it, amid the torments of the knife and the protracted agonies of fire. He even takes a savage delight in taunting his persecutors, and provoking their ingenuity of torture; and as the devouring flames prey on his very vitals, and the flesh shrinks from the sinews, he raises his last song of triumph, breathing the defiance of an unconquered heart, and invoking the spirits of his fathers to witness that he dies without a groan.

"Notwithstanding all the obloquy with which the early historians of the colonies have overshadowed the characters of the unfortunate natives, some bright gleams will occasionally break through, that throw a degree of melancholy lustre on their memories. Facts are occasionally to be met with, in their rude annals, which, though recorded with all the colouring of prejudice and bigotry, yet speak for themselves; and will be dwelt on with applause and sympathy, when prejudice shall have passed away.

"In one of the homely narratives of the Indian wars in New-England, there is a touching account of the desolation carried into the tribe of the Pequod Indians. Humanity shudders at the cold-blooded accounts given, of indiscriminate butchery on the part of the settlers. In one place we read of the surprisal of an Indian fort in the night, when the wigwams were wrapped in flames, and the miserable inhabitants shot down and slain, in attempting to escape, "all being despatched and ended in the course of an hour." After a series of similar transactions, "Our soldiers," as the historian piously observes, "being resolved by God's assistance to make a final destruction of them," the unhappy savages being hunted from their homes and fortresses, and pursued with fire and sword, a scanty but gallant band, the sad remnant of the Pequod warriors, with their wives and children, took refuge in a swamp.

"Burning with indignation, and rendered sullen by despair—with hearts bursting with grief at the destruction of their tribe, and spirits galled and sore at the fancied ignominy of their defeat, they refused to ask their lives at the hands of an insulting foe, and preferred death to submission.

"As the night drew on they were surrounded in their dismal retreat, in such manner as to render escape impracticable. Thus situated, their enemy "plied them with shot all the time, by which means many were killed and buried in the mire." In the darkness and fog that precedes the dawn of day, some few broke through the besiegers and escaped into the woods: "the rest were left to the conquerors, of which many were killed in the swamp, like sullen dogs who would rather, in their self-willedness and madness, sit still and be shot through, or cut to pieces," than implore for mercy. When the day broke upon this handful of forlorn, but dauntless spirits, the soldiers, we are told, entering the swamp, "saw several heaps of them sitting close together, upon whom they discharged their pieces, laden with ten or twelve pistol bullets at a time; putting the muzzles of their pieces under the boughs, within a few yards of them; so as, besides those that were found dead, many more were killed and sunk into the mire, and never were minded more by friend or foe."

"Can any one read this plain unvarnished tale, without admiring the stern resolution, the unbending pride, and loftiness of spirit, that seemed to nerve the hearts of these self-taught heroes, and to raise them above the instinctive feelings of human nature? When the Gauls laid waste the city of Rome, they found the nobles clothed in their robes, and seated with stern tranquility in their curule chairs; in this manner they suffered death without an attempt at supplication or resistance. Such conduct in them was applauded as noble and magnanimous; in the hapless Indians it was reviled as obstinate and sullen. How much are we the dupes of show and circumstance! How different is virtue, arrayed in purple and enthroned in state, from virtue, destitute and naked, reduced to the last stage of wretchedness, and perishing obscurely in a wilderness.

"Do these records of ancient excesses fill us with disgust and aversion? Let us take heed that we do not suffer ourselves to be hurried into the same iniquities. Posterity lifts up its hands with horror at past misdeeds, because the passions that urged to them are not felt, and the arguments that persuaded to them are forgotten; but we are reconciled to the present perpetration of injustice by all the selfish motives with which interest chills the heart and silences the conscience. Even at the present advanced day, when we should suppose that enlightened philosophy had expanded our minds, and true religion had warmed our hearts into philanthropy—when we have been admonished by a sense of past transgressions, and instructed by the indignant censures of candid history—even now, we perceive a disposition breaking out to renew the persecutions of these hapless beings. Sober-thoughted men, far from the scenes of danger, in the security of cities and populous regions, can coolly talk of "exterminating measures," and discuss the *policy* of extirpating thousands. If such is the talk in the cities, what is the temper displayed on the borders? The sentence of desolation has gone forth—"the roar is up amidst the woods;" implacable wrath, goaded on by interest and prejudice, is ready to confound all rights, to trample on all claims of justice and humanity, and to act over those scenes of sanguinary vengeance which have too often stained the pages of colonial history.

"These are not the idle suggestions of fancy; they are wrung forth by recent facts, which still haunt the public mind. We need but turn to the ravaged country of the Creeks to behold a picture of exterminating warfare.

"These deluded savages, either excited by private injury or private intrigue, or by both, have lately taken up the hatchet and made deadly inroads into our frontier settlements.—Their punishment has been pitiless and terrible. Vengeance has gone like a devouring fire through their country—the smoke of their villages yet rises to heaven, and the blood of the slaughtered Indians yet reeks upon the earth. Of this merciless ravage, an idea may be formed by a single exploit, boastfully set forth in an official letter that has darkened our public journals.* A detachment of soldiery had been sent un-

* Letter of gen. Coffee, dated Nov. 4, 1813.

der the command of one general Coffee to destroy the Tallushatches towns, where the hostile Creeks had assembled. The enterprise was executed, as the commander in chief* expresses it, *in style*—but, in the name of mercy, in what style! The towns were surrounded before the break of day. The inhabitants, starting from their sleep, flew to arms, with beat of drums and hideous yellings. The soldiery pressed upon them on every side, and met with a desperate resistance—but what was savage valour against the array and discipline of scientific warfare? The Creeks made gallant charges, but were beaten back by overwhelming numbers. Hemmed in like savage beasts surrounded by the hunters, wherever they turned they met a foe, and in every foe they found a butcher. "The enemy retreated firing," says Coffee in his letter, "until they got around and in their buildings, where they made all the resistance that an overpowered soldier could do; they fought as long as one existed, but their destruction was very soon completed; our men rushed up to the doors of the houses, and in a few minutes killed the last warrior of them; the enemy fought with savage fury, and met death with all its horrors, without shrinking or complaining; not one asked to be spared, but fought so long as they could stand or sit. In consequence of their flying to their houses, and mixing with the families, our men in killing the males, without intention, *killed and wounded a few of the squaws and children.*"

"So unsparing was the carnage of the sword, that not one of the warriors escaped to carry the heart-breaking tidings to the remainder of the tribe. Such is what is termed executing hostilities *in style!*—Let those who exclaim with abhor-

* Gen. Andrew Jackson.

rence at Indian inroads—those who are so eloquent about the bitterness of Indian recrimination—let them turn to the horrible victory of general Coffee, and be silent.

"As yet our government has in some measure restrained the tide of vengeance, and inculcated lenity towards the hapless Indians who have been duped into the present war. Such temper is worthy of an enlightened government—let it still be observed—let sharp rebuke and signal punishment be inflicted on those who abuse their delegated power, and disgrace their victories with massacre and conflagration. The enormities of the Indians form no excuse for the enormities of white men. It has pleased heaven to give them but limited powers of mind, and feeble lights to guide their judgments; it becomes us who are blessed with higher intellects to think for them, and to set them an example of humanity. It is the nature of vengeance, if unrestrained, to be headlong in its actions, and to lay up, in a moment of passion, ample cause for an age's repentance. We may roll over these miserable beings with our chariot wheels, and crush them to the earth; but when war has done its worst—when passion has subsided, and it is too late to pity or to save—we shall look back with unavailing compunction at the mangled corses of those whose cries were unheeded in the fury of our career.

"Let the fate of war go as it may, the fate of those ignorant tribes that have been inveigled from their forests to mingle in the strife of white men, will be inevitably the same. In the collision of two powerful nations, these intervening particles of population will be crumbled to dust, and scattered to the winds of heaven. In a little while, and they will go the way that so many tribes have gone before. The few hordes that still linger about the shores of Huron and Superiour, and the tributary streams of the Mississippi, will share the fate of those tribes that once lorded it along the proud banks of the Hudson; of that gigantic race that are said to have existed on the borders of the Susquehanna, and of those various nations that flourished about the Potowmac and the Rappahanoc, and that peopled the forests of the vast valley Shenandoah. They will vanish like a vapour from the face of the earth—their very history will be lost in forgetfulness—and "the places that now know them, will know them no more forever."

"Or if perchance some dubious memorial of them should survive the lapse of time, it may be in the romantic dreams of the poet, to populate in imagination his glades and groves, like the fauns, and satyrs, and sylvan deities of antiquity. But should he venture upon the dark story of their wrongs and wretchedess—should he tell how they were invaded, corrupted, despoiled—driven from their native abodes and the sepulchres of their fathers—hunted like wild beasts about the earth, and sent down in violence and butchery to the grave—posterity will either turn with horror and incredulity from the tale, or blush with indignation at the inhumanity of their forefathers.—"We are driven back," said an old warrior, "until we can retreat no further—our hatchets are broken—our bows are snapped—our fires are nearly extinguished—a little longer and the white men will cease to persecute us—for we will cease to exist!"

INTRODUCTION.

HOWEVER despised the nation of the Hebrews were among the Greeks, Romans and others of their neighbours, during the existence of their civil government, and by all the nations of the earth ever since, there can be no doubt now, that they have been and still are the most remarkable people that have existed since the first century after the flood.

It does appear from their history, and from the holy scriptures, that the great Governor of the Universe, in his infinite wisdom and mercy to our fallen race, did select this nation, from all the nations of the earth, as his peculiar people, not only to hand down to mankind at large, the great doctrine of the unity of his divine nature, with the principles of the worship due to him by intelligent creatures—the universal depravity of man by the fall of Adam, with the blessed means of his restoration to the favour of God, by the shedding of blood, without which there could be no forgiveness of sin. But also that through them the means and manner of the atonement for sin by the promised Messiah, who was to be sent into our world in the fulness of time, for this invaluable purpose, and who was to be a divine person and literally become the desire of all nations, should be propagated and made known to all mankind, preparatory to his coming in the flesh. And that afterwards, this people should be supported and proved in all ages of the world, by means of their miraculous preservation against all the experience of other nations. For while dispersed through the world without a spot of land they could properly call their own, and despised and persecuted in every part of it, yet they have continued a separate people, known by their countenances, while their enemies and conquerors have wasted away and are, as it were, lost from the earth, in fulfilment of the declarations of their prophets, inspired by God, to the astonishment of all nations.

This people was also a living example to the world of the dealings of Divine Providence towards the workmanship of his hands, by rewarding their obedience in a very extraordinary manner, and punishing their wilful transgressions by the most exemplary sufferings.

Though he often declared them *his peculiar—his chosen—his elect people*—nay that he esteemed them as the *apple of his eye*, for the sake of his servants Abraham, Isaac and Jacob, their progenitors, yet he has fully shewn to the world, that however dear a people might be to him as their governor and king, or by adoption, that no external situation or special circumstances would ever lead him to countenance sin, or leave it unpunished, without a suitable atonement and deep repentance.

They also answered, but in a stronger manner, the use of hieroglyphics and figures, as a universal language, to instruct all mankind in the mind and will of God, before letters were in general use, and had this knowledge been properly improved, would have been more effectual, than instruction by word of mouth or personal address.

God has acknowledged them by express revelation—by prophecies, forewarning them of what should befall them in the world, accordingly as they kept his commandments, or were disobedient to them, until their final restoration to the promised land. In short, their long dispersed state, with their severe persecutions, and still continuing a separate people among all nations, are standing, unanswerable and miraculous proofs of their sacred writings, and a complete fulfilment of the many prophecies concerning them, some thousands of years past.

Another essential purpose, in the course of God's providence with his people is also to be produced. The restoration of this suffering and despised nation to their ancient city and their former standing in the favour of God, with a great increase of glory and happiness, are expressly foretold by Christ, his prophets and apostles, as immediately preceding the second coming of our Lord and Saviour Jesus Christ, to this our earth, with his saints and angels, in his own glory as mediator, and the glory of the father, or of his divine nature, plainly distinguished from that humility and abasement attending his first coming in the flesh. Of course, whenever this restoration shall come to pass, it will be so convincing and convicting a testimony of the truth and certainty of the whole plan and predictions of the sacred record, as powerfully to affect all the nations of the earth, and bring them to the acknowledgment of the true God, even our Lord Jesus the Christ.

For, as Bishop Warburton justly asks, "Is the explanation of the œconomy of grace, in which is contained the system of prophecy; that is, the connection and dependance of the prophecies of the several ages of the church of God, of no use? Surely of the greatest, and I am confident nothing but the light which will arise from thence, will support christianity under its present circumstances. But the contending for single prophecies only, by one who thinks they relate to Christ in a secondary sense, only, and who appears to have no high opinion of secondary senses, looks very suspicious."

Had all the great facts of revelation happened several thousand years ago, and the proof of their reality been ever so conclusive at the time, and nothing more done, but barely to hand them down to posterity as then believed in the testimony for their support at a given period from their fulfilment, would have lost all its weight; and the world might justly have been excused for doubting of their credibility. But God, in his great mercy, has now left the children of men without excuse; because he has so ordered it, in his infinite wisdom, that the farther we recede from the facts, the more do the evidences increase upon us. And this existence of the Jews, as a separate people, under all their afflictions and distresses, and that scattered among almost every nation on earth, is not among the least conclusive; but is like the manna, kept in the ark in a state of purity, which was undeniable evidence of the facts related in their history to the succeeding generations, while the temple lasted. So that now, no reasonable man of common abilities, who studies that history, and their present circumstances in the world, with impartiality, care and close attention, attended by a real desire of knowing the truth, can long doubt the divinity of the sacred volume.

To investigate then the present state and circumstances of this extraordinary people—to examine into their general history, in as concise a manner as may answer our general plan—and to enquire after the ten tribes, which formerly constituted the kingdom of Israel, that now appear to be lost from the earth, must be an undertaking (however difficult and unpromising) worthy the time and labour, which may be necessarily expended therein.

The writer of these sheets must acknowledge himself unequal to the task; but having been for years, endeavouring, but in vain, to urge more able hands to turn their attention to this important subject, he has at last determined to attempt it, under all his difficulties and deficiencies, on the principle, that he may possibly, by drawing the outlines, call the aid of some learned and more able pen into this service, being in his opinion of the utmost consequence to the present generation in particular, as that era in which the *latter times*, the *last times* of the scriptures, or the end of the Roman government, seem to be hastening with rapid strides.

This subject receives great additional importance from its prophetic connection, as before mentioned, with the second advent of the glorified Messiah, as son of God, to this our world, in fulfilment of his own gracious promises in his holy word: the signs of the approach of which, he has expressly commanded us to watch, lest when he comes, as he will, in as unexpected a manner as a thief in the night, we may be found sleeping on our post with the foolish virgins, without oil in our lamps.

This subject has occupied the attention of the writer, at times, for more than forty years. He was led to the consideration of it, in the first instance, by a conversation with a very worthy and reverend clergyman of his acquaintance, who, having an independent fortune, undertook a journey (in company with a brother clergyman, who was desirous of attending him) into the wilderness between the Alleghany and Missisippi rivers, some time in or about the years 1765 or 6, before the white people had settled beyond the Laurel Mountain. His desire was to meet with native Indians, who had never seen a white man, that he might satisfy his curiosity by knowing from the best source, what traditions the Indians yet preserved relative to their own history and origin. This, these gentlemen accomplished with great danger, risque and fatigue. On their return one of them related to the writer the information they had obtained, what they saw, and what they heard.

This raised in the writer's mind such an idea of some former connection between these aborigines of our land, and the Jewish nation, as greatly to increase a desire for further information on so interesting and curious a subject.

Soon after, reading (quite accidentally) the 13th chapter of the 2d apochryphal book of Esdras, supposed to have been written about the year 100, of the christian era, his ardour to know more of, and to seek further into the circumstances of these lost tribes, was in no wise diminished. He has not ceased since, to improve every opportunity afforded him, by personal interviews with Indians—reading the best histories relating to them, and carefully examining our public agents resident among them, as to facts reported in the several histories, without letting them know his object, so as not only to gratify his curiosity, by obtaining all the knowledge relating to them in his power, but also to guard against misrepresentation as to any account he might thereafter be tempted to give of them. His design at present is, if by the blessing of Almighty God his life, now far advanced, should be spared a little longer, to give some brief sketches of what he has learned, in this important inquiry, lest the facts he has collected should be entirely lost, as he feels himself culpable for putting off this business to so advanced a period of life, as to leave him but small hopes of accomplishing his intentions.

He does not mean to attempt to solve all the difficulties, or answer all the objections that may very probably attend this investigation. It must be obvious to every attentive reader, who considers the length of time since the first dispersion of the ten tribes of Israel—the wandering and destitute state of the Indian nations—their entire separation from all civilized society—their total want of the knowledge of letters or of writing—the strange inattention of most of the Europeans, who first settled among them, to record facts relating to them, and the falsehood and deception of many of the few who did attempt it—the difficulties attending the obtaining a critical knowledge of their language, customs and traditions, arising from a prudent, though a violent jealousy and fear of the white people, from whom they have received little else but irreparable injuries, wanton destruction and extreme sufferings. It must be allowed that under such untoward circumstances, many unsurmountable difficulties must arise, that cannot be avoided.

In the prosecution of this compilation, the writer will avail himself of the best accounts given by the Spanish writers, he can meet with—the histories written by our own people who first visited this land, or have since made themselves acquainted with the native inhabitants, and recorded any thing relative to their languages, customs, manners and habits, such as Colden, Adair, Brainerd, Edwards, jun. on the language of the Mohegans—also of the information received from the Rev.

Dr. Beatty, Bartram, and others, of their personal observations, while with the Indians.

The writer is aware that sir William Jones, whose character stands so high in the literary world, has endeavoured to shew that he has discovered the tribes of Israel in the *Afghans* of the eastern world, and he produces the account given by Esdras in proof of it—And although the writer would pay the utmost respect to the learning and judgment of that excellent man, and would not dispute the *Afghans* being of Jewish descent; yet sir William himself, in his abridgement of a Persian work, entitled *The secrets of the Afghans,* transmitted to him by Mr. Vansittart, informs us, that this people, in relating their own story, profess to be descended from king Saul. And they say, that *Afghan* lived in the time of David and Solomon, and finally retreated to the mountains, where his descendants became independent, and exterminated the infidels, meaning the heathen. Now, in the first place, Saul was not an Israelite, but the son of *Kish, a Benjamite,* and therefore may well be found in the east; but not of the tribes of Israel.* Secondly.—If we look carefully into the account given by Esdras (and sir William has given authenticity to his account) we find that the ten tribes he speaks of, were carried away by Salmanazar, and it is agreed on all hands, that he sent them unto the countries near the Euxine sea. And Esdras says they determined to go to a place where they might keep their laws and remain undisturbed by the heathen; but if they had gone eastward, they would have been in the midst of them. Thirdly.—They travelled a great way to an uninhabited country, in which mankind never yet dwelt, and

* Vid. I Samuel, 9th chap. 1 & 2.

passed a great water, but the eastern country, even in that early day, was well inhabited. These facts do not agree with the account given of the Afghans, who from their own statement, belong to another tribe and lived in Persia, from whence they can return to Jerusalem without passing by sea or *from the coasts of the earth*.

A

STAR IN THE WEST.

CHAPTER I.

Of the state of the Jews.

ONE would imagine, from reasoning on the importance of this nation to the world at large—from the many clear and precise histories of them from the time of Abraham their great progenitor, and from the many great and glorious promises made to them and their posterity by a God of truth and faithfulness, on condition of strict obedience to his laws as contained in the divine scriptures, that every person of leisure and observation would wish to become intimately acquainted with the minute circumstances attendant upon them from age to age. But such is the nature of man—such his indolence and inattention to things, however important, that relate to distant objects and not present enjoyments, that judging from actual experience, the state of this people, and their hastening restoration to their beloved city, and to more than their former celebrity and happiness, engages but (comparatively) few, even of those whose constant business in propagating the gospel, ought to have led them, with peculiar energy, to have made them their diligent study.

Indeed, the delays the writer himself has made in this business, under a full conviction of the necessity of it, is pretty good evidence of the tendency of the human heart to avoid active usefulness. It is well known to all historians and readers of the old testament, that God brought this nation of the Jews from the land of Egypt in a miraculous manner, with many signs and wonders, through a barren and desolate wilderness, in the space of forty years. That he went before them in a pillar of cloud by day and of fire by night. That he gave them laws, written by the finger of God, and promised them glorious things in case of obedience; but pronounced the most awful threatenings of misery and destruction in case of disobedience and forsaking his laws. That he became their political *king and governor* by express, personal consent, and mutual compact, in a different sense from that in which he stood to the rest of mankind, by which they were put under a complete theocracy. This continued till *Shiloh* came, according to the prophetic declaration, when the government of the universal church of both Jews and Gentiles descended upon him.

It may be said, that the Jews were long governed by judges and kings after their possession of Canaan. But these were not of their appointment, but of the appointment of God under him, as his substitutes or vicegerents.—See 2 Chron. ix. and 8—" Blessed be the Lord thy God, who delighted in thee, to set thee on *his* throne to be king for the Lord thy God."—1 Sam. viii. and 7.—" And the Lord said unto Samuel, hearken unto the voice of the people in all that they say unto thee, for they have not rejected thee; but they have rejected me, that I should not reign over them." Also Chron. xiii. and 8.

"And now ye think to withstand the kingdom of the Lord, in the hands of the sons of David." Yet such was their constitutional obstinacy and hardness of heart, that after experiencing the most unbounded favors from God, by the fullest and most miraculous protection and signal interpositions in their favor, by driving out the Canaanites before them and placing them in the promised land, which is described as flowing with milk and honey, they continually broke their solemn covenant and opposed the express and positive commands of God himself, given and enforced in all the majesty of Jehovah, through the instrumentality of Moses and Aaron. Moses though the meekest man on earth, became wearied out by their perverseness and rebellion. In the words of an excellent writer,* "there is nothing deserves more particular attention than the spirit and behaviour of the Israelites in the wilderness. A very remarkable instance of the wretched effects of servitude upon the human soul. They had been slaves to the Egyptians for about 140 years; their spirits were debased, their judgments weak; their sense of God and religion very low; they were defective in attention, gratitude and generosity; full of distrust and uneasy suspicions; complaining and murmuring under the most astonishing displays of divine power and goodness, as if still under the frowns and scourges of their unjust task-masters; could scarce raise their thoughts to prospects the most pleasing and joyous. They knew not how to value the blessings of liberty—of a taste so mean and illiberal that the flesh and fish, the cucumbers, the melons, the leeks, the onions, garlic, and such good things of

* Taylor's scheme, Watsons Col. 1 Vol. 114.

Egypt, weighed more with them, than the bread from heaven, (Numb. xi. 4—6) And all the divine assurances and demonstrations that they should be raised to the noblest privileges, the highest honours and felicity, as a peculiar treasure to God above all people in the world. In short nothing would do. The ill qualities of slavery were ingrained in their hearts—a grovelling, thoughtless, sturdy, dastardly spirit, fatigued the divine patience, counteracted and defeated all his wise and beneficent measures; they could not be worked up to that sense of God; that esteem of his highest favours; that gratitude and generous dutifulness; that magnanimity of spirit which were necessary to their conquering and enjoying the promised land; and therefore the wisdom of God, determined that they should not attempt the possession of it, till that generation of slaves, namely, all above 20 years of age, were dead and buried. However, this did not lie out of the divine plan. It served a great purpose, namely, to warn that, and all future ages of the church, both Jewish and Christian, that if they despise and abuse the goodness of God, and the noble privileges and prospects they enjoy, they shall forfeit the benefit of them. And the apostle applieth it to this very important use, with great force and propriety, in his epistle to the Hebrews."—ii. chap. 15, to the end—iv. 1—12.

Thus it was that Moses being thoroughly acquainted with their untoward dispositions, and tendency to revolt to the wicked and ridiculous inventions of the nations around them, and being inspired with a spirit of prophecy, he in very sublime language, warned them of their danger, plainly telling them, if they would obey the voice of the Lord their God indeed, and keep his covenant, then they should be a peculiar treasure to him above all people, for that the whole earth was his. And that although God had thus kindly chosen them as his own people, yet their continuing to enjoy his protection and favour, depended on their obedience to the laws he had given them. And after recapitulating the many special and unheard of mercies and extraordinary dealings of the Lord God of their fathers towards them from the beginning, and then giving them many excellent rules for their conduct, he proceeded—"Take heed unto yourselves, lest ye forget the covenant of the Lord your God, which he made with you, and make you a graven image, or the likeness of any thing which the Lord thy God hath forbidden thee. For the Lord thy God is a consuming fire, even a jealous God. When thou shalt beget children and children's children, and shalt have remained long in the land, and shall corrupt yourselves and make a graven image, or the likeness of any thing, and shalt do evil in the sight of the Lord thy God, to provoke him to anger; I call heaven and earth to witness against you this day, that ye shall soon utterly perish from off the land whereunto ye go over Jordan to possess it; ye shall not prolong your days upon it, but shall utterly be destroyed. And the Lord God shall scatter you among the nations; and ye shall be left few in number among the heathen, whither the Lord shall lead you. And ye shall serve other gods, the work of men's hands, wood and stone, which neither see nor hear, nor eat, nor smell. But if *from thence*, thou shalt seek the Lord thy God, thou shalt find him, if thou seek him with all thy heart and with all thy soul. When thou art in tribulation, and all these things are come upon thee, *even in the latter days*, if thou turn to the Lord thy God, and shall be obedient to his voice; for the Lord thy God is a merciful God, he will not forsake thee, neither destroy thee, nor forget the covenant of thy fathers, which he swear unto them." Deut. iv. 23—32. And Moses after giving them a most excellent system of laws (as he had received them from God) in the 26th chap. 30th verse, enumerates a number of extraordinary blessings that God would confer on them, in case of their hearkening diligently to the voice of the Lord their God, to observe and do all his commandments, and then passes the following awful sentence upon them, in case "it should come to pass, that they would not hearken to the voice of the Lord their God," that the extraordinary and dreadful curses, mentioned in the 45th to the 66th verses, which he recapitulates, should come upon them, and then concludes in the 29th chap. 10th verse, "ye stand this day, *all of you* before the Lord your God—*your captains of your tribes, your elders and your officers, with all the men of Israel,* that thou shouldest enter into covenant with the Lord thy God, and into his oath which the Lord thy God maketh with thee this day, that he may establish thee this day for a people unto himself, and that he may be unto thee a God, as he hath said unto thee, and as he hath sworn unto thy fathers, to Abraham, to Isaac and to Jacob. Neither with you only do I make this covenant and this oath; but with him who standeth here with us this day, before the Lord thy God, and also with him who is not here with us this day. Lest there should be with you man or woman, or family or tribe, whose heart turneth away this day, from the Lord your God to go and serve the gods of the nations; lest there should be among you a root that beareth gall and worm-wood, and it come to pass when he heareth the words of this curse and he bless himself in his heart, saying, I shall have peace though I walk in the stubbornness* of my heart, *to add drunkenness to thirst;* the Lord will not spare him; but then the anger of the Lord and his jealousy shall smoke against that man, and all the curses written in this book shall lie upon him, and the Lord shall blot out his name from under heaven. And the Lord shall separate him unto evil, out of all the tribes of Israel according to all the curses of the covenant that are written in the book of the law. And it shall come to pass when all these things are come upon thee, the blessing and the curse, which I have set before thee, and thou shalt call them to mind among all the nations whither the Lord thy God hath driven thee, and shalt return unto the Lord thy God, and shalt obey his voice according to all that I command thee this day, thou and thy children, with all thine heart and with all thy soul; that then the Lord thy God will turn thy captivity and have compassion on thee, and will return and gather thee from *all the nations* whither the Lord thy God *hath scattered thee.* If any of thine *be driven unto the utmost parts of heaven,* from thence will the Lord thy God gather thee, and from *thence* will he fetch thee. And the Lord thy God *will bring thee into the land which thy fathers possessed,* and thou shalt possess it: and he will do to thee good, and multiply thee above thy fathers. And the Lord thy God will circumcise thy heart and the heart of thy seed, to love the Lord thy God with all thine heart and with all thy soul, that thou mayest live. And the *Lord thy God will put all these curses on thine enemies, and on them who hate thee, who persecuted thee.* And thou shalt return and obey the voice of the Lord to do all his commandments, which I com-

* As in the margin of the bible.

mand thee this day. And the Lord thy God will make thee plenteous in every work of thine hand; in the fruit of thy body, and in the fruit of thy cattle, and in the fruit of thy land, for good; for the Lord will again rejoice over thee for good, as he rejoiced over thy fathers. *If thou shalt hearken to the voice of the Lord thy God, to keep his commandments and his statutes which are written in the book of the law; and if thou turn unto the Lord thy God with all thine heart and with all thy soul.*"—But these promises, and particularly that of being received by and placed under the particular and visible protection and government of Almighty God, necessarily required their separation from the nations round about them, who were one and all sunk in the most stupid idolatry. To increase the obligations of this people to God, he had actually condescended (as before observed) to become their king and head, and promised to attend them through the wilderness, during all their travels, as a pillar of cloud by day, and a pillar of fire by night. Their government thus became a complete theocracy, both in their civil and ecclesiastical establishments. So that afterwards, whether they had Moses and Aaron, judges or kings for their immediate rulers, they were but inferior magistrates in their government, appointed by and under him as their supreme head and sovereign.

They were necessarily and expressly to be separated from all the people of the earth, as a nation; by which the nature of their political and religious institutions, thus united, was made known to the world at large, and by the exclusive nature of their principles and practices, however obnoxious and offensive to other nations, who universally held in an intercommunion of gods and divine worship; yet their attention was thereby strongly drawn to consider them as the peculiar characteristic complexion of the Jewish government. Thus Moses understood it when he said to God, "for wherein shall it be known here, that I and thy people have found grace in thy sight? Is it not that thou goest with us? So shall we be separated, I and thy people, from all the people that are on the face of the earth."

After the death of Moses, and Joshua his successor, and the congregation of the Jews having partially enjoyed the land in tolerable peace and quietness, the succeeding generations with their kings and their princes, forgot the covenant of the Lord their God, agreeably to the prediction of Moses, and went after the inventions of the neighbouring nations. Yet God kindly sent his prophets from time to time, to refresh their memories and to warn them of their danger, in case they persisted in their rebellion, and did not repent and return to the Lord their God, with all their heart and with all their soul, but continued in their disobedience. About 700 years before the christian era, near the time of the invasion of Salmanazar, king of Assyria, Isaiah the prophet of God, was sent to them, with this solemn and awful message. "The Lord sent a word unto Jacob and it hath lighted upon Israel, and all the people shall know, even Ephraim and the inhabitants of Samaria, who say in the pride and stoutness of their heart, the bricks are fallen down; but we will build with hewn stones. The sycamore trees are cut down, but we will change them into cedars. Therefore the Lord shall set up the adversaries of Rezin against him, and join his enemies together: the Syrians before and the Philistines behind, and they shall devour Israel with open mouth; for all this his anger is not turned away, but his hand is stretched out still. For the people turneth not unto him who smiteth them, neither do they seek the Lord of Hosts. Therefore the Lord will cut off from Israel, head and tail, branch and rush, in one day. The ancient and honourable, he is the head, and the prophet who teaches lies, is the tail. For the leaders of this people make them to err, and they who are led of them are destroyed. Therefore the Lord shall have no joy in their young men, neither shall have mercy on their fatherless and widows. For every one is an hypocrite and an evil doer, and every mouth speaketh folly. For all this his anger is not turned away, but his hand is stretched out still. For wickedness burneth as the fire; it shall devour the briars and the thorns, and shall kindle in the thickets of the forest: and they shall mount up, like the lifting up of the smoke. Through the wrath of the Lord of Hosts is the land darkened, and the people shall be as the fuel of the fire; no man shall spare his brother. Isaiah ix. 8—19.

"O Assyrian! the rod of mine anger; and the staff in their hand is mine indignation. I will send him (the Assyrian) against an hypocritical nation, and against the people of my wrath will I give him a charge, to take the spoil and to take the prey, and to tread them down like the mire of the street." Isa. x. 5—6.

After grievous sufferings as above described, God in his great mercy, shewed that he would still be gracious to them in all their distress and apparent abandonment, in this consolatory language—"And it shall come to pass in that day (the latter day) that Jehovah shall again, the second time, put forth his hand to recover the remnant of his people who remaineth from Assyria and from Egypt and from Pathros* and

* A country bordering on Egypt.

from Cush† and from Elam‡ and from Shinar§ and from Hamah¶ and *from the western regions*, (as it should have been translated, instead of the islands of the sea*) Isaiah xi. 11—15 Lowth's translation. And he shall lift up a signal to the nations, and shall gather the outcasts of Israel, and the dispersed of Judah shall he collect from the four extremities of the earth. And the jealousy of Ephraim shall cease, and the enmity of Judah shall be no more; Ephraim shall not be jealous of Judah, and Judah shall not be at enmity with Ephraim. But they shall invade the borders of the Philistines, westward; they shall spoil the children of the east together. They shall lay their hand upon Edom and Moab, and the children of Ammon shall obey them. And "Jehovah shall smite with a drought the tongue of the Egyptian sea; and he shall shake his hand over the river with his vehement wind, and he shall strike it into seven streams, and make them pass over it, dry shod, and there shall (also) be a high way, for the *remnant of his people; which shall remain from Assyria*, as it was unto Israel, in the day when he came up from the land of Egypt."

By this representation it plainly appears—

1st. That the people of the Jews, however scattered and lost on the face of the earth, are in the latter day to be recovered by the mighty power of God, and restored to their beloved city Jerusalem in the land of Palestine.

2d. That a clear distinction is made between the tribes of Judah, in which Benjamin is included, and the ten tribes of

† Or Arabia.

‡ Meaning Persia.

§ Where Babylon formerly stood.

¶ In Assyria, to the east of the mountains forming the boundaries of Media.

* Lowth.

Israel, agreeably to their particular states. The first is described as dispersed among the nations in the four quarters of the world—The second as *outcasts from the nations of the earth*.

3d. Thus they shall pass through a long and dreary wilderness from the north country, and finally enter into Assyria, (it may possibly be) by the way of some narrow strait, where they will meet together in a body and proceed to Jerusalem.

4th. That this restoration is said to be accomplished a second time. The first was from Egypt—the second is to be similar to it, in several of its remarkable circumstances.

5th. The places from whence they are to come, are expressly designated. They are to come first from Assyria and Egypt, where it is well known, many of the tribes of Judah and Benjamin were carried captive, and are now to be found in considerable numbers, and from Pathros bordering on *Egypt*—and from Cush and from Elam, different parts of Persia, where the present Jews are undoubtedly of the same tribes, and perhaps mixed with a few of the ten tribes who remained in Jerusalem and were carried away by Nebuchadnezzar. And from Shinar still more east and where some of the same tribes are now found. And from Hamah near the Caspian sea, where some of the ten tribes have remained ever since the time of Salmanazar; and from the *western regions*.*

6th. Thus we have the two tribes of Judah and Benjamin well known to be dispersed throughout the three quarters of the world—But as to the majority of the ten tribes, although every believer in divine revelation has no doubt of their being preserved by the sovereign power of God in some unknown region; yet as the whole globe has been traversed by

* See Lowth.

one adventurer or another, it is a little astonishing that they have not hitherto been discovered. By the representation above, it is clear that we must look for them, and they will undoubtedly, at last be found, in the *western regions*, or some place answering this description as the place of their banishment.

God proceeds in his encouraging prospects, in language of the greatest affection. "But now saith the Lord, who created thee O Jacob, and he who formed thee O Israel. Fear not, for I have redeemed thee; I have called thee by thy name; thou art mine. When thou passest *through the waters*, I will be with thee, and *through the rivers*, they shall not overflow thee; when thou walkest through the fire, thou shalt not be burned, neither shall the flame kindle upon thee. For I am the Lord thy God, the holy one of Israel, thy saviour. I gave Egypt for thy ransom, Ethiopia and Seba for thee. Since thou was precious in my sight, thou hast been honourable, and I have loved thee, therefore will I give men for thee and people for thy life. Fear not, for I am with thee, I will bring thy seed from the *east* and gather thee from the *west;* I will say to the *north* give up, and to the *south* keep not back; bring my *sons from afar* and my daughters *from the ends of the earth.*" Isaiah xliii. 1—6.

Again, "Thus saith the Lord, in an acceptable time I have heard thee, and in a day of salvation helped thee, and I will preserve thee, and give thee for a covenant of the people to establish the earth, to cause them to inherit the desolate heritages. That thou mayest say to the prisoners go forth: to them who are in darkness, show yourselves.* They shall

* Mr. Faber translates this "to them who are in darkness," "Be ye discovered." This is peculiarly applicable to the present state of the Israelites, as we hereinafter suppose them to be.

feed in the ways, and their pastures shall be in all high places. They shall not hunger nor thirst; neither shall the heat or sun smite them; for he who shall have mercy on them shall lead them, even by the springs of water shall he guide them. And I will make all my mountains a way, and my high ways shall be exalted. Behold *these* shall come *from far:* and lo, these from the *north* and from the *west;* and these from the land of *Sinim.*" Isaiah xlix. 8—13. Here again they are described as passing mountains *from far,* or a great distance, and that from the *north* and *west,* or *north-west;* and others are to come from the land of Sinim, or the eastern country. "Moreover, thou son of man, take thee a stick and write upon it, *for Judah and for the children of Israel his companions.* And then another stick, and write upon it, for Joseph, the stick of Ephraim, *and for all the house of Israel, his companions.*" Ezekiel xxxvii. 16.

It appears by this chapter, that there are some few of the Israelites still with Judah; but all are again to become one people at a future day. It also appears that the body of the house of Israel are remote from Judah, and are to be brought from distant countries to Jerusalem, when they are to become one nation again.

Their approach to their own land, is so joyous an event, that Isaiah breaks forth in language of exultation. "Sing O heavens! and be joyful O earth, and break forth into singing O mountains, for the Lord hath comforted his people, and will have mercy upon his afflicted."

"Thus saith the Lord of Hosts, behold! I will save my people from the east country (the tribes of Judah and Benjamin) and from the west country (the ten tribes;) and I will bring them, and they shall dwell in the midst of Jerusalem, and they shall be my people and I will be their God in truth and in righteousness." Zech. viii. 7—8. Ezekiel, also refers to the same event: "As I live saith the Lord, with a mighty hand and an stretched-out arm, and *with fury poured out* will I rule over you. And I will bring you out from the people, and will gather you out of the countries wherein ye are scattered, with a mighty hand, and with a stretched out arm, and with fury poured out. And I will bring you into the wilderness of the people, and there will I plead with you, face to face, like as I pleaded with your fathers in the wilderness of the land of Egypt, so will I plead with you saith the Lord. And I will cause you to pass under the rod; and I will bring you into the bond of the covenant; and I will purge out from among you *the rebels and them who transgress against me.* I will bring them forth out of the country where they sojourn, and *they shall not enter into the land of Israel,* and ye shall know that I am the Lord." Ezekiel xx. 35—43.

Here we see that they are distinguished again, by those *of the east country* and those *of the west country,* and that they are finally to be united under one government again, when they shall be restored to Jerusalem, yet they must suffer greatly by the way, for their sins and continued obstinacy, which would require God's fury to be poured out upon them, for the reluctance with which they will attempt the journey back to Jerusalem. In short their restoration again to the city of God, will in many things be similar to their Exodus from Egypt to Canaan. They will be obstinate and perverse in their opposition to the journey: and on the way will shew much of the same spirit as their fathers did in the wilderness, as they will be attached to the land of their banishment, as their fathers were to that of Egypt. Many of them will have a wilderness to pass through, as Israel of old had. God also will have a controversy with them by the way, and will destroy many of them, so that they shall never see Jerusalem, the beloved city. But those who hold out to the end, in their obedience to the heavenly call and submission to the divine will, shall be accepted, and *these* shall sincerely repent of their past transgressions. Again "I will accept you with your sweet savour, when I bring you out from the people, and gather you out of the countries wherein ye have been scattered, and I will be sanctified in you before the heathen. And ye shall know that I am the Lord, when I shall bring you into the land of Israel, into the country, for the which I lifted up my hand, to give it to your fathers. And there shall ye remember your ways, and all your doings, wherein ye have been defiled, and ye shall loath yourselves in your own sight for all the evils that you have committed." Bishop Warburton's observations on this passage are worthy of notice.—He says, "It is here we see denounced, that the extraordinary providence under which the Israelites had always been preserved, should be withdrawn, or in scripture phrase, that God would not be enquired of by them. That they should remain in the condition of *their fathers in the wilderness*, when the extrordinary providence of God, for their signal disobedience, was, for sometime, suspended. And yet that though they strove to disperse themselves among the people round about, and projected in their minds to be as the heathen and the families of the countries, to serve wood and stone, they should still be under the government of *a theocracy*, which when administered without an extraordinary providence, the blessing naturally attendant upon it, was, and justly, called *the rod and bond of the covenant.*"

Every serious reader, who takes the divine scriptures for his rule of conduct, must believe that these people of God are yet in being in our world, however unknown at present to the nations—and as God once had seven thousand men, who had not bowed the knee to Baal in the days of Elijah, when he thought that he was the only servant of God, left in Israel, so God has preserved a majority of his people of Israel in some unknown part of the world, for the advancement of his own glory. And we plainly see in the quotations above, that they are distinguished again, by those of the east country, and those of the west country, and that though they were finally to be united into one government, when they shall be restored to Jerusalem, yet they must suffer greatly by the way, for their sins and continued obstinate provocations of the divine majesty, who was their king and governor, which would require his fury to be poured out upon them and particularly for the reluctance with which they they should be prevailed on to attempt a return to Jerusalem, when God should set up his standard to the nations for that purpose. In short, their sufferings and perverse conduct on their Exodus from Egypt to the land of Canaan, seems to be a type of their final return to Jerusalem. They will be obstinate and perverse in their setting off and on their way, as they will be greatly attached to the land of their banishment—They, at least a great part of them, will have a wilderness to pass through, as their fathers had. God will have a controversy with them by the way, on account of their unbelief and the customs and habits indulged among them contrary to the divine commandments, as he had with their fathers, and will destroy them in like manner, so that they shall never arrive at their beloved city, as was done to the rebels in the camp of Moses and Joshua. They are to pass through waters and rivers and be baptized therein as their fathers were in the red sea, and will receive the same divine protection.—Those who shall hold out to the end in a line of obedience and submission to the divine will, shall be accepted and safely returned to the land promised to Abraham, Isaac and Jacob, and their seed after them, where they shall sincerely repent and mourn for all their former transgressions.*

We are not left to the predictions and encouraging declarations of one or two prophets of God; but Ezekiel also confirms and continues the divine interference in their favour, for he says, "Thus saith the Lord, behold! I will take the children of Israel from among the heathen, whither they be gone, and will gather them on every side, and bring them into their own land; and I will make them one nation in the land upon the mountains of Israel: and one king shall be king to them all, and they shall no more be two nations, neither shall they be divided into two kingdoms any more at all. Neither shall they defile themselves any more with their idols, nor with their detestable things, nor with any of their transgressions. But I will save them out of all their dwelling places, wherein they they have sinned, and will cleanse them, so they shall be my people, and I will be their God. And David my servant shall be king over them; and they all shall have one shepherd, they shall also walk in my judgments and observe my statutes to do them. And they shall dwell in the

* Some of them are to be carried in ships, by seafaring nations, as a present to the Lord at Jerusalem.

land that I have given unto my servant Jacob, wherein your fathers have dwelt, and they shall dwell therein, even they and their children, and their children's children forever. And my servant David, shall be their prince forever.

" Moreover I will make a covenant of peace with them; it shall be an everlasting covenant with them. And I will place them and multiply them, and will set my sanctuary in the midst of them for evermore. My tabernacle shall also be with them, yea, I will be their God and they shall be my people. And the heathen shall know, that I the Lord, do sanctify Israel, when my sanctuary shall be in the midst of them forever more."

From this representation it appears, that the posterity of Abraham, Isaac and Jacob, are still God's peculiar people— That he brought them with a mighty arm from Egypt, by the way of the wilderness and through the red sea. That he gave them laws and ordinances to which he commanded the most strict obedience. And in case of failure and wilful disobedience, the severest curses were denounced upon them. They were to be divided into two nations—to be scattered among the gentiles, to the north and the south, to the east and the west. They were to be driven by the hand of God, to the utmost parts of the earth—Into Assyria—Egypt—Pathros—Cush—Elam—Shinar—Hama—and into the western regions and the land of Sinim. They were to serve gods, the workmanship of men's hands, of wood and of stone. Israel is heavily charged with stubborn disobedience, and is threatened with being cut off suddenly, as in one day, and with great and accumulated distress and anguish. They are expressly charged with the sin of *drunkenness,* as adding *drunkenness to thirst,* as their prevailing sin.

On the other hand, the promises to them are very great, in case of obedience, or on sincere repentance in case of failure. After great sufferings, in the latter days, that is about the end of the Roman government, if they shall seek the Lord their God, they shall not be entirely forsaken, or totally destroyed.

Moses also, by the command of God, instituted the offices of *high priest* and priests to preside over and govern their religious rights and sacred services. He consecrated Aaron and his sons to these important offices, and vested them with the most extraordinary powers, that were ever conferred on a mere man. Philo, the famous Jewish writer, speaking in a lofty rhetorical way, gives this character of the high priest—"He was something more than human. He more nearly resembled God, than all the rest. That he partook of the divine and human nature. That he was, on the day of expiation, a mediator between God and his people."

The high priest was the greatest person in the state, next to the king or judge, and represented the whole people. His business was to perform the most sacred parts of the divine service, which consisted in offering up the appointed sacrifices, with many washings and carnal ordinances, as particularly established by Moses. He was clothed with the priestly garments, besides those used by the other priests. 1st. The robe of the Ephod, in the hem of which were 72 bells. 2d. The Ephod* itself, which was like a waistcoat without sleeves,

* The Ephod was considered as essential to all the parts of divine worship, and without it, none ever enquired of God.—Clarke.

the hinder part of which reached down to the heels, and the fore part came but a little below the stomach. It was fastened on the shoulders. To each of the shoulder-straps was fastened a precious stone, on which was engraven the names of the twelve tribes of Israel. 3d. He wore on his breast a piece of cloth doubled of a span square, which was termed the breast plate, and in it were set twelve precious stones, which had the names of the twelve patriarchs engraven on them. 4th. He wore a plate of gold on his forehead, which was tied on the lower part of his tiara, with purple and blue ribbands: and on it was engraven, *Holiness to the Lord.* He wore these only when he ministered in the temple.

Moses also gave them special injunctions with regard to circumcision,* and all the furniture of the temple, particularly respecting the ark, which was to be made of shittim wood, or accasia, called an incorruptible wood in the Septuagint. This ark was a kind of chest or box, about four feet five inches long and two feet six inches wide, in which the two tables of the covenant, or law (called the testimony or witness) written by the finger of God himself, with Aaron's rod and the pot of manna were to be laid up. Exodus xxv. 10. On the top of this, was placed the mercy seat, at the ends of which were the two cherubim of gold, between whom the visible appearance of the presence of God, as seated on a throne, was. The ark was the principal of all the holy things belonging to the tabernacle. 2d Samuel, vi. 12. It gave a

* Some of the Jewish doctors observe, "that the number of proselytes in the great day of the Messiah, will be so great that the church, omitting the ceremony of circumcision, will receive them into its bosom by ablution or baptism. 4th vol. Leighton's works, 157.

sanction of holiness to every place where it was brought.* 2d Chronicles viii. 11. Moses also commanded them to keep *a continual fire upon the altar*, of that which first was given from heaven, and to keep the candles burning on the altar. He also appointed three grand, annual religious festivals, in addition to the weekly sabbath, and daily and other sacrifices, which were to be religiously attended *by the males at Jerusalem*, on pain of being cut off from the congregation.† 1st. The Passover or feast of unleavened bread. It continued seven days from the 15th day of March till the 21st. On the eve of the feast, or the 1st day of unleavened bread, being the 14th day of the month, the paschal lamb was killed and eaten. On the seven following days were offered the paschal sacrifices, and they eat unleavened bread. The first and last days were sabbaths, on which they held their holy convocations. On the tenth day of their first month, Abib, every man took a lamb or kid of the first year, without blemish, according to the house of his fathers, unless the household was too small, *then two neighbours joined together*. It was kept four days till the 14th day, when it was killed. They eat the flesh that night roast with fire, with unleavened bread and *bitter herbs*; but not a bone of *it was to be broken*; and nothing of it was suffered to remain until morning; but if any did, it was to be burned with fire. During the seven days of unleavened bread, no leaven was to be found in their houses, and none was to be eaten on pain of death.

* After their return from the captivity of Babylon, they had synagogues throughout the land; and at the east end of each synagogue, they placed an ark or chest in commemoration of the foregoing ark of the covenant in the temple; and in this they lock up the pentateuch written upon vellum with a particular ink. Predeaux Con. 2d. vol. 534.

† But the women did not go up, and seem to have been altogether excluded. Vid. 2d vol. 63—68.

"To meet the letter of this precept in the fullest manner possible, the Jews, on the eve of this festival, institute a most rigorous search through every part of their houses, not only removing all leavened bread, but sweeping every part clean, that no crumb of bread should be left that had leaven in it—leaven was an emblem of sin, because it proceeded from corruption. (Note on the 19th verse of the 12th Exodus, by Dr. Clark.) The next day after, they offered to God, a handful of barley, being the first fruits of the year, which the high priest ground, and putting some oil and frankincense upon it, he presented it to God—Then they offered a lamb for a whole burnt offering—A meat offering was also made, of fine flour mingled with oil—Also a drink offering of wine—*And they were forbidden to eat either bread or parched corn, or green ears, until the offering was brought unto God.*

2d. The *feast of weeks or pentecost or harvest,* being the first fruits of their labours. It was held seven weeks or fifty days after the Passover, or 14th March. The first fruits of the harvest were now offered up to God. They offered up two cakes made of the new wheat. Deuteronomy xvi. 16. This oblation was accompanied with a great number of sacrifices, and several other offerings and libations.

3d. The *feast of ingathering,* at the end of the year, and was the great *day of atonement for sin.* This was held on the 10th day of the 7th month Tizri, answering to our September and October. This was the first month of the civil year, and the 7th of the ecclesiastical.* On the 1st day of this month was held the memorial of blowing of trumpets. On the 15th

* On it was held a holy convocation unto the Lord, to afflict their souls and offer an offering made by fire unto the Lord. Liviticus 23—27.

day of the month was the feast of Tabernacles—it was kept under booths or green tents and arbors made of small limbs of trees, in memory of their dwelling in tents on their journey through the wilderness. All the males were bound to appear at Jerusalem before the Lord, and this was one of their greatest solemnities. The nation was also divided into twelve tribes, governed by a *chief of each tribe*, under Moses and Aaron. They were again arranged in their encampments in four divisions, under four standards, of a *man*, an *eagle*, a *lion* and an *ox*. He also established *six cities of refuge*, for the protection of the man-slayer, who was guilty through accident, or ignorance. He appointed *an avenger of blood*. This was founded on what God says to Noah, Genesis ixth chap. 5—6 ver. "Surely your blood of your lives will I require—at the hand of man—at the hand *of every man's brother* will I require the life of man. Who so sheddeth man's blood, by man shall his blood be shed, *for in the image of God made he man*." And therefore "whosoever killeth his neighbour ignorantly, whom he hated not in time past, he shall flee into one of these cities and live, lest the avenger of blood pursue the slayer *while his heart is hot* and overtake him, and slay him."

Moses chose seventy assistants or counsellors, who were afterwards called the great Sanhedrim, or council of the nation. When met in council, the high priest sat in the middle, and the assistants, or elders, on each hand in a semi circular form. He also appointed, by the command of God, Aaron and his sons, priests to the congregation of Israel; It was the duty of the priests, among other important objects, publicly to bless the people in the name of Jehovah—to attend the daily worship by sacrifice in the tabernacle—to attend the religious festivals—to keep up the sacred fire on the altar, *and to attend the army, when going to war, with the ark of the covenant*, to ask counsel of the Lord,* to sound the trumpet and encourage the troops. Once in a year the high priest, cloathed in his pontifical dress, went into the holy of holies, when he had on the holy linen coat and the linen breeches on his flesh, and was girded with the linen girdle and attired with the linen mitre. Moses also gave them laws as to clean and unclean beasts, birds and fishes; the clean of which, alone, should be eaten or sacrificed. They were particularly and solemnly forbidden to eat of swines flesh, or the blood or fat of the beast. The fat and entrails of the sacrifices were to be burned on the altar, which was to be made of earth, or stones of the brook, on which an instrument was not to come, that is, it was not to be of hewn stone.

In process of time the people grew weary of being governed by their judges, and not only murmured but grew very turbulent and rebellious. They tumultuously demanded a king to rule over them, like the nations round about them. God in his righteous judgment gave them a king, at the same time, by his prophet, foretelling them of their fate under him. However, their change of government made no change in their dispositions. They still continued their transgressions and perverse disobedience, till God wearied, as it were, with their obstinacy, and the gross iniquities of their kings, divided their nation into two distinct kindoms, in the time of Rehoboam, the son of Solomon, to wit, the kingdom of Judah, to which the tribe of Benjamin was united; and the kingdom of

* Vide Numbers x. 33—35-6, and quote it at large. Joshua vi. 8—13. Also 1 Samuel, iv. 5---7. 2 Samuel vi. 6---7.

Israel, consisting of the remaining ten tribes. Even this did not alarm them so as to prevent their rebellious spirit. But they continued for some hundred years in the most stubborn opposition to the laws God had given them by his servant Moses, and idolatry seemed to become a more desirable object with them as the threatenings of God, by his prophets, were pointed with greater severity against it. They went so far as to invite Tiglah Pilnezer, king of Assyria, to aid them against the king of Syria, though so positively forbidden by God; and at Ahaz, king of Israel's particular request, they united with him and took Damascus, and carried the people of it captives to Ker or Keor, the ancient Charboras or Chabar.—2 Kings, xvi. 9. And such was their obstinacy and rebellion, that it is worthy of observation, that Israel had not one single king from the commencement to the end of their kingdom, who feared the Lord or governed agreeably to his commandments. The fate of Israel was fixed. God, in his righteous displeasure, at length cast them off, and gave them into the hands of that very Tiglah Pilnezer who, it is probable, was the same with Arbaxes,* the first king of Assyria after the revolt of the Medes, about seven hundred and forty years before the christian era, who, with *Ahaz*, king of Judah, as we have already mentioned, took Damascus and annexed it to the Assyrian empire; thus removing the barrier between that empire and Palestine, so that both kingdoms, Syria and Palestine, became an easy prey to this powerful monarch. He captured the Reubenites, the Gadites, and the half tribe of Manasseh, who dwelt on the east side of Jordan, and carried them captives, and placed them in *Halah* and *Harbor*, and *Harah*,

* Vide 1st. vol. Predeaux, page 2-13.

and to the river Gozan.*—1 Chronicles, v. 26. It is scarcely possible that the king of Assyria would have placed so turbulent a people, whom he had led away captive from so distant a land, and whom he had reason so greatly to dislike, in any fertile part of his kingdom; it is most likely that be sent the greatest part of them on his northern frontier, as far as possible from a probability of doing him any harm by their restless dispositions. This is confirmed by the express words of the sacred historian, as will appear hereafter. About twenty years after this, or one hundred and thirty-four years before the Babylonish captivity, the remaining tribes, persisting in their impenitence, and neglecting to take warning by the miserable fate of their brethren, and not discovering the least sign of reformation, God raised up Shalmanazar, the successor of Tiglah Pilnezer, who besieged Hoshea, the king of Israel, in Samaria, and after taking the city, and victoriously conquering

* Harah, or as it is called by some, Hara, which in Hebrew signifies bitter, is the root from whence it is used to signify a mountainous tract, and thus gave that name to the country north of Assyria, near to Media, and perhaps ran through it. On the north of this tract runs the river Araxis, now called Aras.—Obarius, 296. Obarius, on whom much dependence may be placed, describes the source of the river Araxis to be in the mountains of Ararat, of Armenia, on the south of which river lies the little province of Arsea, erroneously supposed by him to be the Arsareth of Esdras; so that Harah is no other than the province of Iran, situate between the rivers Charboras or Araxis, as it is called in the Anabasis of Xenophon and Cyrus, now called Aras and Kur. Kur or Ker was the place Tiglah Pilnezer sent the captives of Damascus, and was to the south east of Media.---Prideaux, vol. 1, p. 13. This is mentioned also in Amos, i. 5, and seems to be a distant place even from Syria, and where captives were usually sent---Gozan, and the river of Gozan. Ptolemy places the region of the Gauzanites in the north east of Mesopotamia, with the city Gizana near the river Charboras, at the foot of the mountain Masius, and another region called Gauzania, in Media, in the latitude 40, 15, near the river Cyrus or Ker, mentioned above. The learned Bochart asserts the city Gauzania to lie in the midway between the mountain Chaboras and the Caspian sea, and between the two streams of the river of Cyrus, and says that probably it gave the name of Gozan both to the river and country; and this he takes to be the scripture place, as being the city of the Medes.

the remaining tribes, took all the chief men, with the bulk of the nation, now lost to every principle of gratitude to God, and carried them also captives into Assyria, and placed most of them with their brethren, who had been formerly taken by Tiglah Pilnezer, in *Halah*, and in Harbor, by the river Gozan, in the cities of the Medes; leaving only some poor remains of the people, who continued in the land in a miserable condition, till Ezzarhaddon afterwards removed them to Babylon and other eastern countries which he had conquered.—And to prevent danger from their numbers, part of them were removed into an adjoining district. This was about seven hundred and twenty-one years before the christian era, and nine hundred and forty-seven after their coming out of Egypt. The king of Assyria also replaced in the cities of Samaria inhabitants from Babylon, and from Cutha, a river of Persia,* and Avà, Hamah and Sepharvin.—2 Kings, xvii. 24.

Thus it appears, that the ten tribes, except a few who took refuge in Jerusalem, with the tribe of Judah,† were wholly deprived of their goodly land, and transferred into the northern parts of Assyria, between the Euxine and Caspian seas, among the cities of the Medes, except a part of them, who were settled something more to the south, in Persia, which was then a part of the Assyrian monarchy.

The two tribes and an half on the east side of Jordan, in the days of Jeroboam, king of Israel, amounted to eight hundred thousand mighty men of valour—2 Chronicles, xiii. 3—so that the whole people at the time of their captivity, including those tribes, being about two hundred and thirty-six years after Jeroboam, must have amounted to a very large number indeed.

* Josephus, vol. 2, page 115. † 2 Chronicles, xi. 16.

Here, then, in all likelihood, they must have remained a long time. Besides the scriptures mentioning their being in the cities of the Medes "to this day," as in 2 Kings, xxiii. 41, and in 1 Chronicles, v. 26. Josephus mentions them in his book De Bell. lib. 2, ch. 28, of the Greek—in the Latin 808—and in his preface 705—in his Antiquities, lib. 20, ch. 9—and lib. 11, ch. 5, page 368. And Sulpitius Severus, as quoted by Flemming from lib. 2, ch. 16, page 321, and who wrote about the year 400, says, "the ten tribes dispersed among the Parthians, Medes, Indians and Ethiopians, never returned to their ancient inheritance, but are subject to the sceptres of barbarous princes. The scriptures, however, declare in the most express terms that they shall return and be wholly restored, with the other tribes, to Jerusalem. If, then, the return of these tribes, wherever they may be, should be by the way of the Euxine sea, which is north from Judea, they need not pass over the Euphrates, which lies across and in the middle between these countries. To accomplish this, if they come from the north east, they may pass over the Straits of Kamschatka, either by a literal fulfilment of the promise, as in the case of the Red sea and Jordan, to bring more declarative glory to God, or they may pass from island to island in bark boats, or in ships, or perhaps, as the most likely way, they may cross on the ice. They will be a long time in travelling, perhaps, to prepare them for their, so great a change in life, as in the forty years in the wilderness, during which all the rebellious among them may perish, as they did under like circumstances on their way to Canaan.

The geographical situation of this part of Assyria is worth attending to. Media lay on the northern side of the Caspian sea, bounded by the mountains of Araxis, or *Chaboras*, or Aras, as it is now called, which separate Media on the north from Armenia, and then bounded by the southern shore of the Caspian sea, which is far north, having on the west the river Halys, running into the Black sea, *which territory has been since possessed by the Tartars.* Persia and Susiana are contiguous on the south.* The country is mountainous on the side of Assyria, and a ridge of mountains that runs to the south of the Caspian sea, bounds a vast plain, a great part of which being covered with salt, is uncultivated and desart. Persian Irak extends at present over a great part of ancient Media. There was a time when the Medes shook off the Assyrian yoke, and ruled over that part of Asia which extended towards the west, as far as the river Halys. That part of Media contiguous to Armenia, was distinguished by the name of Atropatena, the capital of which is named Gaza, or Gazaca, since called Ganzak. Persia extends from the frontier of Media on the north, to the Persian Gulph on the south, and westward to the river Halys. The mountains separating Per-

* Ptolemy mentions a mountain, a city and a river, by the name of Charboras, which divides Assyria from Media towards the north west The river arises out of the mountain Massius, in the north of Mesopotamia, and appears to be the same as Ezekiel, i. 1---3, calls Chebar. Habor, or as it is called in Hebrew, Chabor, must have been the city of this name. Ammianus calls the river by the name of Aboras. Benjamin of Tudela, the Jewish traveller, who lived in the latter end of the twelfth century, says, that passing east, he came to the river Chebar, where he found sixty synagogues. He asserts that the prophet Ezekiel was buried here, and his tomb is there to be seen. Rabbi Pelakich gives an account of some Jews he found in Tartary, who did not observe the traditions of the fathers. Upon enquiring why they neglected them, they answered that they had never heard of them. He complains that the Jews were greatly diminished on the banks of the Euphrates, and in the ancient cities, where they were formerly computed to have amounted to nine hundred thousand.---Modern Universal History. Basnage 620. In Thebes he found two thousand Jews engaged in the silk and dying business.---Chilibriand Introd. 15. Perhaps the number of synagogues is exaggerated.

sia from Media, were called Halzardera, or the thousand mountains. The above is supposed to have given name to the river Gozan, which ran still farther north; but the sound has been changed by length of time, which has been the fate of most places in that country.

Soon after the removal of the ten tribes to this country, and about seven hundred years before Christ, the Medes overran the Assyrian empire, which, from remote antiquity, had extended over a great part of Asia. The Scythians, who lay still farther north, about one hundred years afterwards, conquered the Median empire in Upper Asia, who retained the government but about twenty-eight years.—Herodotus, lib. 1, 157.—1 Predeaux, 25, 35-6. Even this was long enough to promote an acquaintance between the northern parts of Media and the still more northern country of Scythia. The ancient Scythia was the general name given to Tartary, which then extended from the mouth of the Obey, in Russia, to the Dnieper; from thence across the Euxine, or Black sea; thence along the foot of mount Caucasus, by the rivers Ker or Kur, and Aras, to the Caspian sea; thence to the White Mountains, including part of Russia, with the districts that lie between the Frozen sea and the Japan sea.—Sir William Jones, Dissert. vol. 1, 142, and onward. It extended farther north than was known to the then neighbouring nations, living to the southward and eastward. From the mouth of the Danube to the sea of Japan, the whole longitude of Scythia, is about one hundred and ten degrees, which, in that parallel, are equal to (rather more) five thousand miles. The latitude reaches from the fortieth degree, which touches the wall of China, above one thousand miles northward to the frozen regions of Siberia.—Robinson's View of the progress of society in Europe, page 335. Mr. Bryant conjectures that the name Scythia, was derived from *Cuthai*, and if so, it casts more light on the prophetic declarations hereinafter mentioned. Sir William Jones, speaking of the language of the Tartars, says, "that their language, like *those of America*, was in perpetual fluctuation, and that more than fifty dialects, as Mr. Hyde was credibly informed, were spoken between Moscow and China, by the many hundred tribes and their several branches." Yet he doubts not but that they all sprang from one common source; excepting always the jargon of such wandering mountaineers as, having long been divided from the main body of the nation, must, in a course of ages, have framed separate idioms for themselves. But need we go farther than the Assyrians and Persians themselves, who conquered the ten tribes? They had an original language of their own; but their successors, if we may believe the best historians, having become a mixture of several different nations, as Saracens, Tartars, Parthians, Medes, ancient Persians, become Mahometans, Jews, and women from Georgia and other countries, transplanted into Persia, have now a debased language, compounded of those of all these different nations.—Hyde. The country into which the ten tribes were thus transplanted, was very thinly inhabited, and extended farther north than we are yet much acquainted with. Those captive Israelites must have greatly encreased in numbers, before their migration more northward and westward. This is confirmed by the names of the towns in that country, which to this day bear witness to their founders. Samarcand, plainly derived from Samaria, is a very large and populous place. They have a city on a very high hill, called *Mount Tabor.* A city built on the river Ardou, is named *Jericho,* which river runs near the Caspian sea, upon the north and north east. There are two cities, called Chorazin the great and the less. The Tartar chiefs are called *Morsoyes,* very like Moyses, as Moses is called by the ancients.

The Tartars boast their descent from the Israelites, and the famous Tamerlane took a pride in declaring that he descended from the tribe of *Dan.*—Vide note in page 62.

The tribes of Judah and Benjamin are dispersed not in the north east country, from whence the passage towards Syria and Palestine lies along the eastern borders of the Euxine sea, but in the western and southern parts of Asia and Africa, from whence the passage to Syria and Palestine lies far wide and distant from it. But all who are in, or come through the north west parts of Persia, near the western shore of the Caspian sea,* and to the eastward in Mesopotamia, must pass the Euphrates to get to Palestine.

After this we have no account of these tribes, except what is mentioned in 2 Kings, xvii. 23—41, and 1 Chronicles, v. 26, wherein it is said, these tribes were carried out of their own land into Assyria, to this day, &c.—until the time of Josephus, the Jewish historian, who mentions them "as then being somewhere beyond the Euphrates," and calls them Adiabenians.† The other two tribes of Judah and Benjamin,

* The Caspian straits are placed by Ptolemy between Media and Parthia. Vide page 67.

† The river Lyens, which runs a little west of Hala, was anciently called Zaba, or Diava, by Ammianus, which signifies a wolf; whence this portion of Assyria was called Adiabane, and the river Lyens was called sometime Ahavah or Adiabane. It may cast some light on this subject to know that Josephus, in his An-

together with a few of the ten tribes interspersed among them, being in Asia and Europe, living in subjection to the Romans." One of the late Jewish writers says, "the Jews relate that the ten tribes were carried away, not only into Media and Persia, *but into the northern countries beyond the Bosphorus.*"—The next author who mentions them is *Ortelius*, who speaks of them as being in Tartary.—Vide note of Benjamin of Tudela, in page 62.

The famous Giles Fletcher, L L. D. in his treatise on this subject, printed in 1677, observes, "as for two of those colonies of the Samaritan Israelites, carried off by Salmanazer, which were placed in Harak and Harbor, they bordered both on the Medians, (where the others were ordered on the north and north east of the Caspian sea, a barren country.) So that those tribes might easily meet and join together when opportunity served their turn, which happened unto them not long after, when all the provinces of Media, Chaldaran, and Mesopotamia, with their governors, *Merodach, Baladin* and *Dejoces*, called in the scriptures Arphaxad, by desertion, fell away from the Assyrians, in the tenth year of Esar-haddon. And that these tribes did, not long after, reunite themselves and join in one nation, as they were before, being induced partly by their own desires, as disdaining even to live commixed with other people, especially such abandoned idolaters, and partly by the violence of the *Medians*, who expelled them thence."

tiquities, Book 20. ch. 5, says, that Helena, queen of Adiabene, who had embraced the Jewish religion, sent some of her servants to Alexandria, to buy a great quantity of corn; and others of them to Cyprus, to buy a cargo of dried figs, which she distributed to the Jews that were in want. This was in the time of the famine, mentioned by Agabus, Acts xi. 28, and took place in Anno Domini 47, or thereabouts. This shews that there were many Jews in that country.

That the ten tribes were transported into some of the northern provinces of the then Assyrian empire, bordering on the Caspian and Euxine seas, and to the northward and north east of them, is universally admitted, and fully pròved by the sacred records. And that they continued there a very considerable time, and became very numerous, can scarcely be doubted; but that they cannot now be found there, in any great numbers, is also very certain. That there should be found some remnant still in that country, adds to the probability of the account already given. In the sudden removal or migration of a nation from one country to another, it is not probable that every individual would be included. Many attached to the soil by long habit, or taste, or birth, or connected with the natives by domestic circumstances, or from various other causes, would naturally remain behind, and their posterity as naturally encreasing by time, would thus prove the fact of their first existence there as a nation. Thus it was in Samaria and Jerusalem, when Salmanazer carried them away captive; some few were left behind, who continued with Judah and Benjamin, and were finally carried away by Ezzarhaddon or Nebuchadnezzar.* It therefore becomes an important question, what became of them? For no believer in revelation, as already observed, can admit that they are lost to the world, while God has made so many promises that he will bring them in the latter days from the ends of the earth, and that they, together with the other two tribes, shall be reinstated in their beloved city. Now, as we know them to have been exposed in the place of their captivity, at differ-

* Josephus, in his enumeration of the Israelites carried away with Judah and Benjamin, to Babylon, says they amounted to six hundred and fifty-two.--Vol. 2, 171.

ent periods, to oppression and the severest calamities; particularly to the continual blasphemous worship of idolaters, it certainly seems reasonable to conclude, independently of any positive testimony which may be alledged on the subject, that so discontented and restless a people, suffering under so severe a captivity, would strive to change their condition, and endeavour to remove as far as possible from their oppressors. This resolution was greatly promoted by the facility with which such a measure might be effected, on so distant a frontier, while the kingdom was involved in desolating wars with the nations around them, and when the people with whom they sojourned, must have rejoiced at their leaving them, being such troublesome inmates. They must have known the success, first of the Scythians, then the Medes, and then the Persians, under Cyrus, which was followed by the easy conquest of the whole of Media and Persia, as Herodotus has shewn in his history, and by which they must bave been encouraged in so important a business. The power of the kingdom was also comparatively weak, at so great a distance from the capital, and distracted with political cabals and insurrections against Astigages, who reigned over both Media and Persia, and who was conquered by his grandson, Cyrus. And it is not improbable but that a removal more north, by which such restless subjects would leave their improvements and real property to the other inhabitants, and extend the territory of their governors, would not have been disagreeable either to the princes or people of that country. Again, "the usual route from the Euxine sea to the northward of the Caspian sea, through Tartary and Scythia, to Serica and the northern parts of China, by which the merchants carried on a great trade, might enable the tribes to travel northward and eastward, towards Kamschatka." At least this is the assertion of that able geographer D'Anville, in his ancient geography, written before the late discoveries of Cook and others.—Vol. 2, 521-3.

But the most minute and last account we have of them, is in the thirteenth chapter of the second apochryphal book of Esdras, 39—50. Esdras had a dream or vision—An angel appeared and interpreted it to him, in the following detail: "And whereas thou sawest that he, Jesus the Christ, gathered another peaceable multitude unto him; those are the ten tribes, who were carried away prisoners out of their own land in the time of Hosea, the king, whom *Salmanazar*, the king of Assyria, led away captive. And he carried them *over the waters*, and so they came into another land. But they took this counsel among themselves, that they would leave the multitude of the heathen, and go forth *into a further country, where never mankind dwelt*, that they might there keep their statutes, which they never kept in their own land. And they entered into *Euphrates by the narrow passages of the river*; for the Most High then shewed signs for them, and held still the flood, till they were passed over; for through that country there was a great way to go, namely, of a year and an half. And the same region is called Arsareth." Here was a great river to go through, called Euphrates, as all great rivers were called by the Jews. It could not be the river of the east known by that name, because it was in a further country, where mankind never dwelt. But the river Euphrates lay to the southeastward of them, and runs through an inhabited country. They were also put to great difficulties to pass this river, until God shewed signs to them, and held still the flood, which is a very expressive term for the passage being frozen over, to enable them to pass in safety. But to proceed with the vision: "Then dwelt they there, *until the latter times.* And now when they shall begin to come, the *Highest* shall stay the springs of the stream again, that they may go through —therefore sawest thou the multitude in peace. But *those who be left behind of thy people,* are they who are found within my borders. *Now, when he destroyeth the multitude of the nations* that are gathered together, he shall defend his people who remain. *And then he shall shew them great wonders.*" Hear the words of Isaiah, xi. 15, 16, and compare them with the above. "And the Lord shall utterly destroy the tongue of the Egyptian sea, and with his mighty wind shall he shake his hand over the river, and shall smite it in the seven streams, and make men go over dry shod. And there shall be an highway for the remnant of his people, who shall be left from Assyria; like as it was to Israel in the day that he came up out of the land of Egypt." This sea and river cannot mean the Euphrates, the Nile, or the Red sea, as neither is in the way from the northern parts of ancient Media, which were once part of Assyria, where these tribes dwelt. The Caspian or Circasian strait, through the mountains of Caucasus, lies about midway between the Euxine sea to the west, and the Caspian sea to the east, through Iberia. After passing through the strait from the north, by keeping a little west, you pass on in the neighbourhood of the Euxine sea, through Armenia Minor, into Syria Proper, and by the head of the Mediterranean sea to Palestine, without going over the Euphrates. But all who are in Persia, in Armenia Major, and to the eastward in Mesopotamia, and beyond Babylon, must pass the Euphrates to get there. But as before observed, the Jews called all great rivers by the name of the Euphrates, or of some large river well known to them. Nay, they called the invasion of a formidable enemy by the name of a large river, when they came from the north. "Now therefore behold the Lord bringeth up upon them the waters of the river, strong and many, even the king of Assyria, and all his glory —and he shall come up over all his channels and go over all his banks." "Thus saith the Lord, behold waters rise up out of the north, and shall be an overflowing flood, and shall overflow the land, and all that is therein, the city, and them who dwell therein; then the men shall cry, and all the inhabitants of the land shall howl, at the noise of the stamping of the hoofs of his strong horses, at the rushing of his chariots." —Isaiah viii. 7.—Jeremiah xlvii. 2, 3.

By the above story out of Esdras, it appears, as it does in the bible, that these tribes were taken by Salmanazar, in the time of Hoshea, their king, and carried away over the waters into a strange land, that is, transplanted into Media and Persia. *There*, after suffering a long time, how long is not known, but it is pretty clear that it must have been for some hundred years, they repented of their former idolatry, and became discontented and restless, being distressed and wearied out with the folly and wicked practices of their idolatrous neighbours around them. They consulted with their brethren in the northwestern parts of Persia, in the cities of the Medes, who were not far from them, and took counsel together, and resolutely determined to leave the multitude of the heathen, and travel farther north, in search of a country uninhabited and not claimed by any one, and of course free from the troublesome, dangerous neighbourhood and example of the heathen—nay, a country, wherein mankind never yet dwelt. It is not uncommon for men to run into extremes; though it is not improbable but that they might have had some divine direction in the business. They resolved to risk every danger and inconvenience, to avoid opposition to, and temptation from, keeping the statutes of the Lord, which they had so totally neglected in their own holy land, having been led away by the awful examples of the nations around them.

The foregoing extract from the apochryphal book of Esdras, is not quoted as having divine authority; but merely as the historic work of some Jew of an early day. *Bengelius* and *Basnage*, both assert that it is generally admitted by the learned, that those books of Esdras were written in the beginning of the second century. They are held uncanonical by all protestants, not having been ever quoted by the fathers, or any early christian writer, as of divine authority. The Church of England, by her sixth article, permits them to be read for example of life and instruction of manners; but does not allow them to establish any doctrine of religion. The Roman Catholics consider them as of divine authority. This quotation from the first book of Esdras is used here, as any other account of an early transaction, by an author living near the time of the event, would be. This Jew seems to be a serious and devout writer, on a subject he appears to be acquainted with, and from his situation and connections, might be supposed to know something of the leading facts. And whether he wrote in a figurative style, or under the idea of similitudes, dreams or visions, he appears to intend the communication of events that he believed had happened, and as far as they are corroborated by subsequent facts, well attested, they ought to have their due weight in the scale of evidence.

These Israelites, then, accordingly executed their purpose, and left their place of banishment in a body, although it is hardly to be doubted but some, comparatively few, from various motives, as before observed, remained behind; although their places may have been filled up by many natives, who might prefer taking their chance with them in their emigrations, which were common to the people of that region, especially the old inhabitants of Damascus removed to the river Ker, by Tiglah Pilnezer, some time before the taking of Samaria, and the removal of the ten tribes. They proceeded till they came to a great water or river, which stopped their progress, as they had no artificial means of passing it, and reduced them to great distress and almost despair. How long they remained here, cannot now be known; but finally, God again appeared for them, as he had done for their fathers of old at the Red sea, by giving them some token of his presence, and encouraging them to go on; thus countenancing them in their project of forsaking the heathen. God stayed the flood, or perhaps froze it into firm ice, and they passed over by the narrow passages of the river, which may have been occasioned by the islands, so that they might go from island to island, till they landed on the opposite side in safety. They might have been a long time exploring the banks of this water, as some of the nations of Europe, with all their means of knowledge, have since done, before they discovered these narrow passages, which gave them hopes of success.

Here, then, they found a desart land, of a better soil and climate, and went on, and in process of time travelled so far as to take a year and an half, which, construed according to the prophetic rule of their ancestors, a year for a day, would make upwards of five hundred years, and thus literally found a country wherein mankind never yet dwelt.

But although these Children of Israel might have passed over the straits of Kamschatka, and peopled the northeast parts of America, and so went on to the southward and eastward, and left some settlers wherever they remained any time; yet it does not follow that they might not have been attended by many of the inhabitants of Scythia or Tartary, who were willing to try their fortunes with them. Neither does it follow, that some persons of other nations might not have been driven by storms at sea on the American coasts, and made settlements there. All these might have contributed to establish customs among them, different from their own, and also might adulterate and change their language in some instances, as was done in Babylon.

In this land, then, they are to remain till the latter time, when Jehovah will "put forth his hand again a second time, to recover the remnant of his people that remaineth from Assyria, from *Hamah* or *Hala*, and *the western regions*;* *and he will set up an ensign for the nations, and will assemble the outcasts of Israel.*" "And the Lord with his mighty wind will shake his hand over the river, and will strike it into seven streams, and make them pass over dry shod, and there shall be a high way for the remnant of his people, who remain from Assyria, as it was unto Israel in the day that he came out of

* Lowth's translation.

the land of Egypt."—Isaiah xi. 16—as we have before mentioned.

These tribes have been thus lost for more than two thousand years. Those of Judah and Benjamin being, a considerable time after the conquest of Samaria, carried away captives to Babylon, by Nebuchadnezzar, and perhaps with some of their brethren of the ten tribes, who might have remained with them in Jerusalem, were settled in Babylon during seventy years, when they returned to Jerusalem again by the consent of their conquerors, and remained in possession of their beloved country till the coming of the Messiah, whom they perversely put to death on the cross, and voluntarily imprecated that his blood might rest on them and their children; which has since been awfully verified, by their misery and dispersion, having been led away again into captivity by the Romans, who burned their city and made their land a desolation and a curse. From this awful and tremendous fate, the ten tribes, by their previous captivity and banishment, have been happily delivered, having had no hand in this impious transaction.

It was about forty years after the crucifixion, that the conquest of the Romans, and the burning of their temple and city took place. The Romans ploughed up the scite of the city according to the Messiah's prediction, and drove the tribes of Judah and Benjamin as slaves and criminals into every country of the east. They sold thousands of them as they do cattle, and they literally became a bye-word and a hissing with all nations. But at this time their brethren the ten tribes of Israel, were in their state of banishment on the frontiers of Persia and Media, from whence they have disappeared and are generally supposed to be lost. And were it not for the promises of that God, who cannot deceive, a God of holiness and truth, we should give up any enquiry after them as hopeless. But he whose word is truth itself has said, "that in the latter days, he will bring again the captivity of his people Israel and Judah, and will cause them to return to the land that he gave to their fathers, that they should possess it. Go and proclaim these words *towards the north,* and say return thou backsliding Israel, saith the Lord. At that time they shall call Jerusalem the throne of the Lord. And all the nations shall be gathered to it, to the name of the Lord, to Jerusalem; neither shall they walk any more after the stubbornness of their evil heart. In those days the house of Judah shall walk with the house of Israel, and they shall come together out of the land of the north, to the land that I have given for an inheritance unto your fathers." Jeremiah iii. 12—18. "For thus saith the Lord, sing with gladness for Jacob, and shout among the chief of the nations—publish ye—praise ye —and say, O Lord save thy people, the remnant of Israel. Behold! I will bring them from the *north country,* and gather them *from the coasts of the earth,* and with them the blind and the lame, the woman with child and her who travaileth with child together, a great company shall return thither." Jeremiah iii. 7—8.

"Therefore behold! the days come saith the Lord, that they shall no more say, the Lord liveth who brought up the children of Israel out of the land of Egypt; but the Lord liveth who brought up and led the seed of the house of Israel out of the *north country,* and from all countries whither I have driven them, and they shall dwell in their own land." Jeremiah xxiii. 7—8. "Behold! the days come saith the Lord, that the ploughman shall overtake the reaper; and the treader of grapes, him who soweth seed: And the mountain shall drop new wine, and all the hills shall melt. And I will bring again the captivity of my people Israel, and they shall build the waste cities and inhabit them. And they shall plant vineyards and drink of the wine thereof: they shall also make gardens and eat the fruit thereof, and I will plant them upon their land, and they no more shall be pulled up out of the land, which I have given them saith the Lord thy God." Amos ix. 13, &c. "For they shall abide many days without a king and without a prince, without a sacrifice and without an image (the word means a pillar, or chief support, and may be translated, an altar, which suits the context) and without an ephod and without a teraphim; but afterwards shall the children of Israel return and seek the Lord their God, and David their king, and shall fear the Lord and his goodness, in the latter days." Hosea, iii. 4—5.

"God calls to his people—Ho! Ho! come forth and flee from the *land of the north*, for I have spread you abroad as the four winds of the heavens, saith the Lord." Thus saith the Lord of Hosts, behold! I will save my people from the *east country* and from the *west country, or the country of the going down of the sun.*" Zechariah, ii. 6—viii. 7, as it is in the margin of the bible.

We say, if it was not for these and such like promises, it might be thought presumption and folly, for any one to waste his time in enquiring after this long lost people, as it would then have been most natural to conclude that they had passed into oblivion, with the nations of the east and the west, their conquerors, as Babylon, Nineveh, Assyria and Egypt. But as Jehovah cannot deceive, but is the same yesterday, to day and forever, whose words are yea, and amen, who hath said, "yet now thus saith Jehovah, who created thee O Jacob! and who formed thee O Israel! fear thou not, for I have redeemed thee—I have called thee by thy name—thou art mine—fear thou not for I am with thee—from the *east* I will bring thy children, and from the *west* I will gather thee together. I will say to the *north* give up, and to the *south* withhold not, bring my sons *from afar*, and my daughters *from the ends of the earth*." Isaiah, xliii. 1—6.

From all this it plainly appears from whence the Jews are to be gathered a second time, when they shall be brought home again. They are to come from *Assyria* and *Egypt*, where it is well known very many of the tribes of Judah and Benjamin are now to be found, and from *Pathros*, and from *Cush*, and from *Elam*, (different parts of Persia, where they are of the same tribes, with perhaps a small remnant of the Israelites) and from Shinar, still more east, consisting wholly of the two before mentioned tribes, and may include the black Jews, and from *Hamah* near the Caspian sea, where some of the ten tribes may have remained behind, on the departure of their brethren to the northward, and from the *western regions*.

Thus we are to look to some western region, for a number, rather for the main body, of this dispersed nation. Now as no other part of the world has yet been discovered where the body of the Israelites as a nation, have been found, it may be justly concluded, that they must at last be discovered in some western region, not yet taken notice of, where they are kept till the day of their deliverance.

To a believer in the divinity of the bible, there can be no hesitation, but that all this will most assuredly come to pass in the most literal and extensive sense. These lost tribes must be some where on our earth, answerable to the *north* and the *west* from Jerusalem—*a far off*; even in *the ends of the earth*. And as from the present signs of the times, particularly of the Roman government and the reign of antichrist, we may rationally conclude that these are the latter times, the last times of the Roman government, and that the great things foretold in the word of God, are fast accomplishing, it becomes a duty now, to search diligently into these great subjects of christian consideration, and attend to what the spirit of God has revealed of these eventful times, lest the language of Christ to the Pharisees, may become applicable to us—"Ye hypocrites! ye can discern the face of the sky and of the earth; but how is it, that (notwithstanding all your light and knowledge from revelation) ye do not discern this time." Luke, xii. 56.

We will therefore proceed in the attempt, to collect together what may be yet known of this favoured, though sinful and suffering people, once so dear to the God of all the earth, and who still remain a standing and unanswerable monument and pooof of the truth of prophecy to all nations. And if we can do no more than call the attention of christians, of learning and leisure, to this important subject, it will not be lost labour.

CHAPTER II.

An enquiry into the question, on what part of the globe is it most likely, that these descendants of Israel may be now found, arising from late discoveries and facts, that have not come to the knowledge of the civilized world, till of late years.

EVERY quarter of the world has been so traversed and explored by the hardy and adventurous seamen of modern Europe and America, as well as by travellers whose curiosity and indefatigable labours, have scarcely left any considerable tract of the globe unnoticed, that we can scarcely presume on making the least discovery in any hitherto unknown part of the world. We must look to the histories of countries already known to the geographer and traveller, and apply to the divine scriptures for the compass which is to direct our course. Hence it must answer to the following particulars—

1. It must be a country to the north and west from Judea. Jeremiah, iii. 17—18, xxiii. 7—8. Zechariah, ii. 6.

2. It must be a far country from Judea. Isaiah, xliii. 6—xlvi. 11.*

* Remember the former things of old time, verily I am God and none else; I am God and there is none like unto me. From the beginning, making known the end, and from ancient times the things that are not yet done, saying, my council shall stand, and whatever I have willed I will effect. Calling from the east, the eagle, and from a land far distant the man of my council. As I have spoken, so will I bring it to pass; I have formed the design and I will execute it. Lowth's translation.

3. It must answer the term, from the ends of the earth. Isaiah, xliii. 1—6.

4. It must be in the western regions, or the country of the going down of the sun. Zecharia, viii. 7.

5. It must be a land, that at the time of the tribes going to, was without inhabitants, and free from heathen neighbours. 2 Esdras, xiii. 41.

6. It must be beyond the seas from Palestine, the country to which part of them are to return in ships. Isaiah, lx. 9—xvii. 2.

The scriptures are very positive in four of the above particulars, the fifth is founded on the text from 2d Esdras, and although it is not pretended that the apochryphal books bear any comparison as to divine inspiration, with the bible, yet as that book was written by a Jew, somewhere about the year 100, it may, as has already been observed, be used as evidence of an historic fact, equally with any other historian, and if corroborated by other facts, will add to the testimony.

As to the sixth particular, this is not only supported by the text, but it is the opinion of that great and judicious writer, the Rev. Mr. Faber, on the whole representation of the scriptures, who certainly deserves the attention of every serious christian. He seems very positive "that some prevailing maritime power of faithful worshippers, will be chiefly instrumental in converting and restoring a part of the Jewish nation. This seems to be declared in scripture, more than once, with sufficient plainness." "Who are these? like a cloud they fly, and like doves to their holes. Surely the Isles shall wait for me, and the ships of Tarshish, among the first, to bring thy sons from afar; their silver and their gold with them, unto the name of the Lord thy God, unto the holy one of Israel, because he hath glorified me." Isaiah, lx. 8—9. Again it is expressly said, they are to be gathered from the coasts of the earth, implying that they were to have some connection with the sea, and the address which God makes to them puts it out of doubt. "Ho! land spreading wide the shadow of thy wings, which are *beyond the rivers of Cush*, or Cuthai, accustomed to send messengers by sea, even in Bulrush vessels upon the surface of the waters. Go swift messengers unto the nation dragged away and plucked; unto a people wonderful from the beginning hitherto; a nation expecting, expecting and trampled underfoot; whose lands the rivers have spoiled. Isaiah, xviii. 1—2. At that season, a present shall be led to the Lord of Hosts; a people dragged away and plucked; even a people wonderful from the beginning hitherto; a nation expecting, expecting and trampled under foot; whose land, rivers have spoiled, unto the place of the name of the Lord of Hosts, Mount Zion." Isaiah, xviii. 7. Mr. Faber has given a paraphrase of part of the foregoing texts, thus, (3d vol. 94) "Go swift messengers, unto a nation, long apparently forsaken by God; a nation dragged away from their own country and plucked; a nation wonderful from their beginning hitherto; a nation perpetually expecting their promised Messiah, and yet trampled under foot; a nation whose land the symbolical rivers of foreign invaders have for ages spoiled. Go swift messengers! You who by your skill in navigation, and your extensive commerce and alliances, are so qualified to be carriers of a message to people in the remotest countries; go with God's message unto a nation dragged away; to the dispersed Jews; a nation dragged away from its proper seat, and plucked of its wealth and power; a people wonderful from its beginning to this very time for the special providence which has ever attended them and directed their fortunes; a nation still lingering in expectation of the Messiah, who so long since came and was rejected by them and *now is coming again in glory*; a nation universally trampled under foot; whose land, rivers, armies of foreign invaders, the Assyrians, Babylonians, Syromacedonians, Romans, Saracens, and Turks, have over-run and depopulated." Letter on Isaiah, 18.

"My worshippers beyond the river Cush, (which must be to the northward and westward of Jerusalem) shall bring as an offering to me, the daughters of my dispersion." Zeph. iii. 10. And Zechariah treating on the same subject, says, "I will hiss for them (the tribes of Ephraim and his children, mentioned in the former verses) for I have redeemed them; and they shall increase as they have (heretofore) increased. And I will sow them among the people, and *they shall remember me in far countries*, and they shall live with their children and turn again. And I will bring *them* again *also* (that is besides those from far countries) out of the land of Egypt, and gather them out of Assyria, and I will bring them into the land of Giliad and Lebanon, and place shall not be found for them. And he (that is Ephraim) shall pass through *the sea* with affliction, and shall smite *the waves in the sea*, and all the deeps of the river shall dry up, and the pride of Assyria shall be brought down, and the sceptre of Egypt shall pass away, and I will strengthen them in the Lord, and they shall walk up and down in his name, saith the Lord." Zechariah, x. 8—12.

Here is an explicit difference made between the return of Judah and Ephraim, that is, between the Jews and Israelites—the latter is to come from a far country—he is to pass through a great water, or over the seas, or both. The words here made use of, may be very applicable, to people, who have no knowledge or experience of passing over the sea in ships, whose sickness is generally extremely distressing.

Mr. Faber supposes that the land spreading wide the shadow of her wings, may be some maritime nation, the sails of whose ships, and the protection given by them, are here prophesied of. He seems to think, this may refer to Great Britain, in like manner, as she may be designated by Tarshish, which was formerly a great trading and maritime country. Yet he thinks it possible it may refer to some other maritime nation—but it is asked, why not to a union of maritime nations, on so important and difficult an undertaking.

From a serious consideration of all the foregoing circumstances, we seem naturally led to have recourse to the late discovered continent of America, which the first visitants found filled with inhabitants, and though called savages, differed essentially from all the savages ever known to the people of the old world before. In the first place they resembled (considerably) in appearance, the people of the oriental nations. Mr. Penn, who saw and communicated with them in a particular manner, on his first arrival in America, while in their original, uncontaminated state, before they were debased and ruined by their connection with those who called themselves civilized and christians, was exceedingly struck with their appearance. In one of his letters to his friends in England, he says, "I found them with like countenance with the Jewish race; and their children of so lively a resemblance to them, that a man would think himself in Duke's-place or Berry-street, in London, when he seeth them." (Penn's Works, 2d vol. 704, year 1682.) They wore ear-rings and nose jewels; bracelets on their arms and legs; rings on their fingers; necklaces made of highly polished shells found in their rivers and on their coasts. Their females tied up their hair behind, worked bands round their heads, and ornamented them with shells and feathers, and are fond of strings of beads round several parts of their bodies. They use shells and turkey spurs round the tops of their mocasins, to tinkle like little bells, as they walk." Isaiah proves this to have been the custom of the Jewish women, or something much like it. "In that day, says the prophet, the Lord will take away the bravery of their tinkling ornaments about their feet, and their cauls, and their round tires like the moon. The chains and the bracelets and the muflers. The bonnets and the ornaments of the legs, and the head-bands, and the tablets, and the ear rings; the rings and the nose jewels." Isaiah, iii. 18. They religiously observed certain feasts, and feasts very similar to those enjoined on the Hebrews, by Moses, as will hereinafter more particularly be shewn. In short, many, and indeed, it may be said, most of the learned men, who did pay any particular attention to these natives of the wilderness at their first coming among them, both English and Spaniards, were struck with their general likeness to the Jews. The Indians in New-Jersey, about 1681, are described, as persons straight in their limbs, beyond the usual proportion in most nations; very seldom crooked or deformed; their features regular; their countenances some times fierce, in common rather resembling a Jew, than a christian. (Smith's History of New-Jersey, 14.)

It shall now be our business to collect those facts in their history, that are well attested, with those which may be known of them from personal knowledge of men of character, or from their present manners, customs and habits; although we are well advised, and it should be constantly borne in mind, that the corruption of both principle and practice, introduced amongst them, by their connection with Europeans, has so debased their morals and vitiated all their powers of mind, that they are quite degenerated from their ancestors.

An old Charibbee Indian, in a very early day, thus addressed one of the white people. "Our people are become almost as bad as yours. We are so much altered since you came among us, that we hardly know ourselves, and we think it is owing to so melancholy a change, that hurricanes are more frequent than formerly. It is the evil spirit, who has done all this—who has taken our best lands from us, and given us up to the dominion of christains. Edward's History West-Indies, 1 vol. 28. And yet we very gravely assert that we have benefited the Indian nations, by teaching them the christian religion.

The Indians have so degenerated, that they cannot at this time give any tolerable account of the origin of their religious rites, ceremonies and customs, although religiously attached to them as the commands of the great spirit to their forefathers. Suppose a strange people to be discovered, before wholly unknown to the civilized world, and an enquiry was instituted into their origin, or from what nation they had sprung, what mode of examination would be most likely to succeed and lead to a rational solution of the question?

In our opinion, a strict enquiry into the following particulars, would be the best means of accomplishing this valuable purpose.

Their language.

Their received traditions.

Their established customs and habits.

Their known religious rites and ceremonies.

And, lastly, their public worship and religious opinions and prejudices.

Therefore to commence this enquiry, with some degree of method, we shall confine ourselves to these five particulars, as far as we can find well authenticated data to proceed upon.

CHAPTER III.

An enquiry into the language of the American Indians.

WHEN we consider how soon the family of Noah, scattered throughout Asia, Africa and Europe, lost almost every trace of their original language, so far at least, as not to be easily understood by the nations into which they became divided—established different manners and customs peculiar to each nation or people—and finally formed for themselves respectively, such absurd and wholly differing modes of religious worship, as well as principles and doctrines, and finally became, at different times, to bear the most inveterate hatred to each other, we could no longer, at this remote period, hope for much success in looking for convincing testimony to prove the fact very satisfactorily, though we should stumble on the actual descendants of those children of Abraham, the lost ten tribes of Israel, after so long a dispersion and entire separation from the rest of the world. And if we do find any convincing testimony on this subject, we must attribute it to the over-ruling providence of that God who is wonderful in council, and true to all his promises. Hear Sir William Jones, whose authority will have great influence on all who know his character. In his discourse on the origin of the East Indians or Hindoos, Arabs, Tartars, &c. he says, "hence it follows, that the only family after the flood, established itself in the northern parts of *Iran*, now Persia. That as the family multiplied, they were divided into three distinct branches, each retaining little, at first, and loosing the *whole* by degrees, of their common primary language; but agreeing severally on new expressions for new ideas."

Father Charlevoix, a famous French writer, who came over to Canada very early, and paid particular attention to the Indian natives, says, "that the only means (which others have neglected) to come at the original of the Indian natives, are the knowledge of their languages, and comparing them with those of the other hemisphere, that are considered as primitives. Manners very soon degenerate by means of commerce with foreigners, and by mixture of several nations uniting in one body—and particularly so, amongst wandering tribes, living without principle, laws, education or civil government, especially where absolute want of the necessaries of life takes place, and the necessity of doing without, causes their names and uses to perish together. From their dialects, we may ascend to the mother tongues themselves. These are distinguished by being more nervous than those derived from them, because they are formed from nature, and they contain a greater number of words, imitating the things whereof they are the signs. Hence he concludes that if those characteristical marks which are peculiar to any oriental nation are found in the Indian languages, we cannot reasonably doubt of their being truly original, and consequently, that the people who speak them, have passed over from that hemisphere."

This then must be an enquiry into facts, the investigation of which, from the nature of the subject, must be wholly founded on well authenticated accounts recorded by writers of character, who may be consulted on this occasion; or from the information of such persons who have been long domesticated with particular nations, suspected to have originated from the other hemisphere; or of persons whose occupation or mode of life has led them to visit parts of the globe, the most likely to afford some light on this abstruse subject. And even here our assistance cannot be expected to be great; but whatever we are able to discover, we will put together, in hopes that by pursuing this enquiry, though we should arise no farther than bare rudiments, the curiosity of the more learned and persevering, may produce some further and more adequate discovery, to enlighten mankind. The difficulties attending this attempt must be great. The Indian languages, having never been reduced to any certainty by letters, must have been exposed to great changes and misconceptions. They are still a wandering people, having no knowledge of grammar or of the arts and sciences. No monuments of antiquity—no mechanical trades—oppressed and distressed on all hands—driven from their original residence into a wilderness, and even there not suffered to remain stationary; but still driven from place to place—debased and enervated by the habitual use of intoxicating spirits, afforded them by traders for the double purpose of profit and imposition—vitiated by the awful example of white people, we are at this day confined to the few traces of their original language, their religion, rites and customs, and a few common traditions that may yet with labour be collected, to form our opinions upon. The Indian languages in general, are very copious and expressive, considering the narrow sphere in which they move; their ideas being few in comparison with civilized nations. They have neither cases nor declensions. They have few or no prepositions—they remedy this, by affixes and suffixes, and their words are invariably the same in both numbers.

All this, if the writer's information be correct, is very similar to the Hebrew language. He has been informed from good authority, and the same is confirmed by a writer well acquainted with the subject, that there is no language known in Europe, except the Hebrew, without prepositions; that is, in separate and express words. The Indians have all the other parts of speech, except as above. They have no comparative or superlative degrees of comparison more than the Hebrews. They form the last, by some leading vowel of the divine name of the *great spirit*, added to the word. It is observed by some Jewish, as well as christian interpreters, that the several names of God, are often given as epithets by the Hebrews to those things which are the greatest, the strongest, and the best of their kind, *as ruach elohim*, a mighty wind. 1 vol. Stackhouse's History of the Bible, page 8, in a note. Both languages are very rhetorical, nervous and emphatical. Those public speeches of the Indians, that the writer of these memoirs has heard or read, have been oratorical and adorned with strong metaphors in correct language, and greatly abound in allegory. About the year 1684, the governor of New-York, sent an accredited agent to the Onondagos, on a dispute that was likely to arise with the French. The agent (one Arnold) behaved himself very haughtily towards the Indians, at delivering his commission. One of the chiefs then answered him in a strain of Indian eloquence, in which he said among other things, "I have two arms—I extend the one towards Montreal, there to support the tree of peace; and the other towards *Corlaer*, (the governor of New-

York) who has long been my brother. *Onontlis* (the governor of Canada) has been these ten years my father. *Corlaer* has been long my brother, with my own good will, but neither the one or the other is my master. *He who made the world,* gave me this land I possess. *I am free.* I respect them both; but no man has a right to command me, and none ought to take amiss, my endeavouring all I can, that this land should not be troubled. To conclude, I can no longer delay repairing to my father, who has taken the pains to come to my very gate, and who has no terms to propose, but what are reasonable." 1 Wynne's History America, 402—3.

At a meeting held with the President, General Washington, in 1790, to prevail upon him to relax the terms of a treaty of peace, made with commissioners under the old confederation, relative to an unreasonable cession of a large part of their country, which they had been rather persuaded to make to the United States, for the sake of peace, and which afterwards they sincerely repented of, *Cornplant* who had long been a steady friend to the United States, in the most perilous part of the revolutionary war, delivered a long, persuasive and able speech, which the writer of this preserved, and has now before him, and from which are extracted the following sentences, as a proof of the above assertion. "Father, when your army entered the country of the six nations, we called you the *town destroyer,* and to this day, when your name is heard, our women look behind them and turn pale; our children cling close to the necks of their mothers; but our councillors and warriors being men, cannot be afraid; but their hearts are grieved by the fears of our women and children, and desire that it may be buried so deep, as to be heard of no more. Father, we will not conceal from you, that the great spirit and not man, has preserved *Cornplant* from the hands of his own nation. For they ask continually, where is the land, on which our children and their children, are to lie down upon? You told us, say they, that a line drawn from Pennsylvania to Lake Ontario, would mark it forever on the east; and a line running from Beaver Creek to Pennsylvania, would mark it on the west. But we see that it is not so. For first one and then another comes and takes it away by order of that people, who you told us, promised to secure it to us forever. *Cornplant* is silent, for he has nothing to answer. When the sun goes down, *Cornplant* opens his heart before the great spirit; and earlier than the sun appears again upon the hills, he gives thanks for his protection during the night, for he feels, that among men become desperate by the injuries they sustain, it is God only that can preserve him. *Cornplant* loves peace—all he had in store, he has given to those, who have been robbed by your people, lest they should plunder the innocent, to repay themselves.

"The whole season which others have employed in providing for their families, *Cornplant* has spent in endeavors to preserve peace, and at this moment, his wife and children are lying on the ground, and in want of food.—His heart is in pain for them; but he perceives, that the *great spirit*, will try his firmness, in doing what is right. Father! innocent men of our nation are killed one after another, though of our best families; but none of your people, who have committed these murders, have been punished. We recollect that you did promise to punish those who should kill our people; and we ask, was it intended that your people should kill the Seneca's, and not only remain unpunished, but be *protected from the next of kin.* Father! these to us are great things. *We know that you are very strong—We have heard that you are wise,* but *we shall wait to hear your answer to this, that we may know that you are just.*"

Adair records a sentence of a speech of an Indian captain to his companions, in his oration for war. Near the conclusion of his harangue, he told the warriors, "he feelingly knew that their guns were burning in their hands—their tomahawks were thirsty to drink the blood of their enemy, and their trusty arrows were impatient to be upon the wing; and lest delay should burn their hearts any longer, he gave them the cool refreshing word, "*join the holy ark,*" and away to cut off the devoted enemy."

But a speech made by *Logan,* a famous Indian chief, about the year 1775, was never exceeded by Demosthenes or Cicero. In revenge for a murder committed by some unknown Indians, a party of our people fired on a canoe loaded with women and children, and one man, all of whom happened to belong to the family of *Logan,* who had been long the staunch friend of the Americans, and then at perfect peace with them. A war immediately ensued, and after much blood-shed on both sides, the Indians were beat, and sued for peace. A treaty was held, but *Logan* disdainfully refused to be reckoned among the suppliants; but to prevent any disadvantage from his absence, to his nation, he sent the following talk, to be delivered to lord Dunmore at the treaty. "I appeal to any white man to say, if he ever entered Logan's cabin hungry, and he gave him not meat—if ever he came cold and naked, and Logan clothed him not. During the course of the last long and bloody war, Logan remained idle in his cabin, an advocate for peace. Such was his love for the white men, that my countrymen pointed as they passed, and said, *Logan is the friend of white men.* I had thought to have lived with you, but for the injuries of one man. Colonel —— the last spring, in cold blood, and unprovoked, murdered all the relations of *Logan*, not sparing even my woman and children. There runs not a drop of his blood in the veins of any living creature. This called on me for revenge. I have sought it. I have killed many. I have fully glutted my vengeance. For my country, I rejoice at the beams of peace. But do not harbor a thought that mine is the joy of fear. *Logan* never felt fear. He will not turn on his heel to save his life. Who is there to mourn for *Logan?* No, not one."

Great allowance must be made for translations into another lauguage, especially by illiterate and ignorant interpreters. This destroys the force as well as beauty of the original.

A writer (Adair) who has had the best opportunities to know the true idiom of their language, by a residence among them for forty years, has taken great pains to shew the similarity of the Hebrew, with the Indian languages, both in their roots and general construction; and insists that many of the Indian words, to this day, are purely Hebrew, notwithstanding their exposure to the loss of it to such a degree, as to make the preservation of it so far, little less than miraculous.

Let any one compare the old original Hebrew, spoken with so much purity by the Jews before the Babylonish captivity, with that spoken by the same people on their return, after the comparatively short space of seventy years, and he will find it had become a barbarous mixture of the Hebrew and Chaldaic languages, so as not to be understood by an ancient

Hebrew, and in a great measure, has continued so to this day. We say such a consideration will show an almost miraculous intervention of Divine Providence, should a clear trace of the original language be discoverable among the natives of our wilderness at this day. "Their words and sentences are expressive, concise, emphatical, sonorous and bold." Father Charlevoix, in his history of Canada, paid more attention to the Indian languages than most travellers before him, and indeed he had greater opportunities, and was a man of learning, and considerable abilities. He says, "that the *Algonquin* and *Huron* languages, have, between them, *that* of almost all the savage nations of Canada we are acquainted with. Whoever should well understand both, might travel without an interpreter, more than fifteen hundred leagues of country, and make himself understood by an hundred different nations, who have each their peculiar tongue. The *Algonquin* especially has a vast extent. It begins at Acadia and the Gulph of St. Lawrence, and takes a compass of twelve hundred leagues, twining from the south-east by the north, to the south-west. They say also, that the Wolf Nation, or the Mohegans, and the greatest part of the Indians of New-England and Virginia, speak the Algonquin dialects. The *Huron* language has a copiousness, an energy, and a sublimity, perhaps not to be found in any of the finest languages we know of: and those whose native tongue it is, though now but a handful of men, have such an elevation of soul, as agrees much better with the majesty of their language, than with the state to which they are reduced. Some have fancied they found a similarity with the Hebrew, others have thought it had the same origin with the Greek." "The Algonquin language has not so much force as the Huron; but has more sweetness and elegance. Both have a richness of expression, a variety of turns, a propriety of terms, a regularity which astonishes—but what is more surprising, is, that among these barbarians, who never study to speak well, and who never had the use of writing, there is never introduced a bad word, an improper term, or a vicious construction. And even their children preserve all the purity of the language in their common discourse. On the other hand, the manner in which they animate all they say, leaves no room to doubt of their comprehending all the worth of their expressions, and all the beauty of their language."

Mr. Colden, who wrote the History of the Wars of the Five Nations, about the year 1750, and was a man of considerable note, speaking of the language of those nations says, "they are very nice in the turn of their expressions, and that a few of them are so far masters of their language, as never to offend the ears of their Indian auditory by an unpolite expression. They have, it seems, a certain urbanity or atticism in their language, of which the common ears are very sensible, though only their great speakers attain to it. They are so given to speech-making, that their common compliments to any person they respect, at meeting or parting, are made in harangues. They have a few radical words, but they compound them without end. By this their language becomes sufficiently copious, and leaves room for a good deal of art to please a delicate ear. Their language abounds with gutturals and strong aspirations, which make it very sonorous and bold. Their speeches abound with metaphors, after the manner of the eastern nations." It should be noted, that Mr. Colden, though a sensible man, and of excellent character, could not speak their language, and not having any considerable communication with them, took his information from others.

The late Rev. Dr. Jonathan Edwards, of Connecticut, son of the late President Edwards, who was a man of great celebrity, as a well read, pious divine, and of considerable erudition, was intimately associated with the Indians at Stockbridge, of the Mohegan tribe in that state, from the age of six years. He understood their language equally with his mother tongue. He also had studied that of the Mohawks, having resided in their nation about six months for that purpose. He informs us that the name *Mohegan* is a corruption of *Mukkekaneaw,* arising from the English pronunciation. This is a very common thing, and occasions much confusion, and great difficulties, in tracing the languages of the different tribes. For we have not only to contend with a different pronunciation and spelling of both English and French, but the corruption and ignorance of interpreters and traders, especially in an early day; and also the different modes of writing the same word by different people, arising from their different conceptions of the word as pronounced by the Indians.* As for instance, in the same words by the English and French—

English.	*French.*
Owenagunges.	Abenaguies.
Maques.	Aniez.
Odistastagheks.	Mascoaties.
Makihander.	Mourigan.

* The different sounds given by different tribes to the same letters, is also a source of difficulty. Those who write, often use the letter a, where the sound is oh, so that owoh is used in the Mohegan where a or au is used in other languages, as Moquoh for Mauquah, a bear. The sound of these two are alike, when spoken by an Indian. The e final, is never sounded in any word, but a monosyllable.

English.	*French.*
Oneydoes.	Oneyonts.
Utawawas.	Outawies.
Todericks.	Tateras.
Satana's.	Shaonons.

The Mohegan language was spoken by all the various tribes of New-England. Many of the tribes had a different dialect, but the language was radically the same. Mr. Elliot, called the Indian Apostle, who was among the first settlers of Massachusetts, and died in 1691, translated the bible into Indian, which is found to be in a particular dialect of the Mohegan language. Dr. Edwards says it appears to be much more extensive than any other language in North-America. The language of the *Delawares*, in Pennsylvania, of the *Penobscots*, bordering on Nova-Scotia, of the *Indians of St. Francis*, in Canada, of the *Shawanese*, on the Ohio, and of the *Chippewas*, at the westward of Lake Huron, were all radically the same with the *Mohegan*. The same is said of the *Ottowas*, *Nanticokes*, *Munsees*, *Menomonies*, *Messisagas*, *Saukies*, *Ottagaumies*, *Killistinoes*, *Nipegons*, *Algonkins*, *Winnebagoes*, &c.

Dr. Edwards asserts, that for the pronouns common in other languages, they express the pronouns both substantive and adjective, by affixes or letters, or syllables added at the beginnings or ends, or both, of their nouns. In this particular, the structure of their language coincides with that of the Hebrew, in an instance in which the Hebrew differs from all the languages of Europe, ancient and modern, with this only difference, that the Hebrews always joined the affixes to the ends of the words, whereas the Indians, in pronouns of the singular number, prefix the letter or syllable; but in the plural number, they add others as suffixes. Also as the word is increased, they change and transpose the vowels, as in *tmohhecan*, an hatchet; *ndumhecan*, my hatchet: the o is changed into u, and transposed after the manner of the Hebrews; likewise in some instances, the *t* is changed into *d*.

Besides what has been observed concerning *prefixes* and *suffixes*, there is a remarkable analogy, says Dr. Edwards, between some words of the Mohegan language, and the correspondent words in the Hebrew. In the Mohegan *niah* is *I*. In Hebrew it is *ani*, which is the two syllables of *niah* transposed. Keah, thou or thee. The Hebrews use *Ka* the suffix. *Uwoh*, is this man, or this thing; very analagous to the Hebrew *Hu*, or *Huah*, ipse. *Necaunuh* is *we:* in Hebrew it is nachnu or anachnu. In Hebrew *ni* is the suffix for me, or the first person. In the Mohegan, *n*, or *ne*, is prefixed to denote the first person, as *nmeetseh*, or nimeetseh, I eat. In Hebrew k or ka, is the suffix for the second person, and is indifferently either a pronoun, substantive or adjective. *K* or *ka*, has the same use in the Mohegan language as *kmeetseh* or kameetseh, thou eatest. *Knish*, thy hand. In Hebrew the *vau*, and the letter *u* and *hu*, are the suffixes for he or them. In the Indian the same is expressed by *u*, or *uw*, and by *oo*, as in uduhwhunnw, I love him. *Pumissoo*, he walketh. In Hebrew, the suffix to express our, or us, is nu. In Mohegan, it is *nuh*, as *noghnuh*, our father. Nmeetschnuh, we eat, &c.

To elucidate this subject still farther, a list of a few words in the different Indian dialects shall be added, with the same words in Hebrew and Chaldaick.

English.	*Charibbee.*	*Creeks.*	*Mohegan,* and Northern Languages.	*Hebrew.*
His wife	Liani			Li hene
My wife	Yene-nori			Hene herranni
Come hither	Hace-yete			Aca-ati (Samaritan)
The heavens	Chemim			Shemim
Jehovah	Jocanna	Y. He. Ho. wah		Jehovah
Woman	Ishto			Ishto
Man or chief	Ish	Ishte		Ish
I			Niah	Ani, the 2 syllables transposed as ahni
Thou or thee			Keah	Ka
This man			Uwoh	Huah
We			Necaunuh	Nachnu
Assembly or walled house	Kurbet			Guir, or gra bit
Necklace or collar	Enea			Ong
My necklace	Yene kali			Vongali
Wood	Hue			Oa (Chaldaic)
My skin	Nora			Ourni
I am sick	Nane guaete			Nanceheti
Good be to you	Halea tibou			Ye hali ettuboa
To blow	Phoubac			Phouhe
Roof of the house	Toubana ora			Debona our
Go thy way	Bayou boorkaa			Boua Bouak
Eat	Baika			Bge Chaldaic
To eat	Aika			Akl do.
The nose	Nichiri			Neheri
Give me nourishment*	Natoni boman			Natoui bamen
The great first cause		Yo hewah		Jehovah

* Edward's West-Indies.

English.	*Charibbee.*	*Creeks.*	*Mohegan,* and Northern Languages.	*Hebrew.*
Praise the first cause		Halleluwah		Hallelujah
Father		Abba		Abba
Now, the present time		Na		Na
Very hot, or bitter upon me		Heru, hara, or hala		Hara hara
To pray		Phale		Phalac
The hind parts		Kesh		Kish
One who kills another		Abe, derived from Abele Gruf		Abel
The war name who kills a rambling enemy		Noabe, compounded of Noah & Abe		
Canaan		Kenaai		Canaan
Wife		Awah		Eve or eweh
Winter		Kora		Cora
Another name for God		Ale		Ale or alohim
Do		Iennois*		Iannon†
			Indians of Penobscot	
Arrarat, a high mountain			Arrarat, a high mountain.	Arrarat, a high mountain

As the writer of this does not understand either the Hebrew or Indian languages, so as to be a judge of their true idioms or spelling, he would not carry his comparisons of one language with the other, too far. Yet he cannot well avoid mentioning, merely as a matter of curiosity, that the Mohawks, in confederacy with the Five Nations, as subsisting at the first arrival

* Barlow.

† Litterally he shall be called a son. Christian Observer for June 1813, p 349.

of the Europeans in America, were considered as the law-givers, or the interpreters of duty, to the other tribes. Nay, this was so great, that all paid obedience to their advice. They considered themselves as supreme, or first among the rest. Mr. Colden says, that he had been told by old men in New-England, that when their Indians were at war, formerly, with the Mohawks, as soon as one appeared, their Indians raised a cry from hill to hill, a Mohawk! a Mohawk! Upon which all fled like sheep before a wolf, without attempting to make the least resistance. And that all the nations around them, have for many years, entirely submitted to their advice, and pay them a yearly tribute of wampum. The tributary nations dare not make war or peace, without the consent of the Mohawks. Mr. Colden has given a speech of the Mohawks, in answer to one from the governor of Virginia, complaining of the other confederate nations, which shows the Mohawks superiority over them, and the mode in which they corrected their misdoings. Now it seems very remarkable, that the Hebrew word Mhhokek, spelled so much like the Indian word, means a law-giver, (or leges interpres) or a superior.

Blind chance could not have directed so great a number of remote and warring savage nations to fix on, and unite in so nice a religious standard of speech, and even grammatical construction of language, where there was no knowledge of letters or syntax. For instance, A, oo, EA, is a strong religious Indian emblem, signifying, I *climb*, *ascend*, or *remove* to another place of residence. It points to A-no-wah, the first person singular, and O E A, or Yah, He, Wah, and implies putting themselves under the divine patronage. The beginning of that most sacred symbol, is by studious skill, and a thorough knowledge of the power of letters, placed twice, to prevent them from being applied to the sacred name, for vain purposes, or created things.

Though they have lost the true meaning of their religious emblems, except what a very few of the more intelligent traders revive in the retentive memories of the old inquisitive magi, or beloved man; yet tradition directs them to apply them properly. They use many plain religious emblems of the divine name, as Y, O, he, wah—Yah and Ale, and these are the roots of a prodigious number of words, through their various dialects. It is worthy of remembrance, that two Indians, who belong to far distant nations, without the knowledge of each other's language, except from the general idiom, will intelligibly converse together, and contract engagements without any interpreter, in such a surprising manner, as is scarcely credible. In like manner we read of Abraham, Isaac and Jacob, travelling from country to country, from Chaldea into Palestine, when inhabited by various differing nations—thence into Egypt and back again, making engagements, and treating with citizens wherever they went. But we never read of any difficulty of being understood, or their using an interpreter.

The Indians generally express themselves with great vehemence and short pauses, in their public speeches. Their periods are well turned, and very sonorous and harmonious. Their words are specially chosen, and well disposed, with great care and knowledge of their subject and language, to show the being, power and agency of the great spirit in all that concerns them.

To speak in general terms, their language in their roots, idiom and particular construction, appears to have the whole genius of the Hebrew, and what is very remarkable, and well worthy of serious observation, has most of the peculiarities of that language, especially those in which it differs from most other languages; and "often, both in letters and signification, synonimous with the Hebrew language." They call the lightning and thunder, Eloha, and its rumbling noise Rowah, which may not, improperly, be deduced from the Hebrew word *Ruach,* a name of the third person in the holy Trinity, originally signifying "the air in motion, or a rushing wind." —Faber.

The Indian compounded words are generally pretty long, but those that are radical or simple, are mostly short; very few, if any of them, exceed three or four syllables. And as their dialects are guttural, every word contains some consonants, and these are the essential characteristics of language. Where they deviate from this rule, it is by religious emblems, which obviously proceeds from the great regard they pay to the names of the Deity, especially to the great four lettered, divine, essential name, by using the letters it contains, and the vowels it was originally pronounced with, to convey a virtuous idea; or by doubling or transposing them, to signify the contrary. In this all the Indian nations agree. And as this general custom must proceed from one primary cause, it seems to assure us, that this people was not in a savage state when they first separated, and varied their dialects with so much religious care and exact art.

Souard, in his Melanges de Literature, or Literary Miscellanies, speaking of the Indians of *Guiana,* observes, "on the authority of a learned Jew, *Isaac Nasci*, residing at Surinam," we are informed that the language of those Indians, which he calls the *Galibe dialect,* and which is common to all the tribes of *Guiana*, is soft and agreeable to the ear, abounding in vowels and synonims, and possessing a syntax as regular as it would have been, if established by an academy. This Jew says that all the substantives are Hebrew. The word expressive of the soul in each language, means *breath*. They have the same word in Hebrew to denominate God, which means master, or lord."

It is said there are but two mother tongues among the northern Indians, and extending thence to the Missisippi, the Huron and Algonquin, and there is not more difference between these, than between the Norman and French. Dr. Edwards asserts that the language of the Delawares, in Pennsylvania—of the Penobscots, bordering on Nova-Scotia—of the Indians of St. Francis, in Canada—of the Shawanese, on the Ohio—of the Chippewas, to the westward of Lake Huron—of the Ottawas, Nanticokes, Munsees, Minoniones, Messinagues, Saasskies, Ottagamics, Killestinoes, Mipegoes, Algonquins, Winnebagoes, and of the several tribes in New-England, are radically the same, and the variations between them are to be accounted for from their want of letters and of communication. Much stress may be laid on Dr. Edwards' opinion. He was a man of strict integrity, and great piety. He had a liberal education—was greatly improved in the Indian languages, which he habituated himself to from early life, having lived long among the Indians.

CHAPTER IV.

The Indian Traditions as received by their Nations.

AS the Indian nations have not the assistance afforded by the means of writing and reading, they are obliged to have recourse to tradition, as Du Pratz, 2 vol. 169, has justly observed, to preserve the remembrance of remarkable transactions or historical facts; and this tradition cannot be preserved, but by frequent repetitions; consequently many of their young men are often employed in hearkening to the old beloved men, narrating the history of their ancestors, which is thus transmitted from generation to generation. In order to preserve them pure and incorrupt, they are careful not to deliver them indifferently to all their young people, but only to those young men of whom they have the best opinion. They hold it as a certain fact, as delivered down from their ancestors, that their forefathers, in very remote ages, came from a far distant country, by the way of the west, where all the people were of one colour, and that in process of time they moved eastward to their present settlements.

This tradition is corroborated by a current report among them, related by the old *Chickkasah* Indians to our traders, that now about 100 years ago, there came from Mexico, some of the old *Chickkasah* nation, or as the Spaniards call them *Chichemicas*, in quest of their brethren, as far north as the *Aquahpah* nation, above one hundred and thirty miles above the Natchez, on the south-east side of the Missisippi river;

but through French policy, they were either killed or sent back, so as to prevent their opening a brotherly intercourse with them, as they had proposed. It is also said, that the *Nauatalcas* believe that they dwelt in another region before they settled in Mexico.—That their forefathers wandered eighty years in search of it, through a strict obedience to the commands of the great spirit; who ordered them to go in quest of new lands, that had such particular marks as were made known to them, and they punctually obeyed the divine mandate, and by that means found out and settled that fertile country of *Mexico*.

Our southern Indians have also a tradition among them which they firmly believe, that of old time, their ancestors lived beyond a great river. That nine parts of their nation, out of ten, passed over the river, but the remainder refused, and staid behind. That they had a king when they lived far to the west, who left two sons. That one of them, with a number of his people, travelled a great way for many years, till they came to Delaware river, and settled there. That some years ago, the king of the country from which they had emigrated, sent a party in search of them. This was at the time the French were in possession of the country on the river Alleghany. That after seeking six years, they found an Indian who led them to the Delaware towns, where they staid one year. That the French sent a white man with them on their return, to bring back an account of their country, but they have never been heard of since.

It is said among their principal, or beloved men, that they have it handed down from their ancestors, that the book which the white people have was once theirs. That while they had it they prospered exceedingly; but that the white people bought it of them, and learnt many things from it; while the Indians lost their credit, offended the great spirit, and suffered exceedingly from the neighbouring nations. That the great spirit took pity on them and directed them to this country. That on their way they came to a great river, which they could not pass, when God dried up the waters and they passed over dry shod. They also say that their forefathers were possessed of an extraordinary divine spirit, by which they foretold future events, and controuled the common course of nature, and this they transmitted to their offspring, on condition of their obeying the sacred laws. That they did by these means bring down showers of plenty on the beloved people. But that this power, for a long time past, had entirely ceased.

The reverend gentlemen mentioned in the introduction, who had taken so much pains in the year 1764 or 5, to travel far westward, to find Indians who had never seen a white man, informed the writer of these memoirs, that far to the northwest of the Ohio, he attended a party of Indians to a treaty, with Indians from the west of the Missisippi. Here he found the people he was in search of—he conversed with their beloved man who had never seen a white man before, by the assistance of three grades of interpreters. The Indian informed him, that one of their most ancient traditions was, that a great while ago, they had a common father, who lived towards the rising of the sun, and governed the whole world. That all the white people's heads were under his feet. That he had twelve sons, by whom he administered his government. That his authority was derived from the great spirit, by virtue of some special gift from him. That the twelve sons behaved very bad and tyrannized over the people, abusing their power to a great degree, so as to offend the great spirit exceedingly. That he being thus angry with them, suffered the white people to introduce spirituous liquors among them, made them drunk, stole the special gift of the great spirit from them, and by this means usurped the power over them, and ever since the Indians heads were under the white people's feet. But that they also had a tradition, that the time would come, when the Indians would regain the gift of the great spirit from the white people, and with it their ancient power, when the white people's heads would be again under the Indian's feet.

Mr. M'Kenzie in his History of the Fur Trade, and his journey through North-America, by the lakes, to the South-Sea, in the year ——, says, "that the Indians informed him, that they had a tradition among them, that they originally came from another country inhabited by wicked people, and had traversed a great lake, which was narrow, shallow and full of islands, where they had suffered great hardships and much misery, it being always winter, with ice and deep snows —at a place they called the Copper-mine River, where they made the first land, the ground was covered with copper, over which a body of earth had since been collected to the depth of a man's heighth. They believe also that in ancient times their ancestors had lived till their feet were worn out with walking, and their throats with eating. They described a deluge, when the waters spread over the whole earth, except the highest mountain, on the top of which they were preserved. They also believe in a future judgment." M'Kenzie's history, page 113.

The Indians to the eastward say, that previous to the white people coming into the country, their ancestors were in the habit of using circumcision, but latterally, not being able to assign any reason for so strange a practice, their young people insisted on its being abolished.

M'Kenzie says the same of the Indians he saw on his route, even at this day. History, page 34. Speaking of the nations of the Slave and Dog-rib Indians, very far to the northwest, he says, "whether circumcision be practised among them, I cannot pretend to say, but the appearance of it was general among those I saw."

The Dog-rib Indians live about two or three hundred miles from the straits of Kamschatka.

Dr. Beatty says, in his journal of a visit he paid to the Indians on the Ohio, about fifty years ago, that an old christian Indian informed him, that an old uncle of his, who died about the year 1728, related to him several customs and traditions of former times; and among others, that circumcision was practised among the Indians long ago, but their young men making a mock at it, brought it into disrepute, and so it came to be disused. Journal, page 89. The same Indian said, that one tradition they had was, that once the waters had overflowed all the land, and drowned all the people then living, except a few, who made a great canoe and were saved in it. Page 90. And that a long time ago, the people went to build a high place. That while they were building of it, they lost their language, and could not understand one another. That while one, perhaps, called for a stick, another brought him a stone, &c. &c. and from that time the Indians began to speak different languages.

Father Charlevoix, the French historian, informs us that the Hurons and Iroquois, in that early day, had a tradition among them that the first woman came from heaven and had twins, and that the elder killed the younger.

In an account published in the year 1644, by a Dutch minister of the gospel, in New-York, giving an account of the Mohawks, he says, "an old woman came to my house and told the family, that her forefathers had told her that the great spirit once went out walking with his brother, and that a dispute arose between them, and the great spirit killed his brother." This is plainly a confusion of the story of Cain and Abel. It is most likely from the ignorance of the minister in the idiom of the Indian language, misconstruing, Cain being represented as a great man, for the great spirit. Many mistakes of this kind are frequently made.

Mr. Adair, who has written the History of the Indians, and who deserves great credit for his industry and improving the very great and uncommon opportunities he enjoyed, tells us, that the southern Indians have a tradition, that when they left their own native land, they brought with them a sanctified rod, by order of an oracle, which they fixed every night in the ground; and were to remove from place to place on this continent, towards the rising sun, till it buded in one night's time. That they obeyed the sacred oracle, and the miracle at last took place, after they arrived on this side of the Missisippi, on the present land they possess. This was the sole cause of their settling there—of fighting so firmly for their reputed holy land and holy things—that they may be buried with their beloved forefathers."

This seems to be taken from Aaron's rod.

Col. James Smith, in his Journal of Events, that happened while he was prisoner with the Caughnewaga Indians, from 1755 to 1759, says, "they have a tradition that in the beginning of this continent, the angels or heavenly inhabitants, as they call them, frequently visited the people, and talked with their forefathers, and gave directions how to pray, and how to appease the great being, when he was offended. They told them they were to offer sacrifice, burn tobacco, buffaloe and deer's bones, &c. &c." Page 79.

The Ottawas say, "that there are two great beings that rule and govern the universe, who are at war with each other; the one they call *Maneto*, and the other *Matchemaneto*. They say that *Maneto* is all kindness and love, and the other is an evil spirit that delights in doing mischief. Some say that they are equal in power; others say that *Maneto* is the first great cause, and therefore must be all powerful and supreme, and ought to be adored and worshipped; whereas *Matchemaneto* ought to be rejected and despised." "Some of the Wyandots and Caughnewaga's profess to be Roman Catholics; but even these retain many of the notions of their ancestors. Those who reject the Roman Catholic religion, hold that there is one great first cause, whom they call Owaheeyo, that rules and governs the universe, and takes care of all his creatures rational and irrational, and gives them their food in due season, and hears the prayers of all those who call upon him; therefore it is but just and reasonable to pray and offer sacrifice to this great being and to do those things that are pleasing in his sight. But they widely differ in what is pleasing or displeasing to this great being. Some hold that following nature or their own propensities is the way to happiness. Others reject this opinion altogether, and say, that following their own propensities in this manner is neither the means of happiness, or the way to please the deity. My friend, Tecaughretanego, said, our happiness depends on our using our reason, in order to suppress these evil dispositions; but when our propensities neither lead us to injure ourselves nor others, we may with safety indulge them, or even pursue them as the means of happiness. Page 80.

Can any man read this short account of Indian traditions, drawn from tribes of various nations, from the west to the east, and from the south to the north, wholly separated from each other, written by different authors of the best characters, both for knowledge and integrity, possessing the best means of information, at various and distant times, without any possible communication with each other, and in one instance from occular and sensible demonstration; written on the spot in several instances, with the relators before them; and yet suppose that all this is either the effect of chance, accident or design, from a love of the marvellous or a premeditated intention of deceiving, and thereby ruining their own well established reputations?

Charlevoix was a clergyman of character, who was with the Indians some years, and travelled from Canada to the Missisippi, in that early day.

Adair lived forty years entirely domesticated with the southern Indians, and was a man of learning and great observation. Just before the revolutionary war he brought his manuscript to Elizabeth-Town, in New-Jersey, to William Livingston, Esq. (a neighbour of the writer) to have it examined and corrected, which was prevented by the troubles of a political nature, just breaking out. The Rev. Mr. Brainerd was a man of remarkable piety, and a missionary with the Crosweek Indians to his death. Dr. Edwards was eminent for his piety and learning, and was intimately acquainted with the Indians from his youth. Dr. Beatty was a clergyman of note and established character. Bartram was a man well known to the writer, and travelled the country of the southern Indians as a botanist, and was a man of considerable discernment, and had great means of knowledge; and M'Kenzie, in the employment of the northwest company, an old trader, and the first adventurous explorer of the country, from the lake of the woods to the southern ocean.

It is now asked, can any one carefully and with deep reflection, consider and compare these traditions with the history of the ten tribes of Israel, and the late discoveries of the Russians, capt. Cook and others, in and about the peninsula of Kamschatka and the northeast coast of Asia and the opposite shore of America, of which little was before known by any civilized nation, without at least drawing strong presumptive inferences, in favour of these wandering nations being descended from some oriental nation of the old world, and most probably, all things considered, being the lost tribes of Israel.

Let us look into the late discoveries, and compare them with the Indian traditions.

Kamschatka is a large peninsula on the north eastern part of Asia—It is a mountainous country, lying between fifty-one and sixty-two degrees of north latitude, and of course a very cold and frozen climate. No grain can be raised there, though some vegetables are. Skins and furs are their chief exports. The natives are wild as the country itself, and live on fish and sea animals, with their rein-deer. The islands in this sea, which separate it from the northwest coast of America, are so numerous that the existence of an almost continued chain of them between the two continents is now rendered extremely probable. The principal of them are the Kurile Islands, those called Bherings and Copper Islands, the Alentian Islands and Fox Islands. Copper Island which lies in fifty-four degrees north, and in full sight of Bhering's Island, has its name from the great quantities of copper with which the northeast coast of it abounds. Mr. Grieve's history. It is washed up by the sea, and covers the shores in such abundance, that many ships might be loaded with it very easily. These islands are subject to continual earthquakes, and abound in sulphur. Alaska is one of the most eastwardly islands, and probably is not far from the American coast. The snow lies on these islands till March, and the sea is filled with ice in winter. There is little or no wood growing in any part of the country, and the inhabitants live in holes dug in the earth. Their greatest delicacies are wild lily and other roots and berries, with fish and other sea animals. The distance between the most northeastwardly part of Asia and the northwest coast of America, is determined by the famous navigator capt. Cook, not to exceed thirty-nine miles. These straits are often filled with ice, even in summer and frozen in winter, and by that means might become a safe passage for the most numerous host to pass over in safety, though these continents had never been once joined, or at a much less distance than at present. The sea from the south of Bhering's Straits to the islands, between the two continents, is very shallow. From the frequent volcanoes that are continually happening, it is probable, not only that there has been a separation of the continent at Bhering's Straits, but that the whole space from the island to that small opening was once filled up by land; but that it had by the force and fury of the waters, perhaps actuated by fire, been totally sunk and destroyed, and the islands left in its room. Neither is it improbable that the first passage of the sea was much smaller than at present, and that it is widening yearly, and perhaps many small islands that existed at the first separation of the continents, have sunk or otherwise have been destroyed. These changes are manifest in almost every country.

Monsieur Le Page du Pratz, in his 2d vol. of his History of Louisiana, page 120, informs us, that being exceedingly desirous to be informed of the origin of the Indian natives, made every enquiry in his power, especially of the nation of the Natchez, one of the most intelligent among them. All he could learn from them was, that they came from between the north and the sun setting—being no way satisfied with this, he sought for one who bore the character of one of their wisest men. He was happy enough to discover one named *Moneachtape*, among the Yazous, a nation about forty leagues from the Natchez. This man was remarkable for his solid understanding and elevation of sentiments, and his name was given to him by his nation as expressive of the man—meaning "*the killer of pain and fatigue.*" His eager desire to see the country from whence his forefathers came, he obtained directions and set off. He went up the Missouri, where he staid a long time to learn the different languages of the nations he was to pass through. After long travelling he came to the nation of the Otters, and by them was directed on his way, till he reached the southern ocean. After being some time with the nations on the shores of the great sea, he proposed to proceed on his journey, and joined himself to some people who inhabited more westwardly on the coast. They travelled a great way between the north and the sun setting, when they arrived at the village of his fellow travellers, where he found the days long and the nights short. He was here advised to give over all thoughts of continuing his journey. They told him "that the land extended still a long way in the direction aforesaid, after which it ran directly west, and at length was cut by the great water from north to south. One of them added, that when he was young he knew a very old man, who had seen that distant land before it was eat away by the great water; and when the great water was low, many rocks still appeared in those parts." *Moncacht-ape* took their advice and returned home after an absence of five years.

This account given to Du Pratz, in the year 1720, confirms the idea of the narrow passage at *Kamschatka*, and the probability that the continents once joined.

It is remarkable that the people, especially the Kamschatkians, in their marches, never go but in indian file, following one another in the same track. Some of the nations in this quarter, prick their flesh with small punctures with a needle in various shapes, then rub into them charcoal, blue liquid or some other colour, so as to make the marks to become indelible, after the manner of the more eastern nations.

Bishop Lowth in his notes on the 16th verse of the xlixth chapter of Isaiah, says, "this is certainly an allusion to some practice common among the Jews at that time, of making marks on their hands and arms by punctures on the skin, with some sort of sign or representation of the city or temple, to shew their affection and zeal for it. They had a method of making such punctures indelible by fire or staining—and this art is practiced by travelling Jews all over the world at this day—Vid. also his note on chap. xlv. 5th verse.

Thus it is with our northern Indians; they always go in indian file, and mark their flesh just as above represented.

The writer of this has seen an aged christian Indian Sachem, of good character, who sat for his portrait. On stripping his neck to the lower part of his breast, it appeared that the whole was marked with a deep blueish colour in various figures, very discernible. On being asked the reason of it, he answered, with a heavy sigh, that it was one of the follies of his youth, when he was a great warrior, before his conversion to christianity; and now, says he, I must bear it, as a punishment for my folly, and carry the marks of it to my grave.

The people of Siberia made canoes of birch bark, distended over ribs of wood, nicely sewed together. The writer has seen this exactly imitated by the Indians on the river St. Lawrence, and it is universally the case on the lakes. Col. John Smith says, " at length we all embarked in a large birch bark canoe. This vessel was about four feet wide and three feet deep, and about thirty-five feet long; and though it could carry a heavy burthen, it was so artfully and curiously constructed, that four men could carry it several miles, from one landing place to another; or from the waters of the lake to the waters of the Ohio. At night they carry it on the land, and invert it, or turn it bottom up, and convert it into a dwelling-house."

It also appears from the history of Kamschatka, written by James Grieve, that in the late discoveries, the islands which extend from the south point of Kamschatka, amount to thirty-one or thirty-two. That on these islands are high mountains, and many of them smoaking volcanoes. That the passages between them, except in one or two instances, were but one or two days row, at the time of the authors writing that history. They are liable to terrible inundations and earthquakes.

The following is collected from Mr. Steller's journal, as recorded in the above history. "The main land of America lies parallel with the coast of Kamschatka, insomuch that it may reasonably be concluded that these lands once joined, especially at the Techukotskoi Noss, or Cape. He offers four reasons to prove it: 1st. The appearance of both coasts, which seem to be torn asunder. 2d. Many capes project into the sea from thirty to sixty versts. 3d. Many islands are in the sea which divides Kamschatka from America. 4th. The situation of the islands, and the breadth of that sea.— The sea is full of islands, which extend from the north-west point of America to the channel of Anianova. One follows another, as the Kuruloski islands do at Japan. The American coast at sixty degrees of north latitude, is covered with wood; but at Kamschatka, which is only fifty-one degrees, there is none for near fifty versts from the sea, and at sixty-two not one tree is to be found. It is known also, that the fish enter the rivers on the American coast, earlier than they do in the rivers of Kamschatka. There are also plenty of raspberries, of a large size and fine taste, besides honey suckles, cran-berries and black-berries in great plenty. In the sea there are seals, sea-beavers, whales and dog-fish. In the country and in the rivers on the American coast, red and black foxes, swans, ducks, quails, plover, and ten kinds of birds not known in Europe. These particulars may help to answer the question, whence was America peopled; for though we should grant that the two continents never were joined, yet they lie so near to each other, that the possibility of the inhabitants of Asia going over to America, especially considering the number of the islands, and the coldness of the climate, cannot be denied. From Bhering's Island, on its high mountains, you can see mountains covered with snow, that appear to be capes of the main land of America. From all which it appears clearly, here was a probable mean of a people passing from Asia to America, either on the main land before a separation, or from island to island; or on the ice after a separation, by which the continent of America might have been peopled, by the tribes of Israel wandering north-east, and directed by the unseen hand of Providence, and thus they entered into a country wherein mankind never before dwelt.

It is not presumed that the ten tribes of Israel alone did this. Many of the inhabitants might have gone with them from Tartary or Scythia; and particularly the old inhabitants of Damascus, who were carried away in the first place by Tiglah Pilnezer, before his conquest of the Israelites, and were their neighbours, and perhaps as much dissatisfied with their place of banishment, though for different reasons, as the Israelites, as well as from Kamschatka, on their way where they were stopped some time, as the Egyptians did with the Israelites of old. And indeed it is not improbable, as has before been hinted, that some few of other nations, who traded on the seas, might, in so long a course of time, have been driven by stress of weather, and reached the Atlantic shores at different places; but the great body of people settling in North and South-America, must have originated from the same source.

Hence it would not be surprising to find among their descendants, a mixture of the Asiatic languages, manners, customs and peculiarities. Nay, it would appear rather extraordinary and unaccountable if this was not so. And if we should find this to be the case, it would greatly corroborate the fact of their having passed into America from the north-east point of Asia, according to the Indian tradition. We, at the present day, can hardly conceive of the facility with which these wandering northern nations removed from one part of the country to the other. The Tartars at this time, who possess that northern country, live in tents or covered carts, and wander from place to place in search of pasture, &c.

CHAPTER V.

Their general Character and established Customs and Habits.

WE will now proceed to consider the general character of the people of whom we are treating, as preliminary to the enquiring into their customs and habits. It will be necessary to the full understanding our subject, to premise a few particulars. When America was first discovered by Columbus, it was comparatively well peopled by some hundreds, if not thousands of tribes of different nations, from the coast opposite to Kamschatka to Hudson's Bay. Their numbers have not been known, neither can they be known at this day. But to form some general idea of them, by reasoning on the subject, we will give the numbers of the nations that have come to our knowledge at different times*—

A	Abenakias	Aiaouez
Akamsians	Algonkins	Assanpinks
Arrowhatoes	Amelistes	Aurananeaus
Assinnis	Assinaboils	Appalachos
Arathapescoas	Agones	Abeckas
Avoyels	Arkanzas	Aquelou-pissas†
Adaics	Aughquagchs	Atacapas
Appomotacks	Alebamons	Andaslaka
Accotronacks	Attatramasues	Attibamegues
Accomacks	Amdustez	

* Pikes Expedition. No. of Warriors. No. of Women. No. of Children.

† Men who understand and see.

B

Blanes

Bayoue Ogoulas

C

Chatkas* or flat heads

Cuttatawomans

Chickahomines

Chickiaes

Chesapeaks

Connosidagoes

Cohunnewagoes

Chalas

Capahnakes

Coroas

Christinaux

Chilians

Canses

Caddoques

Caonites

Cayugas

Conoies

Chippewas, or Anchipawah, 345, 619, 1624

Cherokees

Chickasaws

Catawbas

Chocktaws

Creeks

Chouanongs†

Chiahnessou

Canzas

Chitemachas

Caonetas

Chatots

Chacci Cumas, or red cray fish

Chaouchas or Ouachas

Cadodaquioux

Conestogoes

Caughnewagoes

Chayennes

Chappunish, or pierced nose Indians

Cantanyans, on the Alleghany river

Ceneseans or Cenis

Cahirmois

Coosades

Cowetas

Cussutas

Chukaws

Colapissas

Caseitas

Chatkas

Conchaes

D

Delawares

Dog-rib Indians

E

Eries

Erigas

F

Foxes, 400, 500, 850

G

Grand Eaux

Gakaos

Ganawoose

H

Hassiniengas

Hurons

Houmas

I

Iroquois

Illinois

Ictans

Icbewas

* They reckoned formerly 25000 warriors, but it is more likely to be only men. Said to be quite peaceable.—Du Pratz.

† A numerous nation of 38 villages, below the Missouri, on the Missisippi.

Ioways, 300, 400, 700.

K

Kecoughtons
Kaskkasies
Killistinoes
Kickapoos
Kappas
Kanoatinas
Kans, 465, 500, 600.

L

Linnilinopes
Lenais
Les Puans

M

Minatarees
Messiasics
Menowa Kautong, or people of the lakes, 305, 600, 1200.
Mantes
Machecous
Mechimacks
Mohiccons
Munsees
Manahoacs
Melotaukes
Monachans, now Tuscaroras, added to the Five Nations in 1712.
Mandans
Monasiceapanoes
Musquaties
Monahassanoes
Massinagues
Mohemonsoes
Mexicans
Moraughtacunds
Mattapomens
Missinasagues
Missouris
Mohocs or Mohawks
Mingoes
Mohuccons
Miamis
Mynonamies 300, 350, 700.
Mascoutons, or Nation of Fire
Messcothins
Mencamis
Mobeluns, or Mouville
Milowacks
Mertowacks
Mohuccories
Mahatons, or Manhattons
Mohegans
Muckhekanies
Ministeneaux
Munseys
Minisinks
Maherins
Massawonaes
Minonionees
Mipegois
Muskoghees
Michigamias
Maquas
Mandans

N

Neshaminas
Narragansetts
Nepiscenicens
Nassamonds
Nottoways
Nanticokes
Natches
Nantaughtacunds
Nepissens
Naudowessies
Natchitoches
Nauatalchas
Nacunes or Greens
Narauwings

O

Omans
Onanikins
Ousasons
Outponies
Onaumanients
Oswagatches
Orundacs
Osages 1252, 1793, 974.
Oneidas
Onondagoes
Oucatonons
Ottowas
Oniscousins
Ottagamies or Foxes
Outimacs
Ousasoys
Otters
Oniyouths
Othouez
Oumas, or Red Nation
Oufe Ogulas, or the Nation of the Dog
Oque-Loussas
Oakfuskees
Ouachibes

P

Piorias
Pequots
Parachuctaus
Prakimines
Pimitconis
Piankishaws
Patowomacks
Pissassees
Padoucas
Pamunkies
Payankatanks
Powhatans
Paspahegas
Panis and White Panis, Black Panis
Pouhatamies
Penobscots
Panemahas
Pacha Oglouas, or the Nation of Bread
Pomptons
Pawnees, 1993, 2170, 2060.
Pemveans
Panoses
Pandogas

Q

Quiocohanses
Quadodaquees

R

Rappahanocks
Round Heads
Rancokas
Ricoras

S

Sokulks
Skillools
Seminoles
Schactikook, or river Indians
Sitons, 360, 700, 1100.
Susquehannas
Satanas
Sankihani
Stegerakies
Shackakonies
Secakoonies
Sivux
Senecas
Sapoonies
Shawanese
Souckelas
Shakies
Saaskies
Shackaxons

Sacs 700, 750, 1400
Shosonees or Snake Indians.

T

Teganatics
Tauxilnanians
Tauxinentes
Tentilves
Tuscaroras
Twightwies
Thomez
Taensas
Tonicas
Theoux
Titones 2000, 3600, 6000
Tomaroas
Tapousoas
Tionontates
Tsouonthousaas, on the Ohio
Tetaus 2700, 3000, 2500.

V

Vermilions

W

Wabingies
Wapings
Wighcocomicoes
Wianoes
Wamasqueaks
Wyandots
Webings
Whonkenties
Winnebagoes 450, 500, 1000.
Washpelong or people of the leaves 180, 350, 530.
Washpeoute 90, 180, 270.

Y

Youghtanunds
Yazous
Yanetongs 900, 1600, 2700.
Yatassees
Other bands generally 1704, 2565, 4420.

Some nations divided and settled at a distance from each other, and after many years, their language so changed, as to form different dialects; as was in our days, the case with the *Erigas*, on the Ohio, who separated from the *Tuscororas*, and formed a distinct dialect in the course of a few years.

Here are then one hundred and ninety different nations, each having a *king* or *sachem* over them, of whom we have had some knowledge, though many of them are not now known; what then must be the number of the nations on this continent could they all be known? Although we cannot with any precision know the number of the nations, on the arrival of Columbus, and much less the number of souls, yet we may as matter of curiosity give the numbers of individual nations of

S

late years as far as the fact can be ascertained—and here our labour will be greatly lessened by a late ingenious and well written pamphlet, entitled, "Discourse delivered before the New-York Historical Society, December 1811," by the honourable Dewitt Clinton, of the city of New-York. To the labours of this gentleman, we are greatly indebted for the substance of many of the following observations, as well as the elegant manner in which he has communicated so much information to the world.

Du Pratz, in his History of Louisiana, (1 vol. 107—123) gives an account of the single nation of the Padoucas, lying west by north-west of the Missouri, in 1724, which may give a faint idea of the numbers originally inhabiting this vast continent. He says "the nation of the *Paduca's* is very numerous, extends almost two hundred leagues, and they have villages quite close to the Spaniards of New Mexico." "They are not to be considered as a wandering nation, though employed in hunting, summer and winter—page 121. Seeing they have large villages, consisting of a great number of cabins, which contain very numerous families. These are permanent abodes; from which one hundred hunters set out at a time with their horses, their bows and a good stock of arrows." "The village where we were, consisted of one hundred and forty huts, containing about eight hundred warriors, fifteen hundred women, and at least two thousand children, some Padoucas having four wives."—page 124. "The natives of North-America, derive their origin from the same country, since at bottom they all have the same manners and usages, as also the same manner of speaking and thinking."

Mr. Jefferson, late President of the United States, in his Notes on Virginia, has also given much useful information to the world on several important subjects relating to America, and among others as to the numbers of the Indians in that then dominion. Speaking of the Indian confederacy of the warriors, or rather nations, in that state and its neighbourhood, called "the Powhatan confederacy," says, it contained in point of territory, as he supposes, of their patrimonial country "about three hundred miles in length, and one hundred in breadth. That there was about one inhabitant for every square mile, and the proportion of warriors to the whole number of inhabitants, was as three to ten, making the number of souls about thirty thousand."

Some writers state the number of their warriors at the first coming of the Europeans to Virginia, to be fifteen thousand. and their population fifty thousand. *La Houtan* says that each village contained about fourteen thousand souls, that is, fifteen hundred that bore arms, two thousand superanuated men, four thousand women, two thousand maids, and four thousand five hundred children. . From all which, it is but a moderate estimate to suppose that there were six hundred thousand fighting men, or warriors, on this continent at its first discovery.

In 1677, col. Coursey, an agent for Virginia, had a conference with the Five Nations, at Albany. The number of warriors was estimated at that time in those nations at the following rate. Mohawks three hundred, Oneidas two hundred, Onondagoes three hundred and fifty, Cayugas three hundred, Senecas one thousand—total two thousand one hundred and fifty, which makes the population about seven thousand two hundred. Vide Chalmer's Political Annals, 606.

Smith, in his History of New-York, says, that in 1756, the number of fighting men were about twelve hundred.

Douglass, in his History of Massachusetts, says, that they were about fifteen hundred in 1760.

In 1764, col. Boquet states the whole number of the inhabitants (he must mean fighting men) at fifteen hundred and fifty.

Captain Hutchins, in 1768, states them at two thousand one hundred and twenty, and Dodge, an Indian trader, in 1779, at sixteen hundred, in the third year of the American revolutionary war. Many reasons may be assigned for the above differences—some may have staid at home for the defence of their towns—some might be absent treating on disputes with their neighbours, or sickness, &c. &c.

During the above war, in 1776—7, the British had in their service, according to the returns of their agent—Mohawks three hundred, Oneidas one hundred and fifty, Tuscororas two hundred, Onondagoes three hundred, Cayugas two hundred and thirty, Senecas four hundred—In the whole fifteen hundred and eighty. The Americans had about two hundred and twenty, making up eighteen hundred warriors, equal to about six thousand souls.

In 1783, Mr. Kirkland, missionary to the Oneidas, estimated the number of the Seneca warriors at six hundred, and the total number of the Six Nations, at more than four thousand.

In 1790, he made the whole number of Indian inhabitants then remaining, including in addition, those who reside on Grand River, in Canada, and the Stockbridge and Brothertown Indians, who had then lately joined them, to be six thousand three hundred and thirty, of which there were nineteen hundred warriors.

In 1794, on a division of an annuity, by order of Congress, to be made among the Six Nations, the numbers appeared with considerable certainty, to be

	In the United States.	*In the British government.*
Mohawks		300
Oneidas	628	460
Cayugas	40	——
Onondagoes	450	760
Tuscaroras	400	
Senecas	1780	
Stockbridge and Brothertown Indians, about	2330	
The above number of British	760	

But what are these to the southern Indians, and especially those of Mexico and Peru. I will give one example. Mons. La Page Du Pratz, in his History of Louisiana, written about the year 1730, assures us, "that the nation of the Natchez, from whom the town of that name on the Missisippi is called, were the most powerful nation in North America—2 vol. 146. They extended from the river Manchas or Iberville, which is about fifty leagues from the sea, to the river Wabash, which is about four hundred and sixty leagues from the sea, and that they had five hundred Sachems in the nation."

He further says, "that the Chatkas or Flat-heads, near the river *Pacha Ogulas*, had twenty-five thousand warriors, but in which number, he supposes many were reckoned who had but a slight title to that name—Page 140.

But a short estimate of the length and breadth of different parts of America, although not pretended to be perfectly accurate, yet having endeavoured to keep within bounds, it may serve to answer the end now proposed.

	Length in miles.	*Breadth in miles.*
Old Mexico	2,000	600
New-Mexico	2,000	1,600
Louisiana	1,600	1,200
Terra Firma	1,400	700
Amazonia	1,200	960
Peru	1,800	500
Chili	1,200	500
Patagonia	700	300
La Plata	1,500	1,000
Brazil	2,500	700
Thirteen United States	1,250	1,040
Esquimaux	1,600	1,200
Canada	1,200	276
Nova Scotia	500	400
Floridas	600	130
Miles	20,850	11,106

Besides this immense territory, on all which there are some Indians to be found, the country from New-Mexico, west to the South seas, which is yet in a state of nature, and abounds in Indian nations, must be added to the vast amount, as more than equal to all the rest.

The Indians, by oppression, diseases, wars and ardent spirits, have greatly diminished in numbers, degenerated in their moral character, and lost their high standing as warriors, especially those contiguous to our settlements.

"The very ancient men who have witnessed the former glory and prosperity of their country, or who have heard from the mouths of their ancestors, and particularly from their beloved men, (whose office it is to repeat their traditions and laws to the rising generations, with the heroic achievements of their forefathers) the former state of their country with the great prowess and success of their warriors of old times, they weep like infants, when they speak of the fallen condition of their nations. They derive however some consolation from a prophecy of ancient origin and universal currency among them, that the man of America, will, at some future period, regain his ancient ascendency and expel the man of Europe from this western hemisphere. This flattering and consolatory persuasion has enabled the Seneca and Shawnese prophets, to arrest, in some tribes, the use of intoxicating liquors, and has given birth, at different periods, to attempts for a general confederacy of the Indians of North America." *Clinton.*

The writer of this was present at a dinner given by general Knox, to a number of Indians in the year 1789, at New-York; they had come to the President on a mission from their nations. The house was in Broadway. A little before dinner, two or three of the Sachems, with their chief or principal man, went into the balcony at the front of the house, the drawing room being up-stairs. From this they had a view of the city, the harbour, Long-Island, &c. &c. After remaining there a short time, they returned into the room, apparently dejected; but the chief more than the rest. General Knox took notice of it, and said to him, brother! what has happened to you?—You look sorry!—Is there any thing to distress you? He answered—I'll tell you brother. I have been looking at your beautiful city—the great water—your fine country—and see how happy you all are. But then, I could not help thinking, that this fine country and this great water were once ours. Our ancestors lived here—they enjoyed it as their own in peace—it was the gift of the great spirit to them and their children. At last the white people came here in a great canoe. They asked only to let them tie it to a tree, lest the waters should carry it away—we consented. They then said some of their people were sick, and they asked permission to land them and put them under the shade of the trees. The ice then came, and they could not go away. They then begged a piece of land to build wigwams for the winter--we granted it to them. They then asked for some corn to keep them from starving—we kindly furnished it to them, they promising to go away when the ice was gone. When this happened, we told them they must now go away with their big canoe; but they pointed to their big guns round their wigwams, and said they would stay there, and we could not make them go away. Afterwards, more came. They brought spirituous and intoxicating liquors with them, of which the Indians became very fond. They persuaded us to sell them some land. Finally they drove us back, from time to time, into the wilderness, far from the water, and the fish and the oysters—they have destroyed the game—our people have wasted away, and now we live miserable and wretched, while you are enjoying our fine and beautiful country. This makes me sorry brother! and I cannot help it."

But to proceed, the colour of the Indians, generally speaking, was red, brown, or copper coloured, differing according to climate, high and low grounds. They are universally attached to their colour, and take every mean in their power to increase it, prefering it to the white. They give a name to the white people, which is highly contemptuous; it is that of an heterogenous animal. Sometimes when they aim at greater severity, that of "*the accursed people.*" The hotter or colder the country is where the Indians have long resided, the greater proportion have they of the white or red colour; this is asserted by Adair from personal experience. He has compared the Shawanoh Indians with the Chikkasaw, and found them much fairer, though their endeavours to cultivate the copper colour were alike. He thinks the Indian colour to be the effect of climate, art and manner of living. Their tradition says, that in the country far west, from which they came, all the people were of one colour; and they are ignorant which was the primitive colour. Adair has seen a white man, who, by his endeavors to change his colour, became as deeply coloured as any Indian in the camp, after he had been in the woods only four years. The Indians to the Southward are often of a deeper hue than those to the northward; in a high country they incline to a lighter tinge; but then those to the northward are more ignorant, and less knowing in their traditions, rites, and religious customs. The like change is not unknown in Europe and Asia. The inhabitants of the northern countries, in many instances, are comparatively fairer than those of the southern countries.

In the south the Indians are tall, erect and robust—their limbs are well shaped, so as generally to form a perfect human figure. They delight in painting themselves, especially with red or vermilion colour. They are remarkably vain, and suppose themselves the first people on earth. The Five Nations called themselves ' *Ongue-honwe,* that is, *men surpassing all others,* the *only beloved people of the great spirit, and his peculiar people.* But as to their common mode of living, they are generally all great slovens—they seldom or ever wash their shirts.

It is a matter of fact, proved by most historical accounts, that the Indians, at our first acquaintance with them, generally manifested themselves kind, hospitable and generous to the Europeans, so long as they were treated with justice and humanity; but when they were, from a thirst of gain, overreached on every occasion, their friends and relations treacherously entrapped and carried away to be sold for slaves; themselves injuriously oppressed, deceived and driven from their lawful and native possessions; what ought to have been expected, but inveterate enmity, hereditary animosity, and a spirit of perpetual revenge. To whom should be attributed the evil passions, cruel practices, and vicious habits to which they are now changed, but to those who first set them the example; laid the foundation, and then furnished the continual means for propagating and supporting the evil.

In a very early day, in the colony of Virginia, the first settlers, by their great imprudence, had soured the Indian temper, raised their jealousies, and provoked their free and independent spirits, so as to lead them to determine on the extirpation of the whole colony—then few, weak and divided.

The Indians managed their intended attack with so much secrecy, that they surprised the colonists in every quarter, and destroyed near one fourth of them. In their turn, the survivors waged a destructive war against the Indians, and murdered men, women and children. Dr. Robertson says, "regardless, like the Spaniards, of those principles of faith, honor and humanity, which regulate hostilities among civilized nations, and set bounds to their rage, the English deemed every thing allowable that tended to accomplish their designs. They hunted the Indians like wild beasts, rather than enemies; and as the pursuit of them to their places of retreat in the woods, was both difficult and dangerous, they endeavoured to allure them from their inaccessible fastnesses, by offers of peace, and promises of oblivion, made with such an artful appearance of sincerity, as deceived the crafty Indian chief, and induced the Indians to return in the year 1623, to their former settlements, and resume their usual peaceful occupations. The behaviour of the two people seemed now to be perfectly reversed. The Indians, like men acquainted with the principles of integrity and good faith, on which the intercourse between nations is founded, confided in the reconciliation, and lived in absolute security, without suspicion of danger, while the English, with perfidious craft, were preparing to imitate savages in their revenge and cruelty.

"On the approach of harvest, when a hostile attack would be most formidable and fatal, the English fell suddenly on all the Indian plantations, murdered every person on whom they could lay hold, and drove the rest to the woods, where so many perished with hunger, that some of the tribes nearest to the English, were totally extirpated."—History of North-America, 96, 97.

Robertson again, speaking of the war in New-England, between Connecticut and Providence, in their first attempt against the Pequod Indians, says, "that the Indians had secured their town, which was on a rising ground in a swamp, with pallisades. The New-England troops, unperceived, reached the pallisades. The barking of a dog alarmed the Indians. In a moment, however, they started to their arms, and raising the war-cry, prepared to repel the assailants. The English forced their way through into the fort, or town, and setting fire to the huts, which were covered with reeds, the confusion and terror quickly became general. Many of the women and children perished in the flames, and the warriors, endeavoring to escape, were either slain by the English, or falling into the hands of the Indian allies, who surrounded the fort at a distance, were reserved for a more cruel fate. The English resolved to pursue their victory, and hunting the Indians from one place of retreat to another, some subsequent encounters were hardly less fatal than the first action. In less than three months, the tribe of the Pequods were extirpated."—Ibid 184—5, 6.

"Thus the English stained their laurels, by the use they made of victory. Instead of treating the Pequods as an independent people, who made a gallant effort to defend the property, the rights and freedom of their nation, they retaliated upon them all the barbarities of American war. Some they massacred in cold blood, others they gave up to be tortured by their Indian allies, a considerable number they sold as slaves in Bermuda, the rest were reduced to servitude among themselves."

What I am about mentioning, may be considered as of little force while standing by itself, yet when connected with so many other circumstances, it is thought worth mentioning. This nation of Pequods were a principal nation of the east, and very naturally reminds one of the similarity of the same name in Jeremiah l. 21, where the inhabitants of Pekod are particularly mentioned; and also in Ezekiel xxiii. 23. The difference in spelling one with a k, and the other with a *q*, is no uncommon thing. The Indian languages being very guttural, the k is generally used where an Englishman would use the q—but many of the first names used by the English in an early day have been corrected. Sir Walter Raleigh says his "first landing in America was at Roanor, which afterwards was found to be called by the Indians, Roanoke. Another trifling observation in itself, yet will add to the presumption already mentioned, is the original name of a point of land on the western part of the Euxine or Black Sea, mentioned by D'Anville, *Nagara.* This is the Abydos of the Greeks, 1 D'Anville, 287, and is much the same with the point in Lake Ontario, in New-York state, well known by the Indian name *Niagara.*

But if this character of the Indians, as originally being kind and hospitable, should be doubted, as I know it will be by many, who think themselves well acquainted with them, from being with the present race around our settlements; let us go back and hear what idea Christopher Columbus formed of them in the very beginning of our knowledge of them. He must be the very best witness that can be produced on this subject. In his account, sent to his royal master and mistress, of the inhabitants, on his first landing in America, he says, "I swear to your majesties, that there is not a better people in the world than these; more affectionate, affable, or mild. They love their neighbours as themselves. Their language is the sweetest, the softest and most cheerful, for they always speaking smiling." In another instance, a venerable old man approached Columbus with great reverence, and presented him with a basket of fruit, and said, "you are come into these countries, with a force against which, were we inclined to resist, resistance would be folly. We are all therefore at your mercy. But if you are men subject to mortality like ourselves, you cannot be unapprised, that after this life, there is another, wherein a very different portion is allotted to good and bad men. If therefore, you expect to die, and believe with us, that every one is to be rewarded in a future state, according to his conduct in the present, you will do no hurt to those who do none to you."—Edwards' West-Indies, 1 vol. 72.

De las Casas, bishop of Chapia, who spent much time and labour among the Indians of New Spain, trying to serve them, says, "I was one of the first who went to America. Neither curiosity, nor interest prompted me to undertake so long and dangerous a voyage. The saving the souls of the heathen was my sole object. Why was I not permitted, even at the expense of my blood, to ransom so many thousands of souls, who fell unhappy victims to avarice and lust. It was said that barbarous executions were necessary to punish or check the rebellion of the Americans. But to whom was this owing? Did not this people receive the Spaniards, who first came among them, with gentleness and humanity? Did they not shew more joy in proportion, in lavishing treasure upon them, than the Spaniards did greediness in receiving it. But our avarice was not yet satisfied. Though they gave up to us their lands and their riches, we would take from them their wives, their children and their liberty. To blacken the characters of these unhappy people, their enemies assert that they are scarce human creatures. But it is *we* who ought to blush for having been less men, and more barbarous than they. They are represented as a stupid people, and addicted to vice. But have they not contracted most of their vices from the examples of christians. But it must be granted that the Indians still remain untainted with many vices usual among Europeans. Such as ambition, blasphemy, swearing, treachery, and many such monsters, which have not yet taken place among them. They have scarce an idea of them. All nations are equally free. One nation has no right to infringe on the freedom of another. Let us do to these people, as we would have them have done to us, on a change of circumstances. What a strange method is this of propagating the gospel; that holy law of grace, which, from being slaves to Satan, initiates us into the freedom of the children of God."

The Abbe Clavigero, another Spanish writer, confirms this idea of the South-Americans. "We have had intimate converse, says he, with the Americans; have lived some years in a seminary destined for their instruction—attentively observed their character—their genius—their disposition and manner of thinking; and have besides, examined with the utmost diligence, their ancient history—their religion—their government—their laws and their customs. After such long experience and study of them, we declare, that the mental qualities of the Americans are not in the least inferior to those of the Europeans."

Among the many instances of provocation given to them by the white people, Neal, in his History of New-England, page 21, says, "one *Hunt*, an early trader with the Indians of New-England, after a prosperous trade with the natives, enticed between twenty and thirty of them on board his vessel, and contrary to the public faith, clapped them under hatches, and took them to Malaga, and sold them to the Spaniards. This the remaining Indians resented, by revenging themselves on the next English vessel that came on their coast."

In the year 1620, a sermon was preached at Plymouth by the Rev. Mr. Cushman, from which the following extract is taken, relative to the treatment they received from the natives. "The Indians are said to be the most cruel and treacherous people in all these parts, even like lions, *but to us* they have been like lambs, so kind, so submissive and trusty, as a man may truly say, many christians are not so kind or sincere. Though when we came first into this country we were few, and many of us very sick, and many died by reason of the cold and wet, it being the depth of winter, and we having no houses or shelter, yet when there were not six able persons among us, and the Indians came daily to us by hundreds, with their sachems or kings, and might in one hour have made despatch of us; yet such fear was upon them, as that they never offered us the least injury in word or deed. And by reason of one *Tisquanto*, that lives among us, and can speak English, we have daily commerce with their kings, and can know what is done or intended towards us among the savages."

The late governor Hutchinson, in his history of New-England, observes, "that the natives shewed courtesy to the English at their first arrival; were hospitable, and made such as would eat their food, welcome to it, and readily instructed them in planting and cultivating the Indian corn. Some of the English who lost themselves in the woods, and must otherwise have perished with famine, they relieved and conducted home."

Mr. Penn, also, at his first coming amongst them, spoke and wrote of them in high terms, as a kind and benevolent people.

The history of New-Jersey informs us, that "for near a century, the Indians of that state had all along maintained an intercourse of great cordiality and friendship with the inhabitants, being interspersed among them, and frequently receiving meat at their houses, and other marks of their good will and esteem."—Smith, page 440.

Father Charlevoix, who travelled early, and for a long time among the Indians, from Quebec to New-Orleans, and had great opportunities, which he made it his business and study to improve, tells us, speaking of the real character of the Indian nations, "that with a mien and appearance altogether savage; and with manners and customs which favour the greatest barbarity, they enjoy all the advantages of society. At first view, one would imagine them without form of government, laws or subordination, and subject to the wildest caprice. Nevertheless, they rarely deviate from certain maxims and usages, founded on good sense alone, which holds the place of law, and supplies in some sort, the want of legal authority. They manifest much stability in the engagements they have solemnly entered upon; patience in affliction, as well as submission to what they apprehend to be the appointment of Providence; in all this they manifest a nobleness of soul and constancy of mind, at which we rarely arrive, with all our philosophy and religion. They are neither slaves to ambition nor interest, the two passions that have so much weakened in us the sentiments of humanity, (which the kind author of nature has engraven on the human heart) and kindled those of covetousness, which are as yet generally unknown among them."

It is notorious, that they are generally kinder to us, though they despise us, than we are to them. There is scarce an instance occurs, but that they treat every white man who goes among them, with respect, which is not the case from us to them. The same author says, "the nearer view we take of our savages, the more we discover in them some valuable qualities. The chief part of the principles by which they regulate their conduct; the general maxims by which they govern themselves; and the bottom of their characters have nothing which appears barbarous. The ideas, though now quite confused, which they have retained of a first Being; the traces, though almost effaced, of a religious worship, which they appear formerly to have rendered to the Supreme Deity, and the faint marks which we observe, even in their most indifferent actions, of the ancient belief, and the primitive religion, may bring them more easily than we think of, into the way of truth, and make their conversion to christianity more easily to be effected, than that of more civilized nations."

But what surprises exceedingly, in men whose whole outward appearance proclaims nothing but barbarity, is, to see them behave to each other, with such kindness and regard, that are not to be found among the most civilized nations. Doubtless this proceeds, in some measure, from the words *mine* and *thine*, being as yet unknown to these savages. We are equally charmed with that natural and unaffected gravity, which reigns in all their behaviour, in all their actions, and in the greatest part of their diversions. Also with the civility and deference they shew to their equals, and the respect of young people to the aged. And lastly, never to see them quarrel among themselves, with those indecent expressions, oaths and curses, so common among us; all which are proofs of good sense and a great command of temper.* In short, to make a brief portrait of these people, with a savage appearance, manners and customs, which are entirely barbarous, there is observable among them, a social kindness, free from almost all the imperfections which so often disturb the peace of society among us. They appear to be without passion; but they do that in cold blood, and some times through principle, which the most violent and unbridled passion produces in those who give no ear to reason. They seem to lead the most wretched life in the world; and yet they were, perhaps, the only happy people on earth, before the knowledge of the objects which so work upon and seduce us, had excited in them, desires which ignorance kept in supineness; but which have not as yet (in 1730) made any great ravages among them. We discover in them a mixture of the fiercest and most gentle manners. The imperfections of wild beasts, and

* Le Page Du Pratz, says, "I have studied these Indians a considerable number of years, and I never could learn that there ever were any disputes or boxing matches among either the boys or men. 2 vol. 165.

the virtues and qualities of the heart and mind which do the greatest honour to human nature.

Du Pratz, in his history of Louisiana, says, "that upon an acquaintance with the Indians, he was convinced that it was wrong to denominate them savages, as they are capable of making good use of their reason, and their sentiments are just. That they have a degree of prudence, faithfulness and generosity, exceeding that of nations who would be offended at being compared with them. No people, says he, are more hospitable and free than the Indians. Hence they may be esteemed a happy people, if that happiness was not impeded by their passionate fondness for spirituous liquors, and the foolish notion they hold, in common with many professing christians, of gaining reputation and esteem by their prowess in war." But to whom do they owe their uncommon attachment to both these evils? Is it not to the white people who came to them with destruction in each hand, while we did but deceive ourselves, with the vain notion, that we were bringing the glad tidings of salvation to them. Instead of this, we have possessed these unoffending people with so horrid an idea of our principles, that among themselves they call us *the accursed people.* And their great numbers, when first discovered, shew that they had, comparatively, but few wars before we came among them.

Mr. William Bartram, a gentleman well known in the state of Pennsylvania, son to the late John Bartram, Esq. so long Botanist to Queen Caroline, of England, before the revolution, in the journal of his travels through the Creek country, speaking of the Siminoles or lower Creek nation, and of their being then few in number, says, "yet this handful of people possess a vast territory, all East Florida and the greatest part of West Florida, which being naturally cut and divided into thousands of islets, knolls and eminences, by the innumerable rivers, lakes, swamps, savannas and ponds, form so many secure retreats and temporary dwelling places, that effectually guard them from any sudden invasion or attacks from their enemies. And being such a swampy, hammoky country, furnishes such a plenty and variety of supplies for the nourishment of every sort of animal, that I can venture to assert, that no part of the globe so abounds with wild game or creatures fit for the food of man. Thus they enjoy a superabundance of the necessaries and conveniences of life with the security of person and property, the two great concerns of mankind. They seem to be free from want or desires. No cruel enemy to dread; nothing to give them disquietude but the gradual encroachments of the white people. Thus contented and undisturbed, they appear as blithe and free as the birds of the air, and like them as volatile and active, tuneful and vociferous. The visage, action and deportment of a Siminole; being the most striking picture of happiness in this life—Joy, contentment, love and friendship without guile or affectation, seem inherent in them, or predominate in their vital principle, for it leaves them but with the last breath of life."

To exemplify their kindness to strangers, he says, that having lost his way in travelling through their towns, he was at a stand how to proceed, when he observed an Indian man at the door of his habitation, beckoning to him, to come to him. Bartram accordingly rode up to him. He cheerfully welcomed him to his house, took care of his horse, and with the most graceful air of respect led him into an airy, cool apartment, where being seated on cabins, his women brought in a refreshing repast, with a pleasant cooling liquor to drink. Then pipes and tobacco. After an hour's conversation, and Mr. Bartram informing him of his business, and where he was bound, but having lost his way, he did not know how to go on. The Indian cheerfully replied, that he was pleased that Mr. B. was come into their country, where he should meet with friendship and protection; and that he would himself lead him into the right path. He turned out to be the prince or chief of Whatoga. How long would an Indian have rode through our country, before he would have received such kindness from a common farmer, much less a chief magistrate of a country? Mr. Bartram adds to the testimony of Father Charlevoix, in favour of their good characters among themselves. He says they are just, honest, liberal and hospitable to strangers; considerate, loving and affectionate to their wives and relations; fond of their children; frugal and persevering; charitable and forbearing. He was weeks and months among them in their towns, and never observed the least sign of contention or wrangling; never saw an instance of an Indian beating his wife, or even reproving her in anger.

Col. John Smith says, "when we had plenty of green corn and roasting ears, the hunters became lazy, and spent their time in singing and dancing. They appeared to be fulfilling the scriptures, beyond many of those who profess to believe them, in that of taking no thought for to-morrow, but in living in love, peace and friendship, without disputes. In this last respect they are an example to those who profess christianity—page 29.

The first and most cogent article in all their *late* treaties with the white people is, "that there shall not be any kind of spirituous liquors brought or sold in their towns; and the traders are allowed but ten gallons for a company, which are esteemed sufficient to serve them on their journey; and if any of this remains on their arrival, they must spill it on the ground." Mr B. met two young traders running about forty kegs of Jamaica spirits into the nation. They were discovered by a party of Creeks, who immediately struck their tomahawks into every keg, and let the liquor run out, without drinking a drop of it. Here was an instance of self denial, seldom equalled by white men, for so fond are they of it, that had they indulged themselves with tasting it, nothing could have prevented them from drinking the whole of it. Mr. B. saw a young Indian who was present at a scene of mad intemperance and folly, acted by some white men in the town. He clapped his hand to his breast, and with a smile looking up, as if struck with astonishment, and wrapt in love and adoration of the Deity, lamented their conduct.

We have thus endeavored to give some ideas of the Indian character, at the first arrival of the Europeans among them, before they were debauched and demoralized by an acquaintance with those who pretend to be their benefactors, by communicating to them the glad tidings of salvation, through Jesus Christ. We have exhibited the testimony of the best writers, from various parts of the continent, acquainted with very different nations, from the south to the north. It is given generally in the authors own words, lest we might be charged with misrepresenting their meaning, by adopting our own language, or putting a gloss on theirs; and our design has been, that the reader may be made acquainted with the people of whom we treat. We must confess, that we have given the fairest part of their character, while at home and among their friends, though a perfectly just one.

The objects which engage their attention, and indeed their whole souls, are war and hunting. Their haughty tempers will not condescend to labour—this they leave to their women. Hence they put on rather a solemn character, except when they divert themselves with their principal amusements, dancing and gaming. But in war, and while opposing the enemies of their nation, they are cruel and revengeful. They make war with unrelenting fury, on the least unatoned affront, equal to any European nation whatever. It is their custom and long continued habit. They kill and destroy their own species without regret. The warrior is the highest object of their ambition. They are bitter in their enmity, and to avenge the blood of a kinsman, they will travel hundreds of miles, and keep their anger for years, till they are satisfied.* They scalp all the slain of their enemies (as many of the Asiatics did) that they get in their power, contrary to the usage of all other savages.† They usually attack their enemies with a most hedious and dreadful yelling, so as to make the woods to ring. Very few of the ablest troops in the world can withstand the horror of it, who are strangers to them, and have not before been acquainted with this kind of reception. They are kind to women and children whom they take

* The murderer shall surely be put to death. The avenger of blood, himself, shall slay the murderer; when he meeteth him, he shall slay him.—Numbers xxxv. 18, 19.

† David speaks of the hoary scalps of his enemies.

prisoners, and are remarkable for their delicacy, in their treatment of the first. To such prisoners as they, by certain rules, doom to death, they are insultingly cruel and ferocious beyond imagination; and their women are most ingenious and artful in the science of tormenting. All this is mutual, and it is distressing to say, with truth, that it is too much like the practice of those who call themselves a more enlightened people. Had the Indians read Lucan's Pharsalia—lib. iii. 400, which contains the description of the Massilian Grove of the Gallic Druids, wherein they would have found every tree reeking with the blood of human victims—or had they been acquainted with the British Druids, "who indeed seem to have exceeded, if possible, their heathen neighbours, in savage ferocity and boundless lust of sacrificial blood, they would have, indeed, been able to settle accounts with their white neighbours. The page of history trembles to relate the baleful orgies of the Druids, which their frantic superstition celebrated, when enclosing men, women and children, in one vast wicker image, in the form of a man, and filling it with every kind of combustible, they set fire to the huge colossus. While the dreadful holocaust was offering to their sanguinary gods, the groans and shrieks of the consuming victims were drowned amidst shouts of barbarous triumph, and the air was rent with the wild dissonance of martial music."—1 vol. of Indian Antiquities. Or had the Indians read of the emperor Maximinian putting to death the Theban legion of six thousand, six hundred and sixty-six christian soldiers, who had served him faithfully, because they refused to do sacrifice to the heathen gods, and persecute their brother christians—Caves primitive christ. 331—or had they been acquainted with the tortures of the martyrs for Christ, for many centuries—or the European practice of burning heretics*—or had they heard of the Waldenses and Albigenses—of St. Bartholomews night, or the Irish massacre. They might be ignorant of the bloody torments of the Inquisition, the tortures of Amboyna, or of a French Republican Baptism—or they may never have been informed of the district of La Vendee—of the Convent of Carmes, or of the proceedings in France on the 12th August—or of the more than diabolical, cowardly murder, by the enlightened citizens of Pennsylvania, from the county of Washington, when a whole town of christian Indians, consisting of about ninety souls, men, women and children, were butchered in cold blood, at Muskingum, in the year 1783; and who had been our tried friends during the whole revolutionary war. If the Indians had known these facts, and written the history of the civilized white people, they might have roused the feelings of a tender conscience in their favour. But whoever reads the history of the eulogized heroes of ancient days, will find them not much better, in this respect. Does Achille's behaviour to Hector's dead body, appear less savage or revengeful? Do the Carthagenians or Phœnicians, burning their own children alive in sacrifice, or the bloody massacres and tortures of the southern Indians, by the learned and civilized Spaniards, claim any great preference in point of humanity and the finer feelings of the enlightened sons of science, and of the pretenders to religious knowledge.

* Will any one again laugh at the strong observation of an eminent divine, 'that man in a state of nature, was half devil and half brute'—Clarkes' Com. 131. Who will not adore the God of heaven with gratitude and thanksgiving, for the light of the gospel, which has not only brought life and immortality to light, but wrought so wonderful a change among the present nations of the earth.

But let us come nearer home. Who set them the example of cruelty and barbarity, even to those whom they invaded and plundered of their property—deprived of their lands, and rendered their whole country a scene of horror, confusion and distress. Wynne, in his history of America, tells us, "that the New-England people, in an early day, as we have already seen, made an attack upon the Pequod Indians, and drove eight hundred of them, with about two hundred of their women and children, into a swamp—a fog arising, the men escaped, except a few, who were either killed or wounded. But the helpless women and children were obliged to surrender at discretion. The sachem's wife, who some time before, had rescued the Weathersfield maidens, and returned them home, was among them. She made two requests, which arose from a tenderness and virtue not common among savages. 1st. That her chastity might remain unviolated. 2d. That her children might not be taken from her. The amiable sweetness of her countenance, and the modest dignity of her deportment, were worthy of the character she supported for innocence and justice, and were sufficient to shew the Europeans, that even barbarous nations, sometimes produce instances of heroic virtue. It is not said by the historian, whether her requests were granted or not, but that the women and children were dispersed through the neighbouring colonies, the male infants excepted, who were sent to the Bermudas"—1 vol. 66. Indeed, had the Indians, on their part, been able to answer in writing, they might have formed a contrast between themselves and their mortal enemies, the civilized subjects of Great-Britain. They might have recapitulated their conduct in the persecution of *Indians, witches* and *quakers* in

New-England—*Indians* and *Negroes* in New-York, and the cruelty with which the aborigines were treated in Virginia.

These invaders of a country, (in the peaceable possession of a free and happy people, entirely independent, as the deer of of the forests) made war upon them, with all the advantage of fire-arms and the military knowledge of Europe, in the most barbarous manner—not observing any rules of nations, or the principles of modern warfare, much less the benign injunctions of the gospel. They soon taught the Indians by their fatal examples, to retaliate with the most inveterate malice and diabolical cruelty. The civilized Europeans, though flying from the persecution of the old world, did not hesitate to deny their professed religion of peace and good will to men, by murdering men, women and children—selling captives as slaves—cutting off the heads, and quartering the bodies of those who were killed, nobly fighting for their liberty and their country, in self defence, and setting them up at various places, in ignoble triumph at their success. Philip, an independent sovereign of the Pequods, who disdained to submit, but died fighting at the head of his men, had his head cut off and carried on a pole with great rejoicings, to New-Plymouth, where, Wynne says, his skull is to be seen to this day.—Vide 1 vol. 106 to 108.

This conduct produced greater violence and barbarity on the part of the other nations of Indians in the neighbourhood, often joined by French Europeans who acted, at times, worse than the native Indians, and by this means, a total disregard of promises and pledged faith on both sides, became common. Ibid. 124—6.

I do not quote these instances of inhuman conduct to justify the Indians, but only to shew that they were not the only savages, and that the blame, as is too common, ought not to fall all on one side, because they were vanquished, but should produce some commiseration and principles of christian benevolence towards these highly injured and suffering sons of the wilderness. In the beginning of the revolutionary war, the Americans were constantly styled by their invaders as rebels; and had we been conquered, I have little doubt but that we should have been treated much as the Indians have been, with the difference of having been hanged, instead of being scalped and beheaded. But as we proved successful, by the good providence of God, we are now glorious asserters of liberty and the freedom of man.

The conduct of the Israelites themselves, while in a state of civilization, and under the government of a king, and with the prophets of God to direct and teach them, did not discover a much better spirit than these supposed Israelites, wretched and forlorn, in the wilderness of America, have done. "When Ahaz, king of Judah, had sinned against God, he delivered him into the hand of the king of Assyria; and he was also delivered into the hand of Pekah, king of Israel, who smote him with a great slaughter, and slew in Judah one hundred and twenty thousand in one day, who were all valiant men—2 Chron. xxviii. 5. And the children of Israel carried away captive, of their brethren, two hundred thousand women, sons and daughters; took also much spoil from them, and brought the spoil to Samaria. But a prophet of the Lord was there, whose name was *Oded,* and he went out before the host that came into Samaria, and said unto them, "behold, because the

Lord God of your fathers was wroth with Judah, and hath delivered them into your hands, and ye have slain them in a rage, that reacheth up to heaven—And now ye purpose to keep under the children of Judah and Jerusalem, for bond-men and bond-women unto you; but are these not with you, even with you, sins against the Lord your God? Now hear me, therefore, and deliver the captives again, which ye have taken captive of your brethren; for the fierce wrath of the Lord is upon you."

Here we cannot have the same hopes of tracing the present practices of the natives of the woods to any certain source, as is in the case of their languages. When a people change from a settled, to a wandering state, especially, if thereby they be totally removed from any connection or intercourse with civilized countries, they must necessarily accommodate their actions to their then pressing wants and necessities.

Their practices must change with their circumstances. Not so their language; for although it may greatly alter, and often degenerate for want of cultivation, or by separating into parties, far removed from each other; yet the roots and principles of the language, may in remote ages, be traced in the different dialects, so as to afford tolerable proof of the original language.

If a people, before their emigration, had any knowledge of the arts and sciences, although this might, and indeed would lead them, even in a wandering state, to discover more ingenuity and method in providing for their wants, yet in after ages, as they separated from each other and colonized into distant parts, they would loose this knowledge, and finally, know nothing of them but by tradition, except so far as should fall within their means and absolute wants; which in the first case must be few, and in the other many and pressing. So that we may reasonably conclude, that the first wanderers would leave much greater evidence of their original, as well as of their knowledge of the mechanical arts, than their posterity could possibly do. And further, that the nearer to the place of their first permanent settlement, the greater would be the remains of those arts.

However, we will endeavour to search into, and enumerate those few customs that we have any account of, which prevailed with them when the Europeans first arrived among them, and some of which they still retain.

We do not mean to take up the silly and ridiculous stories published by many writers on this subject, who either had particular, and often wicked ends to answer by their publications, or they founded their narratives on information received on the most transient acquaintance of a few hours, with the vicious and worthless among the Indians along our frontiers; nor shall we trust to accounts related by ignorant traders, who did not comprehend either the idiom of their language, or the strong metaphorical and figurative mode of expressing themselves. This has led to the most false and absurd accounts of both Indian manners and language. To give one instance of this, though among the best of them, the following fact is extracted from an account given of the Mohawks in 1664, by a reverend gentleman who ought to have known better, and must have had an education, and known the principles of grammar. "This nation, says he, has a very heavy language, and I find great difficulty in learning it, so as to speak and preach to them fluently. There are no christians who understand their language thoroughly. When I am among them, I ask them how things are called. One will tell me a word in the infinitive mood, another in the indicative. One in the first, another in the second person. One in the present, another in the preterperfect tense; so that I stand sometimes and look; but do not know how to put it down. And as they have their declensions and conjugations, so they have their increases, like the Greeks; and I am sometimes, as if I was distracted, and cannot tell what to do, and there is no person to set me right. I asked the commissary of the (Dutch West-India company) what this meant, and he answered he did not know, but imagined they changed their language every two or three years." He had been connected with them twenty years.

The Indians are perfect republicans, they will admit of no inequality among them but what arises from age, or great qualifications for either council or war. Although this is the case in peace, yet in war they observe great discipline, and perfect subordination to their beloved man who carries the holy ark, and to their officers, who are appointed on account of the experience they have had of their prowess in war, and good conduct in the management and surprising of an enemy, or saving their men by a timely retreat; but this subordination ends with the campaign.

As the Israelites were divided into tribes, and had a chief over them, and always marched under ensigns of some animal peculiar to each tribe, so the Indian nations are universally divided into tribes, under a sachem or king, chosen by the people from the wisest and bravest among them. He has neither influence or distinction, but from his wisdom and prudence. He is assisted by a council of *old, wise and beloved men,* as they call their priests and councillors. Nothing is determined (of a public nature) but in this council, where every one has an equal voice. The chief or sachem, sits in the middle, and the council on each hand, forming a semi-circle, as the high priest of the Jews did in the Sanhedrim of that nation.

Mr. Penn, when he first arrived in Pennsylvania, in the year 1683, and made a treaty with them, makes the following observations, in a letter he then wrote to his friends in England. "Every king has his council, and that consists of all the old and wise men of his nation, which perhaps are two hundred people. Nothing of moment is undertaken, be it war, peace, selling of land, or traffic, without advising with them. 'Tis admirable to consider how powerful the chiefs are, and yet how they move by the breath of the people. I have had occasion to be in council with them upon treaties for land, and to adjust the terms of trade. Their order is thus; the king sits in the middle of an half moon, and hath his council, the old and the wise on each hand. Behind them, at a little distance, sit the young fry, in the same figure. Having consulted and resolved their business, the king ordered one of them to speak to me. He came to me, and in the name of his king, saluted me. Then took me by the hand, and told me that he was ordered by his king to speak to me; and that now it was not he, but the king who spoke, because what he should say was the king's mind. During the time this person was speaking, not a man of them was observed to whisper or smile. The old were grave—the young reverend in their deportment. They spoke little, but fervently and with elegance. He will deserve the name of *wise*, who out-wits them in any treaty about a thing they understand. At every sentence they shout, and say amen, in their way."

Mr. Smith, in his history of New-Jersey, confirms this general statement. "They are grave even to sadness, upon any common, and more so upon serious occasions—observant of those in company, and respectful to the aged—of a temper cool and deliberate—never in haste to speak, but wait, for a certainty, that the person who spake before them, had finishished all he had to say. They seemed to hold European vivacity in contempt, because they found such as came among them, apt to interrupt each other, and frequently speak altogether. Their behaviour in public councils was strictly decent and instructive. Every one in his turn, was heard, according to rank of years or wisdom, or services to his country. Not a word, whisper or murmur, was heard while any one spoke: no interruption to commend or condemn: the younger sort were totally silent. Those denominated kings, were sachems distinguished by their wisdom and good conduct. The respect paid them was voluntary, and not exacted or looked for, nor the omission regarded. The sachems directed in their councils, and had the chief disposition of their lands"—page 142, 144.

Every nation of Indians have certain customs, which they observe in their public transactions with other nations, and in their private affairs among themselves, which it is scandalous for any one among them not to observe. And these always draw after them, either public or private resentment, when ever they are broken. Although these customs may, in their detail, differ in one nation, when compared with another; yet it is easy to discern that they have all had one origin. This is also apparent from every nation understanding them. Mr. Colden says "their great men, both sachems and captains, are generally poorer than the common people; for they affect to give away, and distribute all the presents or plunder they get in their treaties, or in war, so as to leave nothing to themselves. There is not a man in the ministry of the Five Nations (of whom Mr. Colden was writing) who has gained his office otherwise than by merit. There is not the least salary, or any sort of profit annexed to any office, to tempt the covetous or the sordid; but on the contrary, every unworthy action is unavoidably attended with the forfeiture of their commission; for their authority is only the esteem of the people, and ceases the moment that esteem is lost. An old Mohawk sachem, in a poor blanket and a dirty shirt, may be seen issuing his orders, with as arbitrary an authority as a Roman dictator."

As every nation, as before observed, has its peculiar standard or symbol, as an eagle, a bear, a wolf or an otter, so has each tribe the like badge, from which it is denominated. When they encamp, on a march, they always cut the representation of their ensign or symbol, on the trees, by which it may be known who have been there. The sachem of each tribe is a necessary party in all conveyances and treaties, to which he affixes the mark of his tribe, as a corporation does that of the public seal.

If you go from nation to nation, you will not find one who doth not lineally distinguish himself by his respective family. As the family or tribe of the *eagle, panther,* (which is their lion) *tyger, buffalo,* (their ox or bull)—and also the *bear, deer, racoon*, &c. &c. So among the Jews, was the *lion* of the tribe of *Judah*—*Dan* was known by a *serpent*—*Issachar* by an *ass*, and *Benjamin* by a *wolf*. But the Indians, as the Jews, pay no religious respect for any of these animals, or for any other whatever.

They reckon time after the manner of the Hebrews. They divide the year into spring, summer, autumn, or the falling of the leaf, and winter. Korah is their word for winter with the Cherokee Indians, as it is with the Hebrews. They number the years by any of these four periods, for they have no name for a year. And they subdivide these, and count the year by lunar months, or moons, like the Israelites, who also counted by moons. They call the sun and moon by the same word, with the addition of day and night, as the day sun, or moon—the night sun, or moon. They count the day by three sensible differences of the sun, like the Hebrews—as the sun coming out—mid-day, and the sun is dead, or sunset. Midnight is half way between the sun going in and coming out of the water—also by mid-night and cock-crowing. They begin their ecclesiastical year at the first appearance of the first new moon of the vernal equinox, according to the ecclesiastical year of Moses. They pay great regard to the first appearance of every new moon. They name the various seasons of the year from the planting and ripening of the fruits. The green eared moon is the most beloved or sacred, when the first fruits become sanctified, by being annually offered up; and from this period they count their beloved or holy things.

The number, and regular periods of the Indian public religious feasts, (as will be seen hereafter) is a good historical proof that they counted time, and observed a weekly Sabbath, long after their arrival on the American continent, as this is applicable to all the nations. Till the seventy years captivity commenced, according to Dr. Prideaux, the Israelites had only numeral names for the solar and lunar months, except two called Abib and Ethanaim. The former signifies a green ear of corn, and the latter robust and valiant. And by the first name the Indians term their passover, as an explicative, and which the trading people call the green corn-dance. These two months were equinoctial. *Abib,* or the present *Nisan* of the Jews, was the sixth month of the civil, and first of the ecclesiastical year, answering to our March or April; and Ethanaim, which began the civil year, was the sixth of the ecclesiastical, the same as our September and October.

Mr. Bartram says, while he was at Attasse, in the Creek nation, on a Sabbath day, he observed a great solemnity in the town, and a remarkable silence and retiredness of the red inhabitants. Few of them were to be seen—the doors of their dwellings were shut, and if a child chanced to stray out, it was quickly drawn in doors again. He asked the meaning of this, and was immediately answered, that it being the white people's sabbath, the Indians kept it religiously sacred to the great spirit. The writer of this being present on the Lord's day, at the worship of seven different nations, who happened (accidentally) to be at the seat of government together, he was pleased to see their orderly conduct. They were addressed by an old sachem, apparently with great energy and address. An interpreter being present, he asked him to explain what the speaker had said. The intrepreter answered that the substance of what he delivered, was a warm representation to his audience, of the love the great spirit had always manifested towards the Indians, more than to any other people. That they were in a special manner, under his government and immediate direction. That it was, therefore, the least return they could make for so much goodness, gratefully to acknowledge his favour, and to be obedient to his laws—to do his will, and to avoid every thing that was evil, and of course displeasing to him.

Just before the service began, the writer of this observed an Indian standing at the window with the intrepreter, looking into a small field adjoining the house, where a great many white children were playing with the Indian children, and making a considerable noise. The Indian spoke much in earnest, and seemed rather displeased. The interpreter answered him with great apparent interest. On being asked the subject of their conversation, he said the Indian was lamenting the sad state of those white children, whom he called poor destitute orphans. The interpreter asked why he thought them orphans? For he believed it was not true. The Indian, with great earnestness, replied, is not this the day on which you told me the white people worshipped the great spirit? If so, surely these children, if they had parents, or any persons to take care of them, would not be suffered to be out there, playing and making such a noise. No! no! they have lost their fathers and their mothers, and have no one to take care of them.

When the Indians travel, they always count the time by sleeps, which is a very ancient custom, and perhaps may have been derived from the Mosaic method of counting time, making the evening and the morning to be the first day, &c.

They have also an ancient custom of setting apart certain houses and towns, as places of refuge, to which a criminal, and even a captive may fly, and be safe from the avenger of blood, if he can but enter it.

Mr. Bartram says, "we arrived at the Apalachuela town, in the Creek nation. This is esteemed the mother town, sacred to peace. No captives are put to death, or human blood spilt here."

The Cherokees, according to Adair, though now exceedingly corrupt, still observe the law of refuge, so inviolably, that they allow their beloved town the privilege of protecting a wilful murderer; but they seldom allow him to return home from it in safety.

The town of refuge called *Choate*, is situate on a large stream of the Missisippi, five miles above where fort Loudon formerly stood. Here some years ago, a brave Englishman was protected, after killing an Indian warrior, in defence of his property. He told Adair, that after some months stay there, he intended returning to his house in the neighbourhood; but the chiefs told him it would prove fatal to him. So he was obliged to continue there, till he satisfied the friends of the deceased, by presents to their full satisfaction. In the upper country of the *Muskoge*, there was an old beloved town called *Koosah*, now reduced to a small ruinous village, which is still a place of safety for those who kill undesignedly.

In almost every Indian nation, there are several peaceable towns, which are called old beloved, holy or white towns. They seem to have been formerly towns of refuge, for it is not within the memory of their oldest people, that ever human blood was shed in them; although they often force persons from them, and put them to death elsewhere.

It may be thought improper here, to say much of the war-like abilities and military knowledge of the Indians, as it is very popular, especially with Europeans, to despise them as warriors, by which means thousands of Europeans and Americans have lost their lives. But as it may shew that they are not quite so ignorant as strangers to them have thought them, a short account of their military conduct, may illucidate our general subject.

I am assisted by col. Smith, who lived long with them, and often fought against them, in what may be said on this occasion.

However despised, they are, perhaps, as well versed in the art of that kind of war, calculated for their circumstances, and are as strict disciplinarians in it, as any troops in Europe; and whenever opposed by not more than two or three to one Indian, they have been generally victorious, or come off with small loss, while they have made their opponents repent their rashness and ignorance of war on their plan. And indeed, they were always victorious over European troops, till sad experience taught foreign officers to pay more respect to the advice of American officers, who, by adopting the Indian principles of war, knew how to meet them with advantage. It is not sufficient for an army to be well disciplined on their own principles, without considering those of the enemy they are to contend with. Braddock, Boquet, and several others of great celebrity in their own country, have been defeated or surprised, by a (comparatively) small number of these inhabitants of the wilderness, and greatly suffered from despising what they thought untutored savages; and to save the honor and military character of those who commanded, have been led to give very false reports of the combats. The following facts will give force to these observations—

"In col. Boquet's last campaign of 1764, I saw, (says col. Smith) the official return made by the British officers, of the number of Indians that were in arms against us in that year, which amounted to thirty thousand. As I was then a lieutenant in the British service, I told them I was of opinion, that there were not above one thousand in arms against us, as they were divided by Broadstreet's army, being then at Lake Erie. The British officers hooted at me, and said that they could not make England sensible of the difficulties they laboured under in fighting them; and it was expected that their troops could fight the undisciplined savages in America, five to one, as they did the East-Indians, and therefore my report would not answer their purpose, as they could not give an honorable account of the war, but by augmenting their numbers."

Smith was of the opinion, that from Braddock's defeat, until the time of his writing, there never were more than three thousand Indians, at any time in arms against us, west of Fort Pitt, and frequently not more than half of that number

According to the Indians' own account, during the whole of Braddock's war, or from 1755 to 1758, they killed and took fifty of our people for one that they lost. In the war of 1763, they killed, comparatively, few of our people, and lost more of theirs, as the frontier inhabitants, especially the Virginians, had learned something of their method of war; yet even in this war, according to their account (which Smith believed to be true) they killed and took ten of our people for one they lost.

The Indians, though few in number, put the government to immense expense of blood and treasure, in the war from 1756 to 1791. The following campaigns in the western country, will be proof of this.

General Braddock's in the year 1755—col. Armstrong's against the Cattaugau town, on the Alleghany, in 1757—gen. Forbes' in 1758—gen. Stanwix's in 1759—gen. Monckton's in 1760—col. Boquet's in 1761—and again in 1763, when he fought the battle of Brushy-Run, and lost above one hundred men; but by taking the advice and assistance of the Virginia volunteers, finally drove the Indians—col. Armstrong's up the west branch of Susquehannah in the same year—gen. Broadstreet's up Lake Erie in 1764—col. Boquet's at Muskingum at the same time—lord Dunmore's in 1774—gen. M'Intosh's in 1778, and again in 1780—col. Bowman's in 1779—gen. Clark's in 1782—and against the Wabash Indians in 1786—gen. Logan's against the Shawanese in the same year, and col. Harmer's in 1790—gen. Wilkinson's in 1791—gen. St. Clair's in 1791, and gen. Wayne's in 1794, which in all are twenty-three campaigns, besides smaller expeditions, such as the French-Creek expedition, colonels Edward's, Loughrie's, &c. All these were exclusive of the numbers of men who were internally employed as scouting parties, in erecting forts, guarding stations, &c. &c.

When we take the foregoing account into consideration, may we not reasonably conclude, that the Indians are the best disciplined troops in the world, especially when we consider, that the ammunition and arms that they are obliged to use, are of the worst sort, without bayonets or cartouch boxes. No artificial means of carrying either baggage or provision, while their enemies have every warlike implement, and other resources, to the utmost of their desire. Is not that the best discipline, that has the greatest tendency to annoy an enemy, and save their own men? It is apprehended that the Indian discipline is better calculated to answer their purpose in the woods of America, than the British discipline in the plains of Flanders. British discipline, in the woods, is the way to have men slaughtered, with scarcely any chance to defend themselves.

Privates.

The Indians sum up their art of war thus—"The business of the private warrior is to be under command, or punctually to obey orders—to learn to march a-breast in scattered order, so as to be in readiness to surround the enemy, or to prevent being surrounded—to be good marksmen, and active in the use of their musket or rifle—to practice running—to learn to endure hunger or hardships with patience and fortitude—to tell the truth at all times to their officers, more especially when sent out to spy the enemy."

Concerning Officers.

They say that it would be absurd to appoint a man to an office, whose skill and courage had never been tried—that all officers should be advanced only according to merit—that no single man should have the absolute command of an army—that a council of officers should determine when and how an attack is to be made—that it is the duty of officers to lay plans, and to take every advantage of the enemy—to ambush and surprise them, and to prevent the like to themselves. It is the duty of officers to prepare and deliver speeches to the men, in order to animate and encourage them, and on a march to prevent the men, at any time, getting into an huddle, because if the enemy should surround them in that position, they would be greatly exposed to the enemy's fire. It is likewise their business, at all times, to endeavour to annoy the enemy, and save their own men; and therefore ought never to bring on an attack without considerable advantage, or without what appeared to them to insure victory, and that with a loss of but few men. And if at any time they should be mistaken in this, and are likely to lose many men in gaining the victory, it is their duty to retreat, and wait for a better opportunity of defeating their enemy, without the danger of losing so many men." Their conduct proves that they act on these principles.

This is the statement given by those who are experimentally acquainted with them, and as long as the British officers despised both Indians and Americans, who had studied their art of war, and formed themselves on the same plan, they were constantly beaten by those soldiers of nature, though seldom one fourth of the number of the British. But the British officers had one advantage of them. That was the art of drawing up and reporting to their superiors, plans of their battles, and exaggerated accounts of their great success, and the immense loss of the Indians, which were never thought of till long after the battle was over, and often while they were smarting under their severe defeat or surprise.

The writer of this could give some instances, if it would an-answer any good end, that came under his own knowledge.

When the Indians determine on war or hunting, they have stated preparatory, religious ceremonies, for purification, particularly by fasting, as the Israelites had.

Father Charlevoix gives an account of this custom in his time. In case of an intention of going to war, he who is to command does not commence the raising of soldiers, till he has fasted several days, during which he is smeared with black—has no conversation with any one—invokes by day and night, his *tutelar spirit,* and above all, is very careful to observe his dreams. The fast being over, he assembles his friends, and with a string of wampum in his hands, he speaks to them after this manner. Brethren! the great spirit authorizes my sentiments, and inspires me with what I ought to do.* The blood of —— is not wiped away—his body is not covered, and I will acquit myself of this duty towards him," &c.

Mr. M'Kenzie in some measure, confirms this account, though among different nations. "If the tribes feel themselves called upon to go to war, the elders convene the people in order to obtain the general opinion. If it be for war, the chief publishes his intention to smoke in the sacred stem (a pipe) at a certain time. To this solemnity, meditation and fasting are required as preparatory ceremonials. When the people are thus assembled, and the meeting sanctified by the

* This shews the mistakes committed by writers who do not intimately understand the idiom of the Indian languages. Above it is said, "that the warrior invoked his tutelar spirit," but by this address, it is plain that it was the great spirit. So the translator of Charlevoix, calls a string of wampum, of which the war-belts are made, a collar of beads. Great allowance should be made for the ignorance of both travellers and writers. The secrecy of Indians, in keeping all their religious rites from the knowledge of white people, lest they should defile them by their presence, adds much to their difficulty. And Charlevoix being a religious Roman Catholic, easily slid into the idea of an attendant spirit.

custom of smoking (this may be in imitation of the smoke of the incense offered on the altar of the Jews) the chief enlarges on the causes which have called them together, and the necessity of the measures proposed on the occasion. He then invites them who are willing to follow him, to smoke out of the sacred stem, which is considered as a token of enrolment." A sacred feast then takes place, and after much ceremony, usual on the occasion, "the chief turning to the east, makes a speech to explain more fully the design of their meeting, then concludes with an acknowledgment for past mercies received, and a prayer for the continuance of them, from the master of life. He then sits down, and the whole company declare their approbation and thanks by uttering the word *Ho!*" (in a very hoarse, guttural sound, being the third syllable of the beloved name, "with an emphatic prolongation of the last letter. The chief then takes up the pipe, and holds it to the mouth of the officiating person," (like a priest of the Jews, with the incense) "who after smoking three whiffs. utters a short prayer, and then goes round with it from east to west, to every person present." The ceremony then being ended, "he returns the company thanks for their attendance, and wishes them, as well as the whole tribe, health and long life."

Do not these practices remind the reader of the many directions in the Jewish ritual, commanding the strict purification, or sanctifying individuals about to undertake great business, or to enter on important offices.

Adair, who had greater opportunities of knowing the real character of the Indians to the southward, than any man that has ever written on the subject, gives the following account. "Before the Indians go to war, they have many preparatory ceremonies of purification and fasting, like what is recorded of the Israelites. When the leader begins to beat up for volunteers, he goes three times round his dark winter house, contrary to the course of the sun, sounding the warwhoop, singing the war song, and beating a drum.* He addresses the croud, who come about him, and after much ceremony, he proceeds to whoop again for the warriors to come and join him, and sanctify themselves for success against the common enemy, according to their ancient religious law. A number soon join him in his winter house, where they live separate from all others, and purify themselves for the space of three days and three nights, exclusive of the first broken day. On each day they observe a strict fast till sunset, watching the young men very narrowly (who have not been initiated in war titles) lest unusual hunger should tempt them to violate it, to the supposed danger of all their lives in the war, by destroying the power of their purifying, beloved physic, which they drink plentifully during that time. They are such strict observers of their law of purification, and think it so essential in obtaining health and success in war, as not to allow the best beloved trader that ever lived among them, knowingly, to enter the beloved ground appropriated to the duty of being sanctified for war, much less to associate with the camp in the woods, at such a time, though he is united with them in the same war design. They oblige him to walk and encamp separately by himself, as an impure, dangerous animal, till the leader hath purified him, according to the usual time and method, with the consecrated things of the ark." With the He-

* The Indians have something in imitation of a drum, made of a wet deer skin drawn over a large gourd or frame of wood.

brews, the ark of *Berith*, (the purifier) was a small wooden chest, as has already been shewn in the first chapter, of three feet nine inches in length, and two feet three inches broad, and two feet three inches in height, and overlaid with pure gold. The Indian ark is of a very simple construction, and it is only the intention and application of it, that makes it worthy of notice, for it is made with pieces of wood, securely fastened together in the form of a square. The middle of three of the sides extend a little out, but the fourth side is flat, for the convenience of the person's back who carries it. This ark has a cover, and the whole is made impenetrably close with hickory splinters. It is about half the dimensions of the Jewish ark, and may properly be called the Hebrew ark imitated. The leader and a beloved waiter carry it by turns. In contains several consecrated vessels, made by beloved, superannuated women, and of such various antiquated forms, as would have puzzled Adam to have given significant names to each. These two carriers are purified longer than the rest, that the first may be fit to act in the religious office of a priest of war, and the other to carry the awful, sacred ark, all the while they are engaged in the act of fighting.

"And it came to pass, when the ark set forward, that Moses said, rise up Lord, and let thine enemies be scattered; and let them that hate thee, flee before thee. And when it rested he said, return O Lord unto the many thousands of Israel"—Numbers x. 35, 36. "But they presumed to go up unto the hill top; nevertheless, the ark of the covenant of the Lord and Moses, departed not out of the camp. Then the Amalekites came down and the Canaanites who dwelt on that hill, and smote them, and discomfited them even unto Hormah"—ibid xiv. 45.

"And David said unto them, ye are the chief of the fathers of the Levites; sanctify yourselves both ye and your brethren, that ye may bring up the ark of the Lord God of Israel unto the place that I have prepared for it"—1 Chron. xv. 12.

The *Hetissu*, or beloved waiter, feeds each of the warriors by an exact stated rule, giving them even the water they drink, out of his own hands, lest by intemperance they should spoil the supposed communicative power of their holy things, and occasion fatal disasters to the war camp. They never place the ark on the ground, nor sit on the bare earth, while they are carrying it against the enemy. On hilly ground, where stones are plenty, they place it on them; but on land, where stones are not to be had, they use short logs, always resting themselves in like manner. The former is a strong imitation of the pedestal on which the Jewish ark was placed, a stone rising three fingers breadth above the floor. They have as strong faith in the power and holiness of their ark, as ever the Israelites had of theirs, ascribing the superior success of the party to their stricter adherence to the law, than the other. This ark is deemed so sacred and dangerous to be touched, either by their own sanctified warriors, or the spoiling enemy, that they will not touch it on any account. It is not to be meddled with by any but the war chieftain and his waiter, who are consecrated for the purpose, under the penalty of incurring great evil. Nor would the most inveterate enemy among their nations, touch it in the woods for the same reason, which is agreeable to the religious opinion and customs of the Hebrews, respecting the sacredness of their ark, as in the case of Uzzah and the Philistines.

A gentleman who was at the Ohio in the year 1756, assured the writer that he saw a stranger there, very importunate to view the inside of the Cherokee ark, which was covered with a dressed deer skin, and placed on a couple of short blocks of wood. An Indian sentinel watched it, armed with a hickory bow, and brass pointed barbed arrow; and he was faithful to his trust; for finding the stranger obtruding, with apparent determination to pollute the supposed sacred vehicle, he drew his arrow to the head, and would have shot him through the body, had he not suddenly withdrawn.

The leader virtually acts the part of a priest of war *pro tempore*, in imitation of the Israelites, fighting under the divine military banner of old.

The Indians will not cohabit with women while they are out at war; they religiously abstain from every kind of intercourse, even with their own wives, for the space of three days and nights, before they go out to war; and so after they return home, because they are to sanctify themselves. So Joshua commanded the Israelites, the night before they marched, to sanctify themselves by washing their clothes, avoiding all impurities, and abstaining from all matrimonial intercourse.

When the Indians return home victorious over an enemy, they sing the triumphal song to *Y. O. He. wah*, ascribing the victory to him, like a religious custom of the Israelites, who were commanded always to attribute their success in war to Jehovah, and not to their swords and arrows.

The Indian method of making peace, carries the face of great antiquity. When the applicants arrive near the town, they send a messenger a head, to inform the enemy of their amicable intentions. He carries a swan's wing in his hand, painted with streaks of white clay, as an expressive emblem of his peaceful embassy. The next day, when they have made their friendly parade, by firing off their guns and whooping, they enter the beloved square. Their chief, who is a-head of the rest, is met by one of the old beloved men of the town. They approach each other in a bowing posture. The former says, *Yo Ish le cher Anggona?* "*Are you come a friend, in the name of the great spirit!*" The other replies, *Yah Orahre O Anggona.* "*The great spirit is with me, I am come a friend in his name.*" The beloved man then grasps the stranger with both his hands, around the wrist of his right hand, which holds some green branches; then again about the elbow; then about the arm close to the shoulder, as a near approach to the heart. Then he waves an eagle's tail over the head of the stranger, which is the strongest pledge of good faith. The writer of this has been witness to this ceremony, performed by an embassy from the Creek nation, with his excellency general Washington, president of the United States, in the year 1789.

The common method of greeting each other is analogous with the above, in a great measure. The host only says, *Ish la chu? Are you a friend?* The guest replies, *Orahre-O. I am come in the name of O. E. A. or Yohewah.*

"They are very loving to one another, if several came to a christian's house, and the master of it gave to one of them victuals, and none to the rest, he would divide it into equal shares amongst his companions If the christians visited them, they would give them the first cut of their victuals. They never eat the hollow of the thigh of any thing they kill; and if a christian stranger came to one of their houses in their towns, he was received with the greatest hospitality, and the best of every thing was set before him. And this was often repeated from house to house."—Smith's history of New-Jersey, page 130.

The Indians are not only religiously attached to their tribe while living; but their bodies, and especially their bones, are the objects of their solicitous care, after they are dead. Among the Mohawks, their funeral rites show they have some notion of a future state of existence. They make a large round hole, in which the body can be placed upright, or upon its haunches, which, after the body is placed in it, is covered with timber, to support the earth, which they lay over it, and thereby keep the body from being pressed, they then raise the earth in a round hill over it. They dress the corpse in all its finery, and put wampum and other things in the grave with it. The relations will not suffer grass, or any weed to grow on the grave, and frequently visit it with lamentations.

Among the French Indians in Canada, as mentioned by Charlevoix, as soon as the sick person expires, the house is filled with mournful cries; and this lasts as long as the family is able to defray the expense, for they must keep open house all the time. In some nations the relatives fast to the end of the funeral, with tears and cries. They treat their visitors—praise the dead, and pass mutual compliments. In other nations, they hire women to weep, who perform their duty punctually. They sing—they dance—they weep without ceasing, always keeping time. He has seen the relatives in distress, walk at a great pace, and put their hands on the heads of all they met, probably to invite them to share in their grief. Those who have sought a resemblance between the Hebrews and the Americans, have not failed to take particular notice of their manner of mourning, as several expressions in scripture give room to such conjectures, and to suppose them much alike to those in use with those people of God. Indeed, do not these customs and practices seem to be derived from those of the Jews burying their dead in tombs hewed out of a rock, wherein were niches, in which the dead were set in an upright posture, and often with much of their property buried with them. Josephus tells us, that from king David's sepulchre, Hyrcanus, the Maccabean, took three thousand talents, about thirteen hundred years after his death, to get rid of Antiochus, then besieging Jerusalem.

The southern Indians, when any of their people die at home, wash and anoint the corpse, and soon bring it out of doors, for fear of pollution. They place it opposite to the door in a sitting posture. They then carry it three times round the house in which he is to be interred, for sometimes they bury him in his dwelling-house, and under his bed. The religious man of the deceased's family, in this procession, goes before the corpse, saying each time, in a solemn tone, *Yah*—then *Ho*, which is sung by all the procession. Again he strikes up *He*, which is also sung by the rest. Then all of them suddenly strike off the solemn chorus, by saying *wah*, which constitutes the divine, essential name, *Yah-Ho-He-wah*. In the Choktaw nation, they often sing, *Hal-le-lu-yah*, intermixed with their lamentations. They put the corpse in the tomb in a sitting posture, with his face towards the east, and his head anointed with bear's oil. He is dressed in the finest apparel, having his gun, pouch, and hickory bow, with a young panther's skin full of arrows, along side of him, and every other useful thing he had been possessed of. The tomb is made firm and clean inside. They cover it with thick logs, so as to bear several tiers of cypress bark, and then a quantity of clay over it.

The graves of the dead are so sacred among the northern nations, that to profane them, is the greatest hostility that can be committed against a nation, and the greatest sign that they will come to no terms with them.

The Indians imagine if a white man was to be buried in the domestic tombs of their kindred, it would be highly criminal; and that the spirits would haunt the eaves of the house at night, and cause misfortunes to their family.

If any one dies at a distance, and they are not pursued by an enemy, they place the corpse on a scaffold, secured from wild beasts and fowls of prey. When they imagine the flesh is consumed, and the bones dried, they return to the place, bring them home, and inter them in a very solemn manner. The Hebrews, in like manner, carefully buried their dead, but on any accident, they gathered their bones, and laid them in the tombs of their fore-fathers. Thus Jacob "charged his sons, and said unto them, I am to be gathered unto my people, bury me with my fathers, in the cave that is in the field of Ephron the Hittite." This was in Canaan. "There they buried Abraham and Sarah his wife; there they buried Isaac and Rebeckah, his wife; and there I buried Leah." "And Joseph took an oath of the children of Israel, saying, God will surely visit you, and ye shall carry my bones from hence." "And Moses took the bones of Joseph with him."* And the bones of Joseph, which the children of Israel brought up out

* Gen. xlix. 29, 31—l. 25—Exod. xiii. 19.

of Egypt, buried they in Shechem," as above mentioned.—Joshua xxiv. 32. The Jews buried near their cities, and sometimes opposite to their houses, implying a silent lesson of friendship, and a caution to live well. They buried families together; but strangers apart by themselves.

When an old Indian finds that it is probable that he must die, he sends for his friends, and with them collects his children and family around him; and then, with the greatest composure, he addresses them in the most affectionate manner, giving them his last council, and advising them to such conduct as he thinks for their best interests. So did the patriarchs of old, and the Indians seem to follow their steps, and with as much coolness as Jacob did to his children, when he was about to die.

A very worthy clergyman, with whom the writer was well acquainted, and who had long preached to the Indians, informed him, that many years ago, having preached in the morning to a considerable number of them, in the recess between the morning and afternoon services, news was suddenly brought, that the son of an Indian woman, one of the congregation then present, had fallen into a mill-dam, and was drowned. Immediately the disconsolate mother retired to some distance in deep distress, and sat down on the ground. Her female friends soon followed her, and placed themselves in like manner around her, in a circle at a small distance. They continued a considerable time, in profound and melancholy silence, except now and then uttering a deep groan. All at once the mother putting her hand on her mouth, fell with her face flat on the ground, her hand continuing on her mouth. This was followed, in like manner, by all the rest, when all cried out, with the most melancholy and dismal yellings and groanings. Thus they continued, with their hands on their mouths, and their mouths in the dust a considerable time. The men also retired to a distance from them, and went through the same ceremony, making the most dismal groanings and yellings.

Need any reader be reminded of the Jewish customs on occasions of deep humiliation, as in Job 21 and 5—Mark me and be astonished, and lay your hand on your mouth. 29 and 9—The princes refrained talking, and laid their hands on their mouths. 40 and 4—Behold! I am vile, what shall I answer thee? I will lay my hand on my mouth. Micah 7 and 16—The nations shall see and be confounded; they shall lay their hands on their mouth. Lament. 3 and 9—He putteth his mouth in the dust, if so be, there may be hope. Prov. 30 and 32—If thou hast thought evil, lay thine hand upon thy mouth.

The Choktaw Indians hire mourners to magnify the merit and loss of the dead, and if their tears do not flow, their shrill voices will be heard to cry, which answers the solemn chorus much better. However, some of them have the art of shedding tears abundantly. Jerem. ix chap. 17, 19—Thus saith the Lord of Hosts, consider ye, and call for the mourning women, that they may come, and send for cunning women, that they may come, for a voice of wailing is heard, &c.

By the Mosaic law, the surviving brother was to raise up seed to a deceased brother, who should leave a widow childless. The Indian custom resembles this in a considerable degree. A widow among the Indians is bound by a strict penal law or custom, to mourn the death of her husband, for the space of three or four years. But if it be known that the elder brother of her deceased husband has lain with her, she is afterwards exempt from the law of mourning—has liberty to tie up her hair, anoint and paint herself, which she could not otherwise do, under pain of being treated as an adultress.

The Indians, formerly on the Juniata and Susquehannah rivers, placed their dead on close or covered cribs, made for the purpose, till the flesh consumed away. At the proper time they gathered the bones, scraped and washed them, and then buried them with great ceremony. There is a tribe called Nanticokes, that on their removal from an old to a new town, carry the bones of their ancestors with them.

This also prevailed in particular cases among the Canada Indians. An officer of the regular troops at Oswego, upwards of sixty years ago, reported the following fact. A boy of one of the westward nations, died at Oswego—the parents made a regular pile of split wood, laid the corpse upon it and burnt it. While the pile was burning, they stood gravely looking on, without any lamentation, but when it was burned down they gathered up the bones, and with many tears, put them into a box, and carried them away with them.* The Indians are universally remarkable for a spirit of independence and freedom beyond any other people, and they generally consider death, as far preferable to slavery. They abhor covetousness, and to prevent it, they burn all the little property an Indian has at the time of his death, or bury it with him in his grave. This necessarily tempts them to frugality and abstemiousness in their manner of living. They are wholly ignorant of all kind of mechanicks, except so far as is pressed on them by necessity. They are free from hypocrisy or any

* Exod. xiii. 19, Josh. xxiv. 12. 2 Sam. xxi. 12—14.

forced civility or politeness; but their general conduct, shows a frank and candid, but plain and blunt hospitality and kindness; with a degree of faithfulness in their dealings, except with their enemies, that often astonishes white people; who although their pretensions are so much higher, cannot, at least do not, reach them in this particular.

The great author of the *divine legation of Moses,* in treating of the government of the Jews, both civil and religious, as necessarily united under one great head, *the God of Abraham, Isaac and Jacob,* states his subject clearly and fully, and then says, "but the poet *Voltaire,* indeed, has had a different revelation. The pride of every individual among the Jews, says he, is interested in believing, that it was not *their detestable policy,* their ignorance in the arts or their unpoliteness, that destroyed them; but that it is God's anger that yet pursues them for their idolatries." This *detestable policy,* (which I would not consider in the most obvious sense of the Mosaic institution, because that might tend to make the poet himself detestable) was a principle of independence. This ignorance in the arts prevented the entrance of luxury; and this unpoliteness, hindered the practice of it. And yet parsimony, frugality and a spirit of liberty, which naturally preserve other states, all tended in the ideas of this wonderful politician to destroy the Jewish." How surprisingly does this observation of bishop Warburton, apply in support of these untutored Indians, and point out from whence they must have drawn their principles of conduct.

CHAPTER VI.

The known Religious Rites and Ceremonies of the Indians.

TO adopt the language of Father Charlevoix, "nothing has undergone more sudden, frequent, or more surprising revolutions, than religion. When once men have abandoned the only true one, they soon lose sight of it, and find themselves entangled and bewildered in such a labyrinth of incoherent errors, inconsistencies and contradictions, that there often remains not the smallest clue to lead us back to the truth. One example. The Buccaniers of St. Domingo, who professed to be christians, but who had no commerce, except among themselves, in less than thirty years, and through the sole want of religious worship, instruction, and an authority capable of retaining them in their duty, had lost all marks of christianity, except baptism alone. Had these people continued only to the third generation, their grand children would have been as void of christianity as the inhabitants of Terra-Australis, or New Guinea. They might, possibly, have preserved some ceremonies, the meaning of which they could not account for."

However, our wandering tribes of Indians have, in a most surprising manner, bordering on something rather supernatural, preserved so many essential parts of their original plan of divine worship, and so many of their primitive doctrines, although they have at present almost wholly forgotten their meaning and their end, as to leave little doubt of their great source.

They are far from being idolaters, although many good men, from want of a knowledge of their language, and often having communion with the most worthless part of them, without making any allowance for their local situation and circumstances, have given terrific accounts of these children of nature. And this is not much to be wondered at. For many of our worthy, over zealous and pious Europeans, and some white Americans, deeply affected with a sense of their unhappy state, and feeling the importance of the gospel to them, have unwisely gone into the woods to them, without proper and preparatory education for so important an undertaking.—I mean, without understanding their language, or being well acquainted with their manners, customs and habits —nay, not even making themselves acquainted with their religious prejudices, or by taking sufficient time and using proper means to gain their confidence.

To people so ignorant of what they ought first to have known, and wholly trusting to a heathen interpreter, unable to feel or express the nature of spiritual things, and having to deal with a most jealous and artful people, rendered so by the experience of more than a century, by the continued impositions and oppression of the nation to which their visitants belonged—it is quite a natural thing, that they were often at first despised by the Indians, and then made a mere butt, for the most worthless to frighten and laugh at. Hence the Indians have often in a frolic dressed themselves in the most terrific manner, and made the most frightful images, with every kind of extravagant emblem about it, to alarm and terrify their new comers, of whom they thought so lightly. We speak now principally of their light, bad people, who inhabit around or near our settlements. That, as a people, they are sensible of propriety, and are careful observers of characters, is well known to those who have been long conversant with them. It is a fact well attested, that a preacher went among them before the revolutionary war, and in a sudden discourse to them, began to tell them that there was a God, who created all things—that it was exceedingly sinful and offensive to him, to get drunk, or lie, or steal—all which they must carefully avoid. They answered him—"Go about your business, you fool! Do not we know that there is a God, as well as you! Go to your own people and preach to them; for who gets drunk, and lies and steals more than you white people?" In short, if the Indians form their ideas of us from the common traders and land speculators, and common people, with whom they usually have to do, they will not run into a greater error than we do, when we form our ideas of the character of Indians from those who generally keep about our settlements, and traffic with the frontier inhabitants.

The Indians are filled with great spiritual pride—we mean their chiefs and best men. They consider themselves as under a theocracy, and that they have God for their governor and head. They therefore hold all other people, comparatively, in contempt. They pay their religious worship, as Mr. Adair assures us, (and he had a great opportunity of knowing) to *Loak-Ishto, Hoolo-Abba*, or the great, beneficent, supreme, holy spirit of fire, who resides above the clouds, and on earth with unpolluted, holy people. They were never known (whatever some Spanish writers may say to the contrary, to cover their own blood-thirsty and more than savage barbarity to the natives they found in Mexico, at their first arrival among them) to pay the least perceivable adoration to images or dead persons, or to celestial luminaries, or evil spirits, or to any created being whatever.

Their religious ceremonies are more after the Mosaic institution, than of pagan imitation. They do not believe the sun to be any larger than it appears to the naked eye. Notwithstanding the various accounts we have had from different authors, greatly exaggerating the reports of the Indian's irreligious conduct, they have taken little or no pains to be well informed (for it is attended with considerable difficulty, from their known secrecy) and have therefore grossly misrepresented them, without designing to mislead. Historians ought not to be trusted, as to detailed accounts of these people, with whom it seems to have been previously agreed among themselves, to charge with being red savages and barbarians, while the Indians, in return, consider as white savages and accursed people, those who thus traduce them. Readers should carefully examine into their means of knowledge—their connections with the Indians, and the length of time and opportunities they enjoyed in a social intercourse with them. Difficulties, and those very great, have arisen from the impracticability of a stranger being well informed, particularly arising from their unconquerable jealousy and great secrecy in every thing relating to their religious character. Again, historians are often fond of the marvellous, and are apt to take up with any information they can get, without examining its source, and are too apt to make up strange stories to answer their private purposes, or to cover base designs. This is fully exemplified in the abominable false accounts published by the Spaniards, relative to Mexico, on their first conquering, or rather carrying destruction and blood-shed through that fine country, to gratify their covetousness and bloody dispositions, when they had not the least foundation in truth for their diabolical accounts.

Adair assures us, that from the experience of forty years, he can say, that none of the various nations from Hudson's bay to the Missisippi, have ever been known by our trading people, to attempt the formation of any image of the *great spirit* whom they devoutly worship. They never pretend to *divine* from any thing but their dreams, which seems to proceed from a tradition, that their ancestors received knowledge of future events from heaven by dreams—vide Job xxxiii. &c.

Du Pratz had a particular intimacy with the chief of the guardians of the temple, in a nation near the Missisippi—2 vol. 173. That on his requesting to be informed of the nature of their worship, he was told that they acknowledged a supreme being, whom they called *Coyo-cop-chill*, or *great spirit*, or the *spirit* infinitely great—or the *spirit* by way of excellence. That the word *chill* in their language, signifies the most superlative degree of perfection, and is added to make that appear, as *oua* is fire, and *oua chill* is the supreme fire, or the sun. Therefore by the word Coyo-cop-chill, they mean a spirit that surpasses other spirits, as much as the sun does common fire. The guardian said, that the great spirit was so great and powerful, that in comparison with him, all other things were as nothing. He had made all that we see—all that we can see—and all that we cannot see. He was so good that he could not do ill to any one, even if he had a mind to do it. They believed that the great spirit had made all things by his will; that nevertheless the little spirits who are his servants, might by his orders, have made many excellent works in the universe, which we admire; but that God himself had formed man with his own hands. They called the little spirits, *free servants.* That those spirits were always before the *great spirit,* ready to execute his pleasure with an extreme diligence.

That the air was filled with other spirits, some good, some wicked, and that the latter had a chief, who was more wicked than all the rest. That the great spirit had found him so wicked, that he had bound him forever, so that the other spirits of the air, no longer did so much harm.

He was then asked, how did God make man? he answered that he kneaded some clay, and made it into a little man—after examining it and finding it well formed, he blew on his work, and forthwith the little man had life—grew—acted—walked and found himself a man, perfectly well shaped. He then was asked about the woman—he said, probably she was made in the same manner as the man, but their ancient speech made no mention of any difference, only that the man was made first—page 174.

The Indians also, agreeably to the theocracy of Israel, think the great spirit to be the immediate head of their state, and that God chose them out of all the rest of mankind, as his peculiar and beloved people.

Mr. Locke, one of the ablest men Great-Britain ever produced, observes, "that the commonwealth of the Jews, differed from all others, being an absolute theocracy. The laws established there, concerning the worship of the one invisible deity, were the civil laws of that people, and a part of their political government, in which God himself was the legislator."

In this, the Indians profess the same thing precisely. This is the exact form of their government, which seems unaccountable, were it not derived from the same orignal source, and is the only reason that can be assigned for so extraordinary a fact.

The Indians are exceedingly intoxicated with religious pride, and hold the white people in inexplicable contempt—the common name they give us in their set speeches, literally means, *nothings*; but in their war speeches, *ottuck ookproose*, the accursed people. But they flatter themselves with the name *Hottuk-ore-too-pate*, the beloved people. This is agreeable to the Hebrew epithet *Ammi*, during the theocracy of Israel. When their high priest (if we may be allowed the term, for their most beloved man) addresses the people, he calls them, "the beloved or holy people." These addresses are full of flourishes on the happiness of their country, calling it a land flowing with milk and honey.

When any of their beloved people die, they soften the thoughts of death, by saying, *he is only gone to sleep with their beloved forefathers*, and usually mention a common proverb among them, "*neitak intahah*," the days appointed, or allowed him, were finished. And this is their firm belief, for they affirm that there is a fixed time and place, when and where every one must die, without any possibility of averting it. They frequently say, "such a one was weighed on the path, and made to be light." They always ascribe life and death to God's unerring and particular providence.

Contrary to the usage of all the ancient heathen world, they not only name God by several strong compounded appellations, expressive of many of his divine attributes, but likewise say *yah* at the beginning of their religious dances, with a bowing posture of body—then they sing *y, y, y, ho, ho, ho, he, he,* and repeat those sacred notes (but not the whole name) on every religious occasion. The religious attendants calling to *Yah,* to enable them humbly to supplicate, seems to point to the Hebrew custom of pronouncing *Jah,* which signifies the divine essence. It is well known, what sacred regard the Jews had to the great four lettered name, scarcely ever to mention it in the whole, but once a year, when the high priest went into the holy sanctuary on the day of expiation of sins. Might not the Indians, have copied from them this sacred invocation, and also their religious forbearance in never mentioning the whole name, but in their sacred songs of praise Their method of invoking the great spirit in solemn hymns, with that reverend deportment, and spending a full breath on each of the first two syllables or letters of the awful divine name, has a surprising analogy to the Jewish custom, and such as no other nation or people, even with the advantage of written records, have retained.

Charlevoix, speaking of the northern Indians, observes, that the greatest part of their feasts, their songs and their dances, appeared to him, to have had their rise from religion, and yet preserve some traces of it. I have met with some persons, says he, who could not help thinking that our Indians were descended from the Jews; and found in every thing, some affinity between them and the people of God. There is indeed a resemblance in some things, as not to use knives at certain meals, and not to break the bones of the beast that they eat at the these times, (and we may add, that they never eat the part under the lower joint of the thigh, but always throw it away.) The separation of their women, at certain periods. Some persons have heard them, or thought they heard them, pronounce the word, *hallalujah*, in their songs. The feast they make, at the return of their hunters, and of which they must leave nothing, has also been taken for a burnt offering, or for the remains of the *passover of the Israelites*: and the rather, they say, because when any one family cannot compass his portion, he may get the assistance of his neighbour, as was practised by the people of God, when a family was not sufficient to eat the whole paschal lamb.

The Israelites of old were ordered by Moses to fix in the tabernacle (as Solomon did afterwards in the temple, all by command of God) Cherubim over the mercy seat. The curtains also which lined the walls and the veil of the temple, had the like figures on them. The Cherubim are said to have represented the names, *yo-he-wah-elohim*, in redeeming lost mankind, and means the similitude of the great and mighty one, whose emblems in the congregational standards, were, "the *bull*, the *lion*, the *man* and the *eagle*." So Ezekiel informs us the Cherubim were uniform and had these four compounded animal emblems. Every one had four faces (appearances, habits or forms.)—x chap. 14, 20, 22. Each of the Cherubim, according to the prophet, had the head and face of a man; the likeness of an eagle about the shoulders, with expanded wings; their necks, manes and breasts resembled those of a lion, and their feet those of a bull or calf; the soles of their feet, were like a calf's foot. Ezek. i. 4, 5, 6. "And I looked and behold a whirlwind came out of the north, a great *cloud and a fire infolding itself*, and a brightness was about it, and out of the midst thereof as the colour of amber, out of the midst of the fire—also out of the midst thereof, the likeness of four living creatures. And this was their appearance :—they had the likeness of a man, and every one had four faces, and every one had four wings," &c. &c.—10th ver. "As for the likeness of their faces, they four had the face of a man and the face of a lion on the right side; and they four had the face of an ox on the left side; and they four also had the face of an eagle—vide ver. 11. These are the terrestial cherubim, and the psalmist represents them as the chariot of divine majesty, and displays his transcendant and glorious title of King of Kings. Psalms xviii. 7, 11—"God sitteth between and rideth upon the cherubim" as a divine chariot—ibid. xcix. 1.

So the American Indians, particularly the Cherokees and Choktaws, have some very humble representation of these cherubimical figures, in their places of worship, or beloved square; where, through a strong religious principle, they dance almost every winter's-night, always in a bowing posture, and frequently singing, *halleluyah*, yo, he, wah. They have in these places of worship, which Adair says he has seen, two white painted eagles, carved out of poplar wood, with their wings stretched out, and raised five feet from the ground, standing in the corner, close to the red and white imperial seats; and on the inner side of each of the notched pieces of wood, where the eagles stand, the Indians frequently paint with a white chalky clay, the figure of a man, with buffalo's horns,* and that of a panther, the nearest animal in America, to that of a lion, with the same colour. These

* It was an ancient custom amongst the eastern nations, to use horns as an emblem of power, which the Indians always do.

figures they paint a-fresh at the first fruit offering, or the annual expiation of sins. Yet it has never been known that the Indians ever substituted the eagle, panther, or the similitude of any thing whatever, as objects of divine adoration, in the room of the great invisible divine essence. Nay, they often give large rewards for killing an eagle, and they kill the panther wherever they find him.

The ideas which a people form of the supreme deity, will direct to the nature of their religious worship. Among the southern Indians, *Ish-to-hoolo* is an appellation for God. It points at the greatness, purity and goodness of the creator, in forming man. It is derived as is said from *Ishto*, great, which you find in all the prophetical writings, attributed to God. Also from the present tense of the infinitive mood of the active verb *ahoolo*, "I love," and from the preter tense of the passive verb *hoolo*, that is sanctifying, sanctified, divine or holy. Women set apart, they term *hoolo*, that is, sanctifying themselves to *Ish-to-hoolo*. So Netakhoolo signifies a sanctified or holy day. So *Okka hoolo*, water sanctified. Thus *Ish-to-hoolo*, when applied to God, in its true radical meaning, imports *the great beloved holy cause*, which is exceedingly comprehensive and more expressive of the true nature of God, than the Hebrew name *Adonai*, which may be applicable to a human being. When they apply the epithet, compounded, to any of their own religious men, it signifies, *the great holy, beloved, sanctified man of the holy one.*

They make the divine name point yet more strongly to the supreme author of nature. For as abba, signifies father, so, to distinguish God, as the king of kings, by his attributes, from their own *Minggo Ishto*, or great chief, they frequently name God *Minggo Ishto Abba, Ishto Abba, Minggo Abba,* &c. and when they strive to move the passions, *Ishto Hoolo Abba.* They have another more sacred appellative, which with them is the mysterious essential name of God. The tetragrammanaton of the Hebrews, or the great four lettered name already mentioned, *Y. O. He.•wah.* This they, like the Hebrews, never mention altogether in common speech. Of the time and place, when and where they mention it, they are very particular, and always with a solemn air.

The Indians have among them orders of men answering to our prophets and priests. In the Muskohge language, *Hitch Lalage,* signifies cunning men, or persons prescient of futurity, much the same with the Hebrew seer. But the Indians in general call their pretended prophets, *Loa-che,* men resembling the holy fire, or elohim. Their tradition says, that their forefathers were possessed of an extraordinary divine spirit, by which they foretold things future, and controled the common course of nature; and this they transmitted to their offspring, provided they obeyed the sacred laws annexed to it. They believe that by the communication of the same divine fire, working in their *Loa-che,* they can yet effect the like. But they say it is out of the reach of *Nana Ookproo,* or bad people, either to comprehend or perform such things, because the holy spirit of fire will not co-operate with or actuate *Hottuch Ookproo,* the accursed people. "A sachem of the Mingo tribe, being observed to look at the great comet which appeared the first day of October, one thousand six hundred and eighty, was asked, what he thought was the meaning of that prodigious appearance? answered gravely, "It signifies that we Indians shall melt away, and this country be inhabited by another people."—Smith's New-Jersey, 136, in a note. How this Indian came by his knowledge, without the learned Whiston's astronomical tables, or whether he had any knowledge, is not so material. He will, however, be allowed as good a right to pretend to it, when the event is considered, as the other had in his conjectures concerning the cause of Noah's flood. At all events, this Indian must have reasoned well, and had pretty clear conceptions of the effects that would naturally follow such causes.

Mr. Beatty gives much the same account of their prophets among the Delaware nations or tribes, above forty-five years ago. They consult the prophets upon any extraordinary occasion—as in great or uncommon sickness, or mortality, &c. This, he says, seems to be in imitation of the Jews of old, enquiring of their prophets. Ishto Hoolo is the name of all their great *beloved men*, and the pontifical office descends by inheritance to the eldest.

It cannot be expected but that the dress of the old Indian high-priest, or rather, their *great beloved man*, or the first and oldest among the *beloved men*, should be different from that of the high-priest of the Jews. The poverty and distressed condition of the Indians, renders such a conformity impossible; but notwithstanding the traces of agreement are really astonishing, considering their circumstances, and their having no means of knowing what it was, but by tradition, being deprived of all records relative to it.

Before the Indian Archi-magus, or high-priest, officiates in making the supposed holy fire, for the yearly atonement for sin, as will soon be shewn, he clothes himself with a white garment, resembling the ephod of the Jews, being made of a finely dressed deer or doe skin, and is a waistcoat without sleeves. When he enters on that solemn duty, a beloved attendant spreads a white dressed buckskin* on the white seat, which stands close to the supposed holiest division of their place of worship, and then puts some white beads on it, that are offered by the people. Then the Archi-magus wraps round his shoulders a consecrated skin of the same sort, which reaching across under his arms, he ties behind his back, with two knots on his legs, in the form of a figure of eight. Instead of going barefoot, he wears a new pair of white buckskin mocasins, made by himself, and stiched with the sinews of the animal. He paints the upper part of them across the toes, with a few streaks of red, made of the red root, which is their symbol of holy things, as the vermilion is of war. These shoes he never wears at any other time, and leaves them with the other parts of his pontifical dress, when the service is over, in the beloved place.

In resemblance of the sacred breast-plate, the American priest wears a breast-plate, made of a white conck-shell, with two holes bored in the middle of it, through which he puts the ends of an otter skin strap, and fastens a buckhorn white button to the outside of each, as if in imitation of the precious stones of urim and thumim, which miraculously blazoned on the high-priest's breast, the unerring words of the divine oracle. Instead of the plate of gold which he wore on his forehead, with the words holy, or separated to God, the Indian wears around his temples either a wreath of swan's feathers, or a long piece of swanskin doubled, so as only the fine snowy down appears

* When the high-priest of the Jews went into the holy of holies, on the day of expiation, he clothed himself in white; and when the service was over, he left those clothes in the tabernacle.—Levit. xvi. 4-23.

on each side. And in likeness of the tiara of the former, the latter wears on the crown of his head a tuft of white feathers, which they call *yaterah*, but the meaning of the word is not known. He also fastens a number of blunted wild turkey cocks' spurs towards the toes of his mocasins, as if in resemblance of the bells which the Jewish high-priest wore on his coat of blue.

Bartram assures us, "that there is in every town or tribe, an high-priest, usually nick-named by the white people, the juggler or conjurer, besides several of inferior rank. But that the oldest high priest or seer presides always in spiritual things, and is a person of great consequence. He maintains and exercises great influence in the state, particularly in military affairs; their senate or great council never determining on an expedition without his council and assistance. These people believe most firmly, that their seer or high priest has communion with powerful invisible spirits, who they suppose have some share in the rule and government of human affairs, as well as in that of the elements. He further adds, that these Indians are by no means idolaters, unless their puffing the tobacco smoke towards the sun, and rejoicing at the appearance of the new moon, may be termed so.* So far from idolatry are they that they have no images among them, nor any religious rite or ceremony relating to them, that I could ever perceive.

"They adore the great spirit, the giver and taker away of the breath of life, with the most profound and respectful hom-

* It is rather supposed that they use the smoke of the sacred stem or pipe, as the Jews did their incense—and as to the new moon, as they reckon their time by it, they are as careful observers of it, as the Jews were.

age. They believe in a future state, where the spirit exists, which they call the world of spirits, where they enjoy different degrees of tranquility and comforts agreeably to their life spent here. They hold their beloved man or priest in great respect, and pay strict obedience to what he directs."

These religious beloved men, are also supposed to be in great favour with the deity, and able to procure rain when they please. In this respect also, we may observe a great conformity to the practice of the Jews. Their records inform us, that in the moon Abib or Nisan, they prayed for the spring or latter rain, to be so seasonable and sufficient as to give them a good harvest; and the Indians have a tradition, that their fore-fathers sought for, and obtained such seasonable rains, as gave them plentiful crops continually; and they now seek them, in a manner agreeable to a shadow of this tradition.

In the year 1747, a Natchez warrior told Adair, that while one of their prophets was using his divine invocations for rain, he was killed by thunder on the spot; upon which account the spirit of prophecy ever after subsided among them, and he became the last of *their* reputed prophets. They believed that the *holy spirit of fire* had killed him with some of his angry darting fire, for wilful impurity; and by his threatening voice, forbad them to renew the like attempt; and justly concluded, that if they all lived well, they should fare well and have proper seasons. This opinion coincides with that of the Hebrews, who esteemed thunder-struck individuals as under the displeasure of heaven, and they also observed and enforced such rules of external purity as none of the nations observed, except the Hebrews.

As the Jewish prophets had oracular answers to their prayers, so the Indian prophets, who invoke *yo-he-wah* and mediate with the supreme holy fire, that he may give seasonable rains, have a transparent stone of supposed great power in assisting to bring down the rain, when it is put in a basin of water agreeably to a reputed divine virtue impressed on one of the like sort, in times of old, which communicates it circularly.

This stone would suffer great injury, as they assert, were it even seen by their own laity; but if by foreigners, it would be utterly despoiled of its divine communicative power. This looks something like a tradition of the blazing stones of Urim and Thumim. As the Jews had a sanctum sanctorum, or most holy place in their tabernacle and temple, so have all the Indian nations, particularly the Muskohge nation. It is partitioned off by a mud wall, about breast high, between the white seat, which always stands to the left hand of the red painted war seat. There they deposit their consecrated vessels and supposed holy utensils, none of the laity daring to approach that sacred place for fear of particular damage to themselves, and a general hurt to the people, from the supposed divinity of the place.

According to Mr. Bartram, the great or public square of the southern towns, generally stands alone, in the centre and highest part of the town. It consists of four square or cubical buildings of one story high—uniform and of the same dimensions, so situated as to form an exact tetragon, encompassing an area of half an acre of ground, more or less, according to the strength and size of the town, or will of the inhabitants. One of these buildings is the council-house, where all public business is done. Another of these buildings differs from the rest—It is closely shut up on three sides, and has a partition wall run through it, longitudinally from end to end, dividing it into two apartments, the back part is dark, having only three small arched apertures or holes opening into it from the front apartment, and are but just sufficient for a man to go in at. This secluded place, appears to be designed as a *sanctuary* or sacred part of the temple, as it is said among them, to be death for any person, but the Mico, or high priest, to enter into it, and none are ever admitted, unless by permission of the priests, who guard it night and day. Here are deposited all the sacred things, as the physic-pot, rattles, chaplets, eagle's tail, calumet or sacred stem, the pipe of peace, &c. But children and females are never admitted.

At this time the people of the town were fasting, taking medicine, and praying to avert a grievous calamity of sickness which then afflicted them. They fasted seven or eight days, during which they neither eat or drank any thing, but a meagre gruel made of corn flour and water, at the same time drinking their black drink or physic, which acts as a severe emetic.

CHAPTER VII.

Their Public Worship and Religious Opinions.

THE Indians, in general, keep the following religious fasts and festivals—

1. Their Feast of First Fruits, and after it, on the evening of the same day, one something like the Passover.
2. The Hunter's Feast, like that of Pentecost.
3. The Feast of Harvest and day of expiation of sin.
4. A daily Sacrifice.
5. A Feast of Love.

1st. Their Feast of First Fruits and Passover.

Mr. Penn, who found them perfectly in a state of nature, and wholly a stranger to their manners and characters, and who could not have had any knowledge of them but from what he saw and heard for some months he remained with them, on his first visit to their country, informs his friends in England, in one of his first letters, in 1683, "that he considered these poor people as under a dark night in things relating to religion; yet that they believed in a god, and immortality, without the help of metaphysics, for they informed him that there was a great king who made them, who dwelled in a glorious country to the southward of them; and that the souls of the good will go thither, where they shall live again. Their worship consists of two parts—*sacrifice* and *cantico.* The first is with their first fruits. The first and fattest buck they kill goeth to the fire, where he is all burnt with a doleful ditty of him who performs the ceremony, but with such marvellous fervency and labour of body, that he will even sweat to a foam.

The other part is their cantico, performed by round dances —sometimes words—sometimes songs—then shouts—two are in the middle, who begin, and by singing and druming on a board, direct the chorus. This is done with equal earnestness and labour, but with great appearance of joy. In the fall when the corn cometh in, they begin to feast one another. There have been two great festivals already, to which all come, who will. Mr. Penn was at one himself.—"Their entertainment was at a great seat by a spring, under some shady trees. It consisted of twenty bucks, with hot cakes made of new corn, with both wheat and beans, which they make up in a square form, in the leaves of the corn, and then bake them in the ashes—they then fall to dancing: But all who go to this feast must take a small present in their money, it might be but six pence, which is made of the bone of a fish. The black is with them as gold, and the white as silver—they call it *wampum*." Afterwards speaking of their agreement in rites with the Hebrews, he says that "they reckon by moons—they offer their first fruits—they have a kind of Feast of Tabernacles—they are said to lay their altars upon twelve stones—they mourn a year—they have a separation of women; with many other things that do not now occur.

From Mr. Adair, the following account, or rather abstract, of his account of the feast and fast of what may be called their Passover, and Feast of First Fruits, is made.

On the day appointed (which was among the Jews, generally in the spring, answering to our March and April, when their barley was ripe, being the first month of their ecclesiastical, and the seventh of their civil year, and among the Indians, as soon as their first spring produce comes in) while the sanctified new fruits are dressing, six old beloved women come to their temple, or sacred wigwam of worship, and dance the beloved dance with joyful hearts. They observe a solemn procession as they enter the holy ground, or beloved square, carrying in one hand a bundle of small branches of various green trees; when they are joined by the same number of beloved old men, who carry a cane in one hand, adorned with white feathers, having green boughs in the other hand. Their heads are dressed with white plumes, and the women in their finest clothes and anointed with bear's grease or oil, having also small tortoise shells and white pebbles fastened to a piece of white dressed deer skin, which is tied to each of their legs. The eldest of the beloved men, leads the sacred dance at the head of the innermost row, which of course is next the holy fire. He begins the dance, after once going round the holy fire, in solemn and religious silence. He then in the next circle, invokes *yah*, after their usual manner, on a bass key and with a short accent. In another circle, he sings *ho, ho*, which is repeated by all the religious procession, till they finish that circle. Then in another round, they repeat *he, he*, in like manner, in regular notes, and keeping time in the dance. Another circle is continued in like manner, with repeating the word *wah, wah* (making in the whole, the divine and holy name of *yah, ho, he, wah.*) A little after this is finished, which takes considerable time, they begin again, going fresh rounds, singing *hal-hal-le-le-lu-lu-yah-yah*, in like manner; and frequently the whole train strike up *hallelu, hallelu, halleluyah, halleluyah,* with great earnestness, fervour and joy, while each strikes the ground with right and left feet alternately, very quick, but well timed. Then a kind of hollow sounding drum, joins the sacred choir, which excites the old female singers to chant forth their grateful hymns and praises to the divine spirit, and to redouble their quick, joyful steps, in imitation of the leader of the beloved men, at their head.

This appears very similar to the dances of the Hebrews, and may we not reasonably suppose, that they formerly understood the psalms and divine hymns, at least those which begin or end with *hallelujah*; otherwise how comes it to pass, that all the inhabitants of the extensive regions of North and South America, have and retain these very expressive Hebrew words, and repeat them so distinctly, applying them after the manner of the Hebrews, in their religious acclamations.

On other religious occasions, and at their Feast of Love, they sing *ale-yo, ale-yo,* which is the divine name by the attribute of omnipotence. They likewise sing *he-wah, he-wah,* which is the immortal soul, drawn from the divine essential name, as deriving its faculties from *yo-he-wah.* These words of their religious dances, they never repeat at any other time, which has greatly contributed to the loss of their meaning; for it is believed they have grown so corrupt, as not now to understand either the spiritual or literal meaning of what they sing, any farther than by allusion to the name of the great spirit.

In these circuitous dances, they frequently also sing on a bass key, *aluhe, aluhe, aluwah, 'aluwah.* Also *shilu-yo, shilu-yo, shilu-he, shilu-he, shilu-wah, shilu-wah,* and *shilu-hah, shilu-hah.** They transpose them also several ways, but with the very same notes. The three terminations make up the four lettered divine name. Hah is a note of gladness and joy. The word preceding it, *shilu,* seems to express the predicted human and divine Shiloh, who was to be the purifier and peace maker. They continue their grateful divine hymns for the space of about fifteen minutes, and then break up. As they degenerate, they lengthen their dances, and shorten the time of their fasts and purifications; insomuch, that they have so exceedingly corrupted their primitive rites and customs, within the space of the last thirty years, (now about eighty years) that, at the same rate of declension, there will not long be a possibility of tracing their origin, but by their dialects and war customs. At the end of this notable religious dance, the old beloved women return home to hasten the feast of the new sanctified fruits. In the mean time, every one at the temple drinks plentifully of the *cussena* and other bitter liquids, to cleanse their sinful bodies, as they suppose. After which, they go to some convenient deep water, and there, according to the ceremonial law of the Hebrews, they wash away their sins with water. They then return with great joy, in solemn procession, singing their notes of praise, till they again enter their holy ground, to eat of the new delicious fruits, which are brought to the outside of the

* Cruden, in his Concordance, says—" All christian commentators agree, that the word Shiloh ought to be understood of the Messiah, of Jesus Christ. Jerome translates it, by qui met bendus est--He who is to be sent; and manifestly reads Shiloach, sent, instead of Shiloh."

square by the old beloved women. They all behave so modestly, and are possessed of such an extraordinary constancy and equanimity in pursuit of their religious mysteries, that they do not shew the least outward emotion of pleasure at the first sight of the sanctified new fruits. If one of them should act in a contrary manner, they would say to him che-hakset-Kanaha—You resemble such as were beat in Kanaha.—Formerly, on the north side of the Susquehannah river, in Pennsylvania, were some old Indian towns, called Kanaa, and now about eighty years ago, there was a remnant of a nation, or a subdivided tribe of Indians, called Kanaai, which greatly resembles the Hebrew name Canaan.

Mr. Smith, in his History of New-Jersey, speaking of the Indians in the year 1681, says—"Very little can be said as to their religion. They are thought to believe in a god and immortality, and seemed to aim at public worship. When they did this, they sometimes sat in several circles, one within another. The action consisted of singing, jumping, shouting and dancing; but mostly performed rather as something handed down from their ancestors, than from any knowledge or enquiry into the serious parts of its origin. They said that the great king who made them, dwelt in a glorious country to the southward, and that the spirits of the best should go there and live again. Their most solemn worship was the sacrifice of the first fruits, in which they burnt the first and fattest buck, and feasted together on what else they had collected. But in this sacrifice broke no bones of any creature they eat. When done, they gathered the bones and buried them very carefully: these have since been frequently ploughed up."—page 140.

Among the Indians on the northwest side of the Ohio, the Feast of the First Fruits is thus described by the Rev. Dr. Charles Beatty, who was an eye witness of the ceremony: Before they make use of any of the first or spring fruits of the ground, twelve of their old men meet, when a deer and some of the first fruits are provided. The deer is divided into twelve parts, according to the number of the men, and the corn beaten in a mortar and prepared for use by boiling or baking into cakes under the ashes, and of course unleavened. This also is divided into twelve parts. Then these men hold up the venison and first fruits, and pray with their faces to the east, acknowledging, as he supposed, the goodness and bounty of heaven towards them. It is then eaten; after which they freely enjoy the fruits of the earth.

On the evening of the same day, they have another public feast, besides that of the First Fruits, which looks somewhat like the Passover; when a great quantity of venison is provided, with other things, dressed in the usual way, and distributed to all the guests; of which they eat freely that evening; but that which is left, is thrown into the fire and burned, as none of it must remain till sun-rise on the next day, nor must a bone of the venison be broken.

The writer of these sheets has made great use of Mr. Adair's history of the Indians, which renders it necessary that something should be further said of him. Sometime about the year 1774, or 1775, Mr. Adair came to Elizabeth-Town, where the writer then lived, with his manuscript, and applied to Mr. Livingston, afterwards governor of the state of New-Jersey, a correct scholar, well known for his literary abilities and knowledge of the belle-lettres, requesting him to correct his manuscript for him. He brought ample recommendations, and gave a good account of himself.

Our political troubles then increasing, Mr. Adair, who was on his way to Great-Britain, was advised not to risk being detained from his voyage, till the work could be critically examined, but to get off as soon as possible. He accordingly took passage in the first vessel that was bound to England.

As soon as the war was over, the writer sent to London and obtained a copy of the work. After reading it with care, he strictly examined a gentleman, then a member with him in Congress, of excellent character, who had acted as our Indian agent to the southward, during the war, (without letting him know the design) and from him found all the leading facts mentioned herein, fully confirmed, by his own personal knowledge.

The Feast of Weeks, or the Hunter's Feast, or Pentecost.

An ancient missionary, who lived a long time with the *Outaowaies*, has written, that among these savages, an old man performs the office of a priest at the feasts. That they begin by giving thanks to the great spirit for the success of the chase, or hunting time. Then another takes a cake, breaks it in two, and casts it in the fire. This was upwards of eighty years ago.

Dr. Beatty says, that once in the year, some of the tribes of Indians beyond the Ohio, choose from among themselves twelve men, who go out and provide twelve deer; and each of them cuts a small saplin, from which they strip the bark, to make a tent, by sticking one end into the ground, bending the tops over one another, and covering the poles with blankets. Then the twelve men choose, each of them, a stone, which they make hot in the fire, and place them together, after the manner of an altar, within the tent, and then burn the fat of the insides of the deer thereon.* At the time they are making this offering, the men within cry to the Indians without, who attend as worshippers, "we pray or praise." They, without, answer, "we hear." Then those in the tent cry *ho-hah*, very loud and long, which appeared to be something in sound like halle-lujah. After the fat was thus offered, some tribes burned tobacco, cut fine, upon the same stones, supposed in imitation of incense. Other tribes choose only ten men, who provide but ten deer, ten saplins, or poles, and ten stones.

The southern Indians observe another religious custom of the Hebrews, as Adair asserts, by offering a sacrifice of gratitude, if they have been successful, and have all returned safe home. But if they have lost any in war, they generally decline it, because, they imagine, by some neglect of duty, they are impure; then they only mourn their vicious conduct, which defiled the ark, and thereby occasioned the loss.

Like the Israelites, they believe their sins are the procuring cause of all their evils, and that the divinity in the ark will always bless the more religious party with the best success. This is their invariable sentiment, and is the sole reason for mortifying themselves in so severe a manner while they are out at war; living very scantily, even in a buffalo range,

* Thou shalt sprinkle the blood upon the altar, and shalt burn their fat for an offering made by fire, for a sweet savour unto the Lord.—Numb. xviii. 17.

under a strict rule, lest by luxury, their hearts should grow evil, and give them occasion to mourn.

The Rev. Dr. Beatty, who went into the Delaware nation so long ago, informed the writer of this, that he was present when there was a great meeting of the nation, consulting on a proposition for going to war with a neighbouring nation. At this time they killed a buck and roasted it, as a kind of sacrifice, on twelve stones, on which they would not suffer any tool or instrument to be used. That they did not eat the middle joint of the thigh. In short, he assured the writer, that he was astonished to find so many of the Jewish customs prevailing among them, and began to conclude that there was some affinity between them and the Jews.

The Muskohgee Indians sacrifice a piece of every deer they kill at their hunting camps, or near home. If the latter, they dip their middle finger in the broth, and sprinkle it over the domestic tombs of their dead, to keep them out of the power of evil spirits, according to their mythology. This seems to proceed from a traditional knowledge, though corrupt, of the Hebrew law of springling with blood.

Charlevoix informs us, that to be esteemed a good hunter among the northern Indians, a man must fast three days together, without taking the least nourishment, having his face smeared with black all the time. When the fast is over, the candidate sacrifices to the *great spirit* a piece of each of the beasts he intends to hunt. This is commonly the tongue and muzzle, which at other times are the hunter's peculiar share, to feast his friends and strangers with. His family and relations do not touch them; and they would as soon die with hunger as eat any of them.

Though the Indians in general believe the upper heavens are inhabited by Ishto-hoolo Aba, and a great multitude of inferior good spirits, yet they are firmly persuaded that the divine omnipresent spirit of fire and light, resides also on earth, in their annual sacred fire, while it is unpolluted, and that he kindly accepts their lawful offerings, if their own conduct is agreeable to the old divine law, which was delivered to their forefathers. The former notion of the deity, is agreeable to those natural images with which the divine penmen, through all the prophetic writings, have drawn of *Yo. He. Wah, Elohim.* When God was pleased with Aaron's priesthood and offerings, the holy fire descended and consumed the burnt offering on the altar, &c. Throughout the Old Testament, this was an emblematic token of the divine presence, and the smoke of the victims ascending towards heaven, is represented as a sweet savour to God—and the incense from the altar is emblematic of the prayers of the saints. And God is said in scripture to be a consuming fire—Deut. iv. 24. He shewed himself to the prophets David, Ezekiel, and his apostle John, in the midst of fire—Psalms civ. 4, Ezekiel i. 4, Daniel vii. 9 and 10, Acts ii. 3. God also appeared surrounded by a flame of fire at the burning bush. And when descending on Mount Sinai, the mountain appeared enveloped in flaming fire—Exodus iii. 2—xix. 18. The people who have lived so long apart from the rest of mankind, are not to be wondered at, if they have forgotten the meaning and end of the sacrifices. They are rather to be pitied for seeming to believe, like the ignorant part of the Israelites of old, that the virtue is either in the form of offering the sacrifice, or in the divinity, who they imagine resides on earth, in the sacred annual fire: likewise, for having forgotten that the blessing was not in the outward sign, but in the thing signified or typified by that sign.

The Feast of Harvest and Day of Expiation of Sin.

We shall now proceed to their most solemn and important feast and fast, answerable to the *Jewish Feast of Harvest and Day of Expiation of Sin.*

The Indians formerly observed this grand festival of the annual expiation of sin, and the offering of the first fruits of the harvest, at the beginning of the first new moon in which their corn became full eared, as we learn from Adair. But for many years past, they are regulated by the season of their harvest. Yet they are as skilful in observing the revolutions of the moon, as ever the Israelites were, at least till the end of the first temple. For during that period, instead of measuring time by astronomical calculations, they knew it only by the phases of the moon.

In like manner the Indians annually observed their festivals and *Nectak-Ya-ah*, or days of afflicting themselves before the great spirit, at a prefixed time of a certain moon.

According to Charlevoix, the harvest among the *Natchez*, on the Missisippi, is in common. The great chief fixes the day for the beginning of the festival of the harvest, which lasts three days, spent in sports and feasting. Each private person contributes something of his hunting, his fishing, and his other provisions, as maize, beans and melons. The great chief presides at the feast—all the sachems are round him, in a respectful posture. The last day, the chief makes a speech to the assembly. He exhorts every one to be exact in the performance of his duties, especially to have a great veneration for the spirit which resides in the temple, and to be careful in instructing their children.

The fathers of families never fail to bring to the temple the first produce of their harvest, and of every thing that they gather, and they do the same by all the presents that are made to their nation. They expose them at the door of the temple, the keeper of which, after presenting them to the spirit, carries them to the king, who distributes them to whom he pleases. The seeds are in like manner offered before the temple, with great ceremony. But the offerings which are made of bread and flour every new moon, are for the use of the keepers of the temple.

As the offerings of the fruits of the harvest precede a long strict fast of two nights and a day, they gormandize such a prodigious quantity of strong food, as to enable them to keep inviolate the succeeding fast. The feast lasts only from morning to sunset.

As we have already seen, this feast with the Hebrews began in the month Tizri, which was the first month of the civil year, answerable to our September and October. The feast took place previous to the great day of expiation, which was the tenth day of the month. So the Indian corn being generally full eared and fit to eat about this time, they are not far from the very time directed in the Mosaic appointment for keeping it.

The feast being over, some of their people are carefully employed in putting their temple in proper order for the annual expiation, while others are painting the white cabin and the supposed holiest with white clay; for it is a sacred and peaceable place, and white is its emblem. Others of an inferior order are covering all the seats of the beloved square with new matrasses, made out of fine splinters of long canes, tied together with flags. Several are busy in sweeping the temple, clearing it of every supposed polluted thing, and carrying out the ashes from the hearth, which, perhaps, had not been cleaned but a few times since the last year's annual offering. Every thing being thus prepared, the chief beloved man, or high-priest, orders some of his religious attendants to dig up the old hearth or altar, and to sweep out the remains, that by chance might either be left or dropped down. He then puts a few roots of the button-snake root, with some green leaves of an uncommon small sort of tobacco, and a little of the new fruits, at the bottom of the fire-place, which he orders to be covered up with white marley clay, and wetted over with clean water. Immediately the magi or priests, order a thick arbor to be made over the altar with green branches of the various young trees, which the warriors had designedly chosen and laid down on the outside of the supposed holy ground. The women in the interim are busy at home, clearing out their houses, putting out all the old fire, renewing the old hearths, and cleansing all their culinary vessels, that they may be fit to receive the pretended holy fire, and the sanctified new fruits, according to the purity of the law, lest by an improper conduct, they should incur damage in life, health, or future crops, &c.

It is fresh in the memory of the old traders, as we are assured by those who have lived long with them, that formerly none of those numerous nations of Indians would eat, or even handle, any part of the new harvest, till some of it had been offered up at the yearly festival by the beloved man or high-priest, or those of his appointment at their plantations,* although the light harvest of the past year should almost have forced them to give their women and children of the ripening fruits to sustain life.

But they are visibly degenerating more and more, both in this and every other religious observance, except what concerns war; yet their magi and old warriors live contentedly on such harsh food as nature affords them in the woods, rather than transgress the divine precept given to their forefathers.

Having every thing in order for the sacred solemnity, the religious waiters carry off the remains of the feast, and lay them on the outside of the square. Others, of an inferior order, carefully sweep out the smallest crumbs, for fear of polluting the first fruit offering; and before sunset, the temple must be cleared, even of every kind of vessel or utensil that had contained any thing, or had been used for any kind of provision during the past year.

Now one of the waiters proclaims with a loud voice, for all the warriors and beloved men, whom the purity of their law admits, to come and enter the beloved square and observe the fast. *He also exhorts the women and children, with those who have not been initiated in war, to keep apart,* according to the law.

Four centinels are now placed, one at each corner of the holy square, to keep out every living creature as impure,

* VideLuke, vi. 1, relating to the second sabbath, but not the seventh-day sabbath, it was the day of offering up the first fruits, before which it was not lawful to eat of the harvest.

except the religious order, and the warriors who are not known to have violated the law of the first fruit offering, and that of marriage, since the last year's expiation. They observe the fast till the rising of the second sun; and be they ever so hungry in that sacred interval, the healthy warriors deem the duty so awful, and disobedience so inexpressibly vicious, that no temptation would induce them to violate it.—They at the same time drink plentifully of a decoction of the button-snake root, in order to vomit and cleanse their sinful bodies.

When we consider their earnest invocations of the divine essence in this solemnity—that they never apply this root only on religious occasions—that they frequently drink it to such excess as to impair their health; and take into consideration its well known property of curing the bite of the rattle snake, must not it be concluded, that this has some reference to the cure of the bite of the old serpent in Eden, or to the serpent lifted up in the wilderness.

In the general fast, the children, and men of weak constitutions, are allowed to eat, as soon as they are certain that the sun has begun to decline from his meridian altitude. This seems to be founded on the principle of mercy before sacrifice—and the snake root used by those in the temple, and the bitter green tobacco, which is eaten by the women and those too wicked to be admitted to the fast held therein, seem to point to eating of the paschal lamb with bitter herbs.

Being great lovers of ripe fruit, and as yet only tantalized with the sight of them, this may, with justice, be said to be a fast to afflict their souls, and to be a sufficient trial of their religious principles. At the end of this solemn fast, the women, by the voice of a crier, bring to the outside of the holy square, a plentiful variety of the old year's food newly dressed, which they lay down and immediately return home. The waiters then go, and reaching their hands over the holy ground, they bring in the provisions and set them down before the famished multitude. They think it wholly out of order to show any joy or gladness for the end of their religious duties. They are as strict observers of their set forms, as the Israelites were of those they received from divine appointment. As soon as the sun is visibly declining from the meridian, the third day of the fast, the chief beloved man orders a religious attendant to cry aloud to the crowded town, that the holy fire is to be brought out for the sacred altar—commanding every person to stay within his house, as becomes the beloved people, without doing the least bad thing; and to be sure to extinguish every spark of the old fire, otherwise the divine fire will bite them severely.

Now every thing is hushed. Nothing but silence all around. The great beloved man, and his beloved waiter, rising up with a reverend carriage, steady countenance, and composed behaviour, go into the beloved place, or holiest, to bring them out the beloved fire. The former takes a piece of dry poplar, willow, or white-oak, and having cut a hole, but not so deep as to reach through it; he then sharpens another piece, and placing that in the hole, and both between his knees, he drills it briskly for several minutes, till it begins to smoke—or, by rubbing two pieces together for a quarter of an hour, he collects, by friction, the hidden fire, which they all consider as proceeding from the holy spirit of fire.

They then cherish it with fine chips, till it glows into a flame, by using a fan of the unsullied wing of a swan. On this the beloved man brings out the fire, in an old earthen vessel, and lays it on the altar, which is under the arbor, thick weaved on the top with green boughs.* They rejoice exceedingly at this appearance of the reputed holy fire, as it is supposed to atone for all their past crimes, except murder. Although the people without, may well know what is doing within, yet by order, a crier informs them of the glad tidings, and orders a beloved old woman to pull a basket full of the new ripened fruits, and bring them to the beloved square. As she is prepared for the occasion, she readily obeys, and soon lays it down at the corner thereof. Then the fire-maker rises from his white seat, and walks northward three times round the holy fire with a slow pace, and in a sedate and grave manner, stopping now and then, and saying some old ceremonial words with a low voice and a rapidity of expression, which none understand but a few of the beloved old men, who equally secrete their religious mysteries, that they may not be profaned. He then takes a little of each sort of the new fruits, rubs some bear's oil over them, and offers them up, together with some flesh, to the bountiful spirit of fire, as a fruit offering and an annual oblation for sin. He likewise pours a little of a strong decoction of the button-snake root, and of the cusseena, into the pretended holy fire. He then purifies the red and white seats with those bitter liquids, and sits down. All culprits may now come forth from their hiding places, dressed in their finest clothes, to pay their thanks, at an awful distance, to the forgiv-

* Even among the Romans, if the sacred fire at any time happened to be extinguished, it could only be lighted again at the rays of the sun

ing *divine fire*. Orders are now given to call the women to come for the sacred fire—They gladly obey. The great beloved man, or high-priest, addresses the warriors and women; giving all the particular positive injunctions and negative precepts they yet retain of the ancient law. He uses very sharp language to the women. He then addresses the whole multitude. He enumerates the crimes they have committed, great and small, and bids them look at the *holy fire* which has forgiven them. He presses on his audience, by the great motives of temporal good and the fear of temporal evil, the necessity of a careful observance of the ancient law, assuring them that the *holy fire* will enable their prophets, the rain-makers, to procure them plentiful harvests, and give their war leaders victory over their enemies. He then orders some of the fire to be laid down outside of the holy ground, for all the houses of the various associated towns, which sometimes lay several miles apart.*

If any are sick at home, or unable to come out, they are allowed one of the old consecrated conch shells full of their sanctifying bitter cusseena, carried to them by a beloved old

* Dr. Hyde says, that the third state of the Persian religion commenced, when, in imitation of the fire preserved upon the altar in the temple at Jerusalem, they kept also a perpetual fire upon an altar. This gave occasion to the common opinion, that the ancient Persians worshipped fire; but Dr. Hyde justifies them from that imputation. He owns that they regarded this fire as a thing sacred, and paid it a kind of service; but he denies that they ever paid to it a proper adoration. One of their priests said, that they did not pay any divine worship to mithra, which is the sun; or to the moon, or the stars, but only turned towards the sun when they prayed, because the nature of it nearly resembled that of fire. They regarded it as an image of God, and some said God resided in it, and others, that it will be the seat of the blessed. On the twenty-fourth March all the inhabitants of a parish in Persia extinguish the fire in their houses, and go to light it again by the fire of the priest, each paying him about six shillings and three pence, which serves for his support. They must have taken this custom from the Jews.

man. This is something like the second Passover of the Jews. At the conclusion, the beloved man orders one of his religious waiters to proclaim to all the people that the sacred annual solemnity is now ended, and every kind of evil averted from the beloved people, according to the old straight beloved speech. They are then commanded to paint themselves, and go along with him, according to ancient custom. They immediately fly about to grapple up a kind of chalkey clay to paint themselves white. They soon appear, all over, as white as the clay can make them. Then they follow on, in an orderly slow procession, to purify themselves in running water. The beloved man, or high-priest, heads the holy train—his waiter next—the beloved men according to their seniority—and the warriors according to their reputed merit. The women follow in the same orderly manner, with all the children who can walk, ranged according to their height.—The very little ones, are carried in the mothers arms. In this manner they move along, singing *halleluyah* to *Y. O. He-wah*, till they get to the water, when the high-priest jumps into it, and all the train follow him.* Having thus purified themselves, and washed away their sins, as they suppose and verily believe, they consider themselves as out of the reach of temporal evil, for their past vicious conduct. They now return

* The Indian women never perform their religious ablutions in presence of the men, but purify themselves, not at appointed times, with the men, but at their discretion. They are also entirely excluded from their temples by ancient custom, except the six old beloved women, who are permitted to sing, dance, and rejoice at their annual expiation for sin; but they must retire before the other solemnities begin.

So the Hebrew women performed their ablutions, separated from the men, by themselves. They also worshipped apart from the men, lest they should attract each others attention in divine worship.

to the centre of the holy ground, where having made a few circles, dancing round the altar, they finish their annual great festival, and depart in joy and peace.

Mr. Bartram, who visited the southern Indians in 1778, gives an account of the same feast, but in another nation. He says that the Feast of First Fruits is their principal festival. This seems to end the old and beigin the new ecclesiastical year. It commences when their new crops are arrived to maturity This is their most solemn celebration.*

When a town celebrates the busk, or first fall fruits, having previously provided themselves with new clothes, new pots, pans, and other household utensils and furniture, they collect all their worn out clothes and other despicable things, sweep and clean their houses, squares, and the whole town, of their filth, which, with all the remaining grain and other old provisions, they cast together in one common heap, and consume it with fire. After taking medicine, and fasting for three days, all the fire in the town is extinguished. During this fast, they abstain from the gratification of every appetite and passion whatever. A general amnesty is proclaimed. All malefactors may return to their town, and they are absolved from their crimes, which are now forgotten, and they are restored to favour. On the fourth morning, the high-priest, or chief beloved man, by rubbing dry wood together, produces new fire in the public square, from whence every habitation in the town is supplied with the new and pure flame. Then the women go forth to the harvest fields and bring from thence new

* This is plainly the great feast on the day of expiation, and that of harvest, when they offer up their fall fruits, and not the spring first fruit feast, and should have been called the new civil year.

corn and fruits, which being prepared in the best manner, in various dishes, and drink withal, is brought with solemnity to the square, where the people are assembled, appareled in their new clothes and decorations. The men having regaled themselves, the remainder is carried off and distributed among the families of the town. The women and children solace themselves in their separate families, and in the evening repair to the public square, where they dance, sing and rejoice, during the whole night, observing a proper and exemplary decorum. This continues three days, and the four following days they receive visits and rejoice with their friends from neighbouring towns, who have also purified and prepared themselves.

The Rev. Mr. Brainerd, in his journal says, he visited the Indians on the 20th of September, 1745, at the Juniata, near the Susquehannah, in Pennsylvania. This is the first month of their civil year, and the usual time of the feast of fruits, or harvest. It ought to be noted, that Mr. Brainerd, though an excellent man, was at this time wholly unacquainted with the Indian language, and indeed with their customs and manners. These Indians in particular, were a set of the lowest grade; the most worthless, of the nations wholly ruined by the example and temptations of the white people. Mr. Brainerd's interpreter was a common Indian, greatly attached to the habits of his countrymen, and much in their interest. He says he found the Indians almost universally busy in making preparations for a great sacrifice and dance. In the evening they met together, to the number of about one hundred, and danced round a large fire, having prepared ten fat deer for the sacrifice. They burned the fat of the inwards in the fire, while they were dancing, and sometimes raised the flame to a prodigious height, at the same time yelling and shouting in such a manner that they might easily be heard two miles off. They continued their sacred dance nearly all night; after which, they eat the flesh of the sacrifice, and then retired each to his lodging. As Mr. Brainerd acknowledges, that he dared not go among them, he could give a very imperfect account of their proceedings, as he must have received it from the interpreter.

The Feast of the Daily Sacrifice.

The next remarkable feasts they religiously observe, are those of the Daily Sacrifice and some occasional ones.

The Hebrews, it is well known, offered daily sacrifices of a lamb every morning and evening, and except the skin and entrails, it was burnt to ashes.

The Indians have a very humble imitation of this rite.—The women always throw a small piece of the fattest of the meat into the fire, before they begin to eat. At times they view it with pleasing attention, and pretend to draw omens from it. This they will do, though they are quite alone, and not seen by any one.

Those who have been adopted by them, and fully considered as belonging to their nation, say, that the Indian men observe the Daily Sacrifice both at home and in the woods, with new killed venison. They also draw their new killed venison, before they dress it, several times through the smoke and flame of fire, both by way of an offering as a sacrifice, and to consume the blood, which, with them, as with the Hebrews, would be a most horrid abomination to eat. They also sacrifice, while in the woods, the melt, or a large fat piece of the first buck they kill.

They imagine that their temples have such a typical holiness, beyond any other place, that if they offered up the annual sacrifice elsewhere, it would not atone for the people, but rather bring down the anger of Ish-to-hoolo Aba, and utterly spoil the power of their holy place and holy things. They who sacrifice in the woods, do it only on particular occasions, allowed by their laws and customs.

Their Feast of Love, &c.

Every spring season, one town or more, of the Missisippi Floridians, keep a solemn Feast of Love, to renew their old friendships. They call this annual feast *Hottuck Aimpa, Heettla Tanaa*, that is, "the people eat, dance and walk, as twined together." The short name of the feast is, "*Hottuk Impanaa*," that is, "eating by a strong religious and social principle." Impanaa signifies, as I am informed, several threads or strands twisted together. They assemble three nights before the feast. On the fourth night they eat together. During the intermediate space, the young men and women dance in circles, from the evening till the morning. When they meet at night, it is professed to be to gladden and unite their hearts before Y. O. He. wah. They sing Y. O. He. wah. shoo—Y. O. He. wah. shoo—Y. O. He. wah. shee—Y. O. He. wah. shee—Y. O. He. wah. shai—Y. O. He. wah. shai—with great energy. The first word is nearly in the Hebrew characters, the name of Joshua or Saviour.

CHAPTER VIII.

Or Miscellaneous Facts omitted.

THE writer of these sheets was himself present at a religious dance of six or seven nations, accidentally meeting together, and having been hospitably entertained by the governor and inhabitants, they gave this dance to the governor and such as he should invite, by way of shewing their gratitude.

The writer was invited, with a very large company of gentlemen and ladies. The following is an exact account of what passed; to every circumstance of which he was critically attentive.

After the company had assembled in a very large room, the oldest sachem of the Senecas, and a beloved man, entered, and took their place in the middle of the room, having something in imitation of a small drum, on which the old sachem beat time at the dance. Soon after, between twenty and thirty Indians came in, wrapped in their blankets. These made a very solemn and slow procession round the room, keeping the most profound silence, the sachem sounding his drum to direct their motion. The second round, they began to sing on a bass key *y. y. y.* till they completed the circle, dancing the whole time, to the sound of the drum, in a very solemn and serious manner. The third round, their ardor increased to such a degree, while they danced with a quicker step, and sang *he-he-he,* so as to make them very warm, and they began to perspire freely, and to loosen their blankets. The fourth round they sang *ho, ho, ho,* with great earnestness, and by dancing with greater violence, their perspiration increased, and they cast off their blankets entirely, which caused some confusion. The next and last round put them in a mere frenzy, twisting their bodies, and wreathing like so many snakes, and making as many antic gestures as a parcel of monkies, singing the whole time, in the most energetic manner, *wah-wah-wah.* They kept time in their dancing, as well as any person could do, who had been taught by a master. Each round took them between ten and fifteen minutes. They then withdrew in indian file, with great silence, except the two with the drum. The company had supposed that they were invited to a war-dance. The writer, desirous of ascertaining the nature of the dance, went to the interpreter, and asked him if what they had seen was intended as a war-dance; he seemed much displeased, and in a pettish manner, answered, a war-dance, no! Indians never entertain civil people with a war-dance. It was a religious dance. In a short time, a considerable bustle being heard at the door, the company came to order, when the Indians re-entered in indian file, and danced one round—then a second, singing, in a more lively manner, *hal-hal-hal* till they finished the round. They then gave us a third round, striking up the word, *le-le-le.* On the next round, it was the word *lu-lu-lu,* dancing naked, with all their might, having again thrown off their blankets. During the fifth round, was sung the syllable *yah-yah-yah.* Then all joining, as it were, in a general, but very lively and joyous chorus, they sang *hal-le-lu-yah,* dwelling on each syllable with a very long breath, in the most pleasing manner.

There could be no deception in all this—the writer was near them—paid great attention—and every thing was obvious to the senses, and discovered great fervor and zeal in the performers. Their pronunciation was very guttural and sonorous, but distinct and clear.

The compiler of these facts, rode in the stage to Elizabeth-Town, sometime about the year 1789, with an Indian sachem from the Creek or Chikkesah nation, and his retinue, who was going, under the care of col. Butler, to New-York, to establish or renew a peace with the United States. He was a strong, tall, well proportioned man, of great gravity in his appearance, and all his behaviour. He was well dressed, and a much better demeanor in his whole conduct, than any Indian the writer had ever seen. Neither he nor one of his attendants could speak English. From the extraordinary respect paid him by his attendants, he was certainly a sachem of high reputation. At dinner, though hard pressed by some of the gentlemen at table, he could not be persuaded to drink more than three glasses of wine, and he would not taste brandy. When in Philadelphia, he drank tea in company with a number of ladies, among whom was a Miss P—e, who painted minature pictures very well. She being prepared for it, took his face with a strong likeness, without his perceiving it. When it was finished, she gave it to the interpreter, who put it into the hands of the chief. He appeared in perfect astonishment; he looked wildly about him, and spoke to the interpreter in Indian, in a very emphatical manner, asking him (as he said) where that had come from, and what was the meaning of it. The interpreter introduced the young lady to him, and told him that she had done it while sitting in the room. He expressed himself very much gratified with it, offered to return it to her, but she desired the interpreter to inform him that she wished to present it to him. He made great acknowledgments for the favour, saying, that he was a poor Indian, and had nothing to give her in return; but that he often spoke to the great spirit, and the next time he did, he would remember her.

When the stage drove up to the tavern at Frankfort, the stage-driver got out to get a dram, the horses took fright and ranaway with the stage and overset it, by which the chief, received a large and very severe cut on his forehead; and col. Butler, was also wounded, but all the rest got off unhurt. The chief jealous that it was done to injure him, seemed terrified and alarmed. But when he observed that col. Butler was also hurt, and that it was an accident, he seemed immediately to become calm and easy—A surgeon soon came in, and sewed up the wound, in a manner that must have given the chief great pain; but he would not acknowledge it, neither did he discover the least symptom of it. As soon as he was dressed, he arose up and addressed col. Butler, which the interpreter explained, saying, "never mind this brother—it will soon be all well. This is the work of the evil spirit—he knows we are going to effect a work of peace—he hates peace and loves war—never mind it—let us go on and accomplish our business—we will disappoint him."

The writer of these sheets, many years ago, was one of the corresponding members of a society in Scotland, for promoting the gospel among the Indians. To further this great work, they educated two young men of very serious and religious dispositions, and who were desirous of undertaking the mission, for this special purpose—when they were ordained and ready to depart, we wrote a letter in the Indian style, to the Delaware nation, then residing on the north-west of the Ohio, informing that we had, by the goodness of the great spirit, been favoured with a knowledge of his will, as to the worship he required of his creatures, and the means he would bless to promote the happiness of man, both in this life and that which was to come. That thus enjoying so much happiness ourselves, we could not but think of our red brethren in the wilderness, and wished to communicate the glad tidings to them, that they might be partakers with us. We had therefore sent them two ministers of the gospel, who would teach them these great things, and earnestly recommended them to their careful attention. With proper passports the missionaries set off and arrived in safety at one of their principal towns.

The chiefs of the nation were called together, who answered them that they would take it into consideration, and in the mean time they might instruct their women, but they should not speak to the men. They spent fourteen days in council, and then dismissed them very courteously, with an answer to us. This answer made great acknowledgments for the favour we had done them. They rejoiced exceedingly at our happiness in thus being favoured by the great spirit, and felt very grateful that we had condescended to remember our brethren in the wilderness. But they could not help recollecting that we had a people among us, who, because they differed from us in colour, we had made slaves of, and made them suffer great hardships and lead miserable lives. Now, they could not see any reason, if a people being black, entitled us thus to deal with them, why a red colour would not equally justify the

2 H

same treatment. They therefore had determined to wait, to see whether all the black people amongst us were made thus happy and joyful, before they could put confidence in our promises; for they thought a people who had suffered so much and so long by our means, should be entitled to our first attention; that therefore they had sent back the two missionaries, with many thanks, promising that when they saw the black people among us restored to freedom and happiness, they would gladly receive our missionaries. This is what in any other case, would be called close reasoning, and is too mortifying a fact to make further observations upon.

The Indians to the northward, are said, by Mr. Colden, a laborious, sensible writer, in the times of their rejoicings, to repeat *yo-ha-han*, which, if true, evinces that their corruption advances in proportion as they are distant from South-America. But Mr. Colden, was an utter stranger to their language and manners, and might have mistaken their pronunciation—or if he wrote from information of others, he has not been accurate, *&c*.

It was a material, or rather an essential mistake to write *yo-ha-han*, as it is confounding their two religious words together. Mr. Adair was assured by Sir William Johnson, who had the management of Indian affairs for many years under the British government, as well as by the Rev. Mr. Ogilvie, a missionary with the Mohawks, that the northern Indians, always pronounced the words of their songs, *y-ho-he, a* or *ah*, and so Mr. Colden altered them in the second edition of his history. He also says, when the northern Indians, at a treaty or conference would give their assent, they answered *y. o. hah*—The speaker called out, *y. o. hah*, the rest answered in a sound, which could not be expressed in English letters, but seemed to consist of two words, remarkably distinguished in their cadence. The sachem of each nation, at the close of their chief's speech, called out severally, *y. o. hah.*

Charlevoix, in his history of Canada, says, that Father Grillon often told him, that after having laboured some time in the missions in Canada, he returned to France and went to China. One day as he was travelling through Tartary, he met a Huron woman, whom he had formerly known in Canada. She told him, that having been taken in war, she had been conducted from nation to nation, till she arrived at the place where she then was.

There was another missionary, passing by the way of Nantz, on his return from China, who related the like story of a woman he had seen from Florida, in America. She informed him, that she had been taken by certain Indians, and given to those of a distant country; and by these again to another nation, till she had been thus successively passed from country to country; had travelled regions exceedingly cold, and at last found herself in Tartary, and had there married a Tartar, who had passed with the conquerors into China, and there settled.

The Cherokees had an honourable title among them, called "the deer-killer of the great spirit, for his people." Every town had one solemnly appointed, who killed deer for the holy feasts. Thus Nimrod is said to have been "a mighty hunter before the Lord"—Gen. x. 9.

The Indian nations, in the coldest weather, and when the ground is covered with snow, practice their religious ablutions.

Men and children turn out of their warm houses, singing their usual sacred notes, at the dawn of day, *Y. O. He-wah*, and thus they skip along, singing till they get to the river, when they instantaneously plunge into it.

The Hebrews also had various washings and anointings. They generally, after bathing, anointed themselves with oil. Their kings, prophets and priests, were anointed with oil, and the Saviour himself is described as "*the Anointed*." The Indian priests and prophets, or beloved men, are always initiated by unction. The Chickesaws some time ago set apart some of their old men. They first obliged them to sweat themselves for the space of three days and nights, in a small hut made for the purpose, at a distance from the town, for fear of pollution, and from a strong desire they all have of secreting their religions mysteries. They eat nothing but green tobacco leaves, and drink only of button-snake wood tea, to cleanse their bodies, and prepare them to serve in the beloved, holy office. After which, their priestly garments are put on, with the ornaments before described, and then bear's oil is poured upon their heads. Like the Jews, both men and women frequently anoint themselves with bear's oil.

It may not be amiss to mention, that Indians never prostrate themselves, nor bow their bodies to each other, by way of salute or homage, except when they are making or renewing peace with strangers, who come in the name of *Yah*; then they bow their bodies in that religious solemnity. Also in their religious dances, for then they sing their hymns addressed to *Y. O. He-wah*.

The Indians would not eat either the Mexican hog, or of the sea-cow, or the turtle, as Gumilla and Edwards inform us;

but they held them in the greatest abhorrence. Neither would they eat the eel; nor of many animals and birds they deemed impure.

It was foretold by Moses, that the Israelites should "*walk in the stubbornness of their own hearts, to add drunkenness to thirst.*" God, by his prophet, threatens them in the severest manner for this abominable crime:

"Wo to the proud crown of *the drunkards of Ephraim*,
And to the fading flower of their glorious beauty!
To those that are at the head of the rich valley, that are stupified with wine!
Behold the mighty One! the exceedingly strong One!
Like a storm of hail, like a destructive tempest;
Like a rapid flood of mighty waters pouring down;
He shall dash them to the ground with his hand.
They shall be trodden under foot,
The proud crown of the *drunkards of Ephraim*.
——In that day shall Jehovah, God of Hosts, become a beauteous crown,
And a glorious diadem to the remnant of his people:
—— But even these have erred through wine, and through strong drink they have reeled;
The priest and the prophet have erred through strong drink;
They are overwhelmed with wine, they have reeled through strong drink;
They have erred in vision, they have stumbled in judgment,
For all their tables are full of vomit;
Of filthiness, so that no place is free."

(*Isaiah* xxviii. 1-8.—*Lowth's translation.*

This is one of the most terrible predictions denounced against them, and has been most awfully verified, should it turn out that the Indians in truth are of the lost ten tribes of Israel. Among all their vices, this seems the most predominant, and destroys every power of soul and body. It is not of this nation or that—of one tribe or another—or of one rank or the other; but it is universal, among men, women and children. In short, it is one, among a great number, of the unnatural returns made them by the Europeans of every nation, for the Indian's kindness at first, and their giving up their lands afterwards, the bringing in ardent spirits among them for lucre of gain, and by this means have reduced their numbers, and driven them into the wilderness. They have themselves long seen their misery in this respect, and have long been struggling to get rid of it; but all in vain, till of late years, many men of virtue and of real religion, have united with them, to aid them, without which it seems impossible that they can withstand this all-conquering enemy.

They will make laws against it—they will determine to expel all spiritous liquors from their towns, and they will with philosophical firmness, destroy large quantities of it, brought in by the traders by stealth. But if they once taste it, all the reasoning of the most beloved man will not prevent them drinking as long as a drop lasts, and generally they transform themselves into the likeness of mad foaming bears.

Mr. Colden says, "there is one vice which the Indians have fallen into since their acquaintance with the christians, and of which they could not have been guilty before that time, that is drunkenness. It is strange how all the Indian nations, and almost every person among them, male and female, are infatuated with the love of strong drink. They know no bounds to their desires, while they can swallow it down, and then, indeed, the greatest men amongst them scarcely deserve the name of a brute."

They complained heavily to the Rev. Mr. Brainerd, that before the coming of the English they knew of no such thing as strong drink. That the English had, by these means, made them quarrel with, and kill one another, and in a word, brought them to the practice of all those vices, that then prevailed among them. In an address, or rather an answer, made by the Delaware Indians in 1768, they say, "brothers! you have spoken to us against getting drunk. What you have said is very agreeable to our minds. We see it is a thing that is very bad, and it is a great grief to us that rum or any kind of strong liquor should be brought among us, as we wish the chain of friendship, which now unites us and our brethren the English together, may remain strong. Brothers! the fault is not all in us. It begins with our brothers, the white people. For if they will bring us rum, some of our people will buy it; it is for that purpose it is brought. But if none was brought, then we could not buy it. Brothers! we beseech you, be faithful and desire our brothers, the white people, to bring no more of it to us. Shew this belt to them for this purpose. Shew it to the great man of the fort (meaning the commandant at Fort Pitt) and to our brothers on the way as you return, and to the great men in Philadelphia, and in other places, from which rum may be brought, and intreat them not to bring any more."

There is a very early record in the history of New-Jersey, to the credit of both Indians and white inhabitants of that day. At a conference held with them, when eight kings or sachems were present, the Indian speaker said, "strong liquors were sold to us by the Swedes and by the Dutch. These people had no eyes. They did not see that it was hurtful to us. Nevertheless, if people will sell it to us, we are so in love with it we cannot forbear. But now, there is a people come to live among us that have eyes. They see it to be for our hurt. They are willing to deny themselves the profit for our good. This people have eyes. We are glad such people have come. We must put it down by mutual consent. We give these four belts of wampum to be witnesses of this agreement we make with you, and would have you to tell it to your children."

Several nominal prophets have lately risen among them, and have become very popular, by taking advantage of their superstition, and declaring themselves messengers from heaven. Whatever they may be in reality, they have done some good. The Onondagoes, greatly addicted to drunkenness, have, by the influence of the brother of Corn-Planter, a Seneca chief, been prevailed on to give up the use of spiritous liquors, and to become comparatively moral. Another of these prophets among the Shawanese and north-western Indians, has been equally successful.

All the promises of a God of truth, to his faithful servants, Abraham, Isaac and Jacob, must be strictly fulfilled, as well as the threatnings of his abused justice. God did make a solemn and special promise to Abraham, which was afterwards repeated to Isaac and Jacob, in very strong and expressive terms. And God said, "by myself have I sworn, saith the Lord, for because thou hast done this thing, and hast not withheld thy son, *thine only son*, that in blessing, I will bless thee, and in multiplying, I will multiply thy seed as the stars of heaven, and as the sand upon the sea shore, and thy seed shall possess the gates of his enemies"—Gen. xxii. 16, 17. Yet this was on condition of their observing the commandments that he had given them, for in case of disobedience, the threatnings were as explicit as the blessings.

"Jehovah hath sent a word against Jacob, and it hath lighted upon Israel—because the people all of them, carry themselves haughtily; Ephraim and the inhabitants of Samaria, and Jehovah, God of Hosts, they have not sought." Yet his mercy will not finally forsake them. For "it shall come to pass in *that day*, no more shall the remnant of Israel, and the escaped of the house of Jacob, lean upon him who smote them, but shall lean upon Jehovah, the holy one of Israel, in truth. A remnant shall return, even a remnant of Jacob unto the mighty God, for though thy people Israel be as the sand of the sea, yet a remnant of them only shall return: the consummation decided shall overflow with strict justice"—Lowth's Isaiah, x. 23. The learned Dr. Bagot, Dean of Christ's Church, Oxford, translates the last clause of the verse thus, "the accomplishment determined, overflows with justice; for it is accomplished, and that which is determined, the Lord of Hosts doth in the midst of the land"—vide Lowth's notes on Isaiah, page 81.

Hosea also repeats the affecting fate of Israel. "And the Lord said unto him, I will cause to cease, the kingdom of the house of Israel, for I will no more have mercy on the house of Israel; but I will utterly take them away. Yet the number of the children of Israel shall be as the sand of the sea, which cannot be measured or numbered; and it shall come to pass, that in the place where it was said unto them, *ye are not my people*, there it shall be said unto them, *ye are the sons of the living God*. Then shall the children of Judah, and the children of Israel be gathered together, and shall *appoint themselves* one head, and they shall come up out of the land, for great shall be the day of Jezreel."

And St. John says, "and the sixth angel poured out his vial on the *great river Euphrates*, and the waters thereof were dried up, that the way of the *kings of the east* might be prepared."

The Indian nations will answer, in a great measure, the description here given. That they have long been confined to wander in the wilderness of America, and that the consumption decreed has been awfully executed on them, cannot be denied. That they have been despised, and considered as barbarians, and children of the devil, is too true.

We have already enumerated one hundred and ninety nations within our scanty means of knowledge, and though many of them are destroyed and done away, for the consumption was decreed, yet if we look at the maps of travellers, and attend to the account given of the nations from Greenland to Mexico, and from thence to the nation of the Dog-ribbed Indians; thence to the Southern ocean, and along its coast northward to the Lake of the Woods, and thence to Hudson's Bay and Greenland, and estimate in addition, the nations of the interior, what nation or people in the world, can so literally answer to the strong figures, of the stars of heaven, and the sands of the sea.

Again, the tribes of Judah and Benjamin, attended by a few of the Israelites among them, scattered throughout Asia, Africa and Europe, have no pretensions to any king among them. But the Indians have a king to every tribe, and as we have seen, the Natchez had once five hundred kings in that one nation. Now if part of the nations to the north-west, should again return over the straits of Kamschatka, and pass on from the north-eastern extremity of Asia, by the way between the Euxine and the Caspian sea, through ancient Media, which formerly extended west to the river Halys, on the Black or Euxine sea* and Asia Minor, into Palestine, then they must pass through the territory of the Grand Porte. Therefore that government must necessarily be destroyed, to make way for these kings from the east, as it is not likely that despotic power would consent to their passing through in peace, to deprive her of the region of Palestine.

Another remarkable circumstance attending the foregoing account is, that before the Babylonish captivity, the Jews had but one temple for public worship, whither the males assembled three times in the year. The Samaritans, after the captivity, observed the same at Samaria, the capital of their kingdom. The ten tribes were carried captives into the north-west parts of Assyria, before the Babylonish captivity, and therefore had no idea of but one place of worship for a nation.

* The different empires of the Lydians and the Medes, were divided by the river Haly's (which has two branches,) which rising in a mountain of Armenia, passing through Celicia, leaving in its progress the Matenians on the right, and Phrygia on the left; then stretching towards the north, it separates the Cappadocian Syrians from Paphlagonia, which is on the left of the stream. Thus the river Halys separates all the lower parts of Asia from the sea, which flows opposite to Cyprus, as far as the Euxine, a space over which an active man could not travel in less than five days—1 Heredotus 112, 113.

The Indians have also but one temple, or beloved square for a nation, whither their males also assemble three times in the year, to wit:—at the Feast of First Fruits, generally the latter end of March and April, it being the beginning of their ecclesiastical year: at the end of which they have another, in imitation of the Passover. The feast for success in hunting, about the time of Pentecost, called the Hunter's Feast; and their great feast for the Expiation of Sin, which is about the time of the ripening of their indian corn and other fall fruit. These form a coincidence of circumstances in important and peculiar establishments, that could not, without a miracle, be occasioned by chance or accident. And though if considered individually, or each by itself, might be said, not to be conclusive evidence, yet taken altogether and compared with many other peculiarities of the Jewish people, they carry strong conviction to the understanding, that these wandering nations have some how or other had intimate connection with those once people of God.

CHAPTER IX.

The testimony of those who had an opportunity of judging, from the appearance and conduct of the Indians at the first discovery of America, as well as of some who have seen them since, in a state of nature.

AND first, that of Spanish authors. And here proper allowance must be made for the prevailing intentions of the first Spanish visitors, in their coming to America, which (with some few exceptions) were principally from the most covetous desires of amassing wealth, and obtaining immense riches at all risques, and by every means. Also it must be remembered, how few concerned themselves about the religious state of the natives, if they could but get their property; neither did they give themselves any trouble to know their history, their origin, customs, or future expectations; but their gold, their silver, their lands, and their furs, were the whole objects of their attention.

We thank God, there were some favourable exceptions. The learned world are by this time pretty well acquainted with the degree of confidence that ought to be put in the Spanish historians in general, further than their accounts are confirmed and supported by after labours of historians of character among other nations.

Few of them conversed with the natives, in such a manner as to gain their confidence, or obtain any intimate knowledge of their customs and manners, with any tolerable degree of certainty. They did not treat them as friends, but as the most inveterate enemies, and despised, hated and murdered them, without remorse or compunction, in return for their kindness and respect. And to excuse their own ignorance, and to cast a mantle over their most shocking, barbarous, cool and premeditated murders, they artfully described them as an abominable swarm of idolatrous cannibals, offering human sacrifices to their false deities, and eating the unnatural victims. Notwithstanding, from even many of these partial accounts, we can trace a near agreement between the civil and martial customs, the religious worship, traditions, dress, ornaments, and other particulars of the ancient Peruvians and Mexicans, and those of the Indians of North-America.

Acosta tells us, that the Mexicans had no proper name for God, yet that they allowed a *supreme omnipotence and providence.* His capacity was not sufficient to discover the former, however, the latter means that very being, and agrees with the religious opinion of their North-American brethren.

Lopez de Gamara, tells us that the Americans were so devout as to offer to the sun and earth, a small quantity of every kind of meat and drink, before any of themselves tasted of it, and that they sacrificed a part of their corn, fruits, &c. in like manner.

Is not this a confused Spanish account of the imitation of the Jewish daily sacrifice, which we have before seen our more northern Indians, in the constant habit of offering to the supreme holy spirit of fire, whom they invoke in their sacred song of *Y. Ho. He-wah,* and loudly ascribe to him, *hal-le-lu-wah,* for his continued goodness to them.

The Spanish writers say, that when Cortes approached Mexico, Montezuma shut himself up, and continued for the space of eight days, in prayer and fasting; but to blacken him, and excuse their own diabolical conduct, they assert, that he offered human sacrifices at the same time, to abominable and frightful idols. These prayers and fastings, were doubtless the same with those of the northern Indians, who on particular occasions, seek to sanctify themselves, and regain the favour of the deity.

Yet these same authors tell us, that they found there, a temple called *Teucalli,* or the house of the great spirit, and a person belonging to it, called *Chacalmua,* that is, a minister of holy things. They likewise speak of the hearth of the great spirit—the continual fire of the great spirit—the holy ark, &c.

Acosta says, that the Peruvians held a very extraordinary feast, called *Ytu,* which they prepared themselves for by fasting two days, not accompanying with their wives, or eating salt meat or garlic, or drinking *chicca* during that period. That they assembled altogether in one place, and did not allow any stranger or beast to approach them. That they had clothes and ornaments which they wore only at that great festival. That they went silently and sedately in procession, with their heads veiled and drums beating; and that this continued one day and night. But the next day they danced and feasted, and for two days successively, their prayers and praises were heard.

This appears no other than our northern Indians' great festival to atone for sin, according to the Mosaic system.

Lericus tells you, that he was present at the triennial feast of the Charibbeans, where a multitude of men, women and children, were assembled. That they soon divided themselves into three orders, a part from each other, the women and children being strictly commanded to stay within, and attend diligently to the singing. That the men sang in one house, he-he-he, while the others, in their separate houses, answered by a repetition of the like notes. Thus they continued a quarter of an hour, dancing in three rings, with rattles. They also tell us, that the *high-priest,* or *beloved man,* was anointed with holy oil, and dressed with pontifical ornaments peculiar to himself, when he officiated in his sacred function.

Ribault Landon describing the annual festival of the Floridians, says, that the day before it began, the women swept out a great circuit of ground, where it was observed with solemnity. That when the main body of the people entered the holy ground, they all placed themselves in good order, decked in their best apparel, when three beloved men, or priests, with different painting and gestures, followed them, playing on musical instruments, and singing with solemn voices, the others answering them. And when they made three circles, the men ran off to the woods, and the women staid weeping behind, cutting their arms with muscle shells, and throwing the blood towards the sun. And when the men returned, the three days were finished.

This is no other than the northern Indians' Passover, or the Feast of Love, badly told, attended with their universal custom of bleeding themselves after great exercise, which the Spaniards foolishly supposed they offered up to the sun

These Spanish writers also assure us, that the Mexicans had a feast and month, which they called Hueitozolti, when the indian corn was ripe. Every man at that time bringing an handful to be offered at the temple, with a kind of drink made out of the same grains. This is no other than the first fruit offering of the northern Indians.

Don Antonio de Ulloa informs us, that some of the South-American natives cut the lobes of their ears, and fasten small weights to them, in order to lengthen them; and others cut holes in their upper and under lips, in which they hang pieces of shells, rings, &c.* This also agrees with the practice of every nation of the northern Indians.

Mr. Bartram says, "their ears are lacerated, separating the border or cartilagenous limb, which is first bound round, very close and tight, with leather strings or thongs, and anointed with fresh bear's oil, until healed. The weight of the lead which they hang to it, extends the cartilage, which after being craped or bound round with brass or silver wire, extends it semi circularly, like a bow or crescent, and it is then very elastic. It is then decorated with a plume of white herons feathers.

Acosta says, that the clothes of the South-Americans are shaped like those of the ancient Jews, being a square little cloak, over a little coat.

Lact, in his description of South-America, as well as *Escarbotus*, assures us, that he often heard the South-Americans repeat the word *hallelujah*. And *Malvenda* says that the na-

* Mr. Bruce in his travels, speaking of a sect of christians called Remmout, says, "their women pierce their ears, and apply weights to make them hang down and enlarge the holes, into which they put ear-rings almost as big as shackles, in the same manner as do the Bedowise, in Syria and Palestine"—4 vol. p. 275.

tives of St. Michael had tomb-stones with several ancient Hebrew characters upon them, as "*why is God gone away?*" and "*he is dead, God knows.*"

The Michuans, one of the original nations of Mexico, held, according to the *Abbe Clavigero's* declaration, this tradition, that "there was once a great deluge, and *Tepzi,* as they call Noah, in order to save himself from being drowned, embarked in a ship formed like an ark, with his wife, his children, and many different animals, and several seeds and fruits. As the waters abated, he sent out the bird, which bears the name of *aura,* which remained eating dead bodies. He then sent out other birds, which did not return, except the little bird called the *flower sucker,* which brought a small branch with it"—Panoplist for June 1813, page 9. From this family of *Tepzi,* the *Michuccans* all believed they derived their origin. Both Malvenda and Acosta affirm that the natives observed a year of jubilee, according to the usage of the Israelites.

Emanual de Moraez, a Portuguese historian, in his history of Brazil, says, "America has been wholly peopled by the *Carthagenians* and *Israelites.* As to the last, he says nothing but circumcision is wanting to constitute a perfect resemblance between them and the Brazilians." And we have seen, that some of the nations practice it to this day.

Monsieur Poutrincourt says, that at an early day, when the Canada Indians saluted him, they said *ho-ho-ho.*

Mr. Edwards, in his history of the West-Indies, says, "that the striking conformity of the prejudices and customs of the Charibbee Indians, to the practices of the Jews, has not escaped the notice of historians, as *Gumella, Du Tertre,* and others."

Adair, who was the most careful observer of the Indians' whole economy, both public and private, and had the best opportunity of knowing it, without much danger of deception, beyond any other writer, gives his opinion in these words. "It is a very difficult thing to divest ourselves of prejudices and favourite opinions, and I expect to be censured for opposing commonly received sentiments. But truth is my object, and from the most exact observations I could make in the long time I traded among the Indian Americans, I was forced to believe them to be lineally descended from the Israelites."

The *Rev. Mr. Beatty* says, "I have before hinted that I have taken great pains to search into the usages and customs of the Indians, in order to see what ground there was for supposing them to be part of the ten tribes of the Jews, and I must own, to my no small surprise, that a number of their customs appear so much to resemble those of the Jews, that it is a great question with me, whether we can expect to find among the ten tribes (wherever they are) at this day, all things considered, more of the footsteps of their ancestors than among the different Indian tribes. It is not forgotten that the Indians are charged, as a barbarous, revengeful, cruel and blood thirsty race—deceitful, ungrateful, and ever ready for murder and rapine. Most of this will not be disputed. They are educated from their infancy to make war in this cruel manner. They scalp their fallen enemy, and most cruelly torment and burn some of those whom they take prisoners. This they think lawful, and often plead the will of the great spirit for it. It is their habitual custom, and they make war on these principles. But they have their virtues too. They pay the greatest respect to female prisoners, and are never known to offer them the least indecency. Whenever they determine to spare their enemies, which is often done, they not only make them free, but they adopt them into their families, and make them a part of their nation, with all the privileges of a native Indian. This is an instance of mildness and generosity known to very few savages in the world, but rather resembles the Romans.

They are generous, hospitable, kind and faithful to their friends or strangers, in as great a degree as they are vindictive and barbarous to their enemies in war.

Col. Smith, in his journal mentions, "that he went a great distance hunting with his patron Tontileaugo, along the shore of Lake Erie. Here we staid several days on account of the high winds, which raised the lake in great billows. Tontileaugo went out to hunt. When he was gone a Wiandot came to the camp—I gave him a shoulder of venison well roasted. He received it gladly—told me he was hungry, and thanked me for my kindness. When my patron came home, I told him what I had done—he answered, it was very well, and supposed I had given him also sugar and bears oil to eat with his venison—I told him I did not, as both were down in the canoe, and I did not go for them. He replied, you have behaved just like a Dutchman. Do you not know, that when strangers come to our camp, we ought always to give them the best that we have. I acknowledged my fault. He said that he would excuse this as I was but young; but I must learn to behave like a warrior, and do great things, and never be found in such little actions."—Page 25, 26.

Smith, in his history of New-Jersey, informs us, "that the Indians long remembered kindnesses families or individuals had shewn them. This also must undoubtedly be allowed, that the original and more incorrupt among them, very seldom forgot to be grateful, where real benefits had been received. And notwithstanding the stains of perfidy and cruelty, which latterly, in 1754, and since, have disgraced the Indians on the frontiers of these provinces, (but which the writer well knows had been produced by the wicked and unjust oppression of these sons of nature, by the white people) even these, by the uninterrupted intercourse of seventy years, had, on many occasions, given irrefragable proofs of liberality of sentiment, hospitality of action and impressions, that seemed to promise a continuation of better things. Witness their first reception of the English—their selling their lands to them afterwards—their former undeviating candor at treaties in Pennsylvania, and other incidents."—Page 144.

But however guilty these unhappy wandering nations may have been, neither Europeans or Americans ought to complain so heavily of Indian cruelties, particularly in scalping their enemies, which is one of their most habitual cruelties, and in which they glory. They are too fully justified in this horrible practice, by the encouragement and example of those who call themselves *civilized*, and even christians. Herodotus informs us that the Scythians scalped their enemies, and used them as trophies of victory. Polybius says, in the war with the Mercenaries, *Gisco,* the Carthagenian general, and seven hundred prisoners were scalped *alive.* Varrus, the Roman general, caused two thousand Jews, whom he had taken prisoners, to be crucified at one time—Josephus, 4 vol. chap. iii. page 12.

Under the mild government of Great-Britain, and that of France, premiums have been promised and given to the Indians, by their governors and generals, for the scalps of their enemies. Nay, even in America, acts of assembly have been passed, giving rewards to the *civilized* inhabitants, for scalps and prisoners, even so high as one hundred pounds for an Indian scalp—2d Colden, 120. If it should be said the government of Great-Britain ought not to be charged with this, it is answered that government not only knew of all this, but during our revolutionary war, the British secretary of state, in the House of Lords, supported its policy and necessity, as they ought to use every means that God and nature had put into their hands.—Belsham. They had in their service at that time, at least fifteen hundred Indian warriors.

Mr. Belsham says, that in the revolutionary war with America, the son of Sir William Johnson, "held a great war feast with the Indians, chiefly Iroquois, when he invited them to banquet upon a Bostonian and to drink his blood." And though I doubt not but this was mere hyperbolical language, yet did it not countenance and encourage the Indians in their customary cruelty and vindictive rage?*

* But are the United States, with all their boasted freedom and philanthropy, free from blame on this subject? The following is an extract from a report from Brigadier General Clayborne, to the Secretary of War, since these sheets have been prepared for the press, even so late as 1st January, 1814. "Sir, on the 13th ultimo, I marched a detachment from this post, with a view of destroying the towns of the inimical Creek Indians, on the Alabama, above the mouth of the Cahaba. After having marched about eighty miles, I was within thirty miles of a town newly erected on ground called holy, occupied by a large body of the enemy." "About noon of the 23d, the right column, commanded by col. Joseph Carson, came in view of the town called Eckanachacu, (or holy ground) and was vigorously attacked"—"Thirty of the enemy were killed, and judging from every appearance, many were wounded." "In the town we found a large quantity of provisions, and immense property of various kinds, which the enemy, flying precipi-

In 1794, the six nations, including a late addition of those of Grand River in Canada, the Stockbridge and Brotherton Indians, consisted of about six thousand souls. They now do

tately, were obliged to leave behind, and which together with two hundred houses were destroyed. They had barely time to remove their women and children across the Alabama, which runs near where the town stood. The next day was occupied in destroying a town consisting of sixty houses, eight miles higher up the river." "The town first destroyed, was built since the commencement of hostilities, and was established as a place of security for the inhabitants of several villages." Three principal prophets resided there---United States Gazette, 15th February, 1814. In Nile's Register, of September 26, 1812, we find this pleasing flight of the imagination of the friends of the war. "Imagination (says the Register) looks forward to the moment, when all the southern Indians [meaning as well in Florida as in Georgia] shall be pushed across the Missisippi." And again in the same paper "fortunately this nation [meaning the Creeks in Georgia] have supplied us with a pretext for dismembering their country." Now the southern Indians had not at that time taken up the hatchet against the United States. In proof of this, we have the assertion of Governor Mitchel, who in his speech to the legislature of Georgia, October 1812, (the next month after the above publication in the Register) said, "as yet those [Indians] within the United States lines, profess peace and friendship." Shortly after this speech the war with the southern Indians was commenced. The radical cause of it is more than broadly hinted at in the letter of the Governor of St. Augustine, to Governor Mitchel, dated December 12, 1812---He, along with other warm expostulations, regarding the conspiracy of the people of Georgia, to expel or destroy the Indians, has the following; "The Indians are to be insulted, threatened and driven from their lands; if they resist, nothing less than extermination is to be their fate; but you deceive yourself sir, if you think the world is blind to your motives; it is not long since the state of Georgia had a slice of Indian lands, and the fever is again at its height." Accordingly, in 1813, Nile's Register sounded the tocsin for their extermination. "All these pleasing prospects, says he, are clouded by blood, and forever blasted by that treacherous people [meaning the Creeks] for whom we have done so much, so that mercy itself seems to demand their extermination. And afterwards, "the fighting continued, with some severity, about five hours, but we continued to destroy many of them, "that is after the fighting was over," who had concealed themselves under the bank of the river, until we were prevented by night. This morning we killed sixteen, who had been concealed."---Poulson's Daily Advertiser, June 24, 1814.

Yet we are the people who remonstrate with zealous warmth and loud recrimination against the barbarism of the British army, in wantonly burning our towns and injuring the defenceless inhabitants, contrary to the rules of civilized warfare---a strange warfare it must be---Civilized warfare, what a contradiction in express terms. Alas! what has not our nation to answer for at the bar of retributive justice. The capitol of Washington, in flames, instructs on this occasion.

not exceed half that number. They have not reserved to them now, above two hundred thousand acres of land out of their immense territory of at least one thousand miles long, and five hundred miles broad.—Clinton 48, 53.

The famous capt. Cook, in his visit to the coast of America, in the south seas, without any reference to this great question, barely gives you the facts that appeared to him during the very short intercourse he had with them—2 vol. 266, 283.

He says that "the inhabitants met them, singing in slow and then quicker time, accompanying their notes with beating time in concert, with their paddles, and regular motions of their hands, and other expressive gestures. At the end of each song, they remained silent, and then began again pronouncing *ho-ho-ah*, forcibly as a chorus. The ship's crew listened with great admiration—the natives behaved well.

"The people of Nootka Sound, keep the exactest concert in their songs, by great numbers together—they are slow and solemn—their variations are numerous and expressive, and the cadence or melody powerfully soothing—their music was sometimes varied from its predominant solemnity of air, and sung in a more gay and lively strain—they have a weapon made of stone, not unlike the American tomahawk, they call it *Taaweesh* and *Tsusknah.*—Page 310.

Their manufactures and mechanic arts are far more extensive and ingenious than the savages of the South Sea Islands, whether we regard the design or the execution. Their flannel and woollen garments, made of the bark of a pine tree beaten into an hempen state, with various figures artificially inserted into them, with great taste, and of different colours of exquisite brightness. They are also famous for painting and carving—ibid 304. Their common dress is a flannel garment or mantle, ornamented on the upper edge by a narrow strip of fur, and at the latter edge by fringes or tassels. Over this, which reaches below the knees, is worn a small cloak of the same substance, likewise fringed at the lower part. Every reader must be reminded by this of the fringes and tassels of the Jews on their garments.

In Prince William's Sound, the common dress is a kind of frock or robe, reaching to the knees, and sometimes to the ankles, made of the skins of animals; and in one or two instances they had woollen garments. All are ornamented with tassels or fringes. A few had a cape or collar, and some a hood. This bears a great resemblance to the dress of the Greenlanders, as described by Crantz—ibid 367—8. The reader will find in *Crantz*, many striking instances, in which the Greenlanders and Americans of this part of America resemble each other, besides those mentioned by capt. Coook"—vol. 1, 136, 138.

Father Joseph Gumella, in his account of the nations bordering on the Oronoko, relates that the Charibbee Indians of the continent, punished their women caught in adultery, like the ancient Jews, by stoning them to death before the assembly of the people—Edward's West-Indies, 1 vol. 39, in a note.

CHAPTER X.

The Indians have a system of morality among them, that is very striking.—They have teachers to instruct them in it—of which they have thought very highly, till of late years, they begin to doubt its efficacy.

WE are indebted to Dobson's Encyclopedia for the following testimony in favour of Indian morality—vol. 1, page 557. It is the advice given from a father to a son, it is believed, taken from a Spanish author. "My son, who art come into the light from the womb, we know not how long heaven will grant to us the enjoyment of that precious gem, which we possess in thee. But however short the period, endeavour to live exactly—praying to the great spirit continually to assist thee. He created thee—thou art his property. He is thy father, and loves thee still more than I do. Repose in him thy thoughts, and day and night direct thy sighs to him. Reverence and salute thy elders, and hold no one in contempt. To the poor and distressed be not dumb, but rather use words of comfort." "Mock not, my son, the aged or the imperfect. Scorn not him who you see fall into some folly or transgression, nor make him reproaches; and beware lest thou fall into the same error, which offends thee in another. Go not where thou art not called, nor interfere in that which does not concern thee." "No more, my son. Enough has been said in discharge of the duties of a father. With these councils I wish to fortify thy mind. Refuse them not, nor act in contradiction to them; for on them, thy life and all thy happiness depend."

Mr. Beatty, when among the Indians on the Ohio, addressed them. In answer, the speaker said, "that they believed that there was a great spirit above, and desired to serve him in the best manner they could. That they thought of him at their rising up, and lying down; and hoped he would look upon them, and be kind to them, and do them good." In the evening several came to their lodging. Among these was one called Neolin, a young man, who used for some time past to speak to his brethren, the Indians, about their wicked ways. He had taken great pains with them, and so far as Mr. Beatty could learn, he had been the means of reforming a number of them. He was informed by a captive, who had been adopted into Neolin's family, that he frequently used to boil a quantity of bitter roots, till the water became very strong—that he drank plentifully of this liquor, and made his family and relatives drink of it. That it proved a severe emetic. The end of which, as Neolin said, was to cleanse them from their inward sins."

The following is an account of their evening entertainment at Altasse, one of the Creek towns, in the year 1778. The writer, after describing the council house, where the Indians met, says, "the assembly being now seated in order, and the house illuminated by their mystical cane fire in the middle; two middle aged men came in together, each having a very large conck shell, full of black drink, advancing with slow, uniform and steady steps, their eyes and countenances lifted up, and singing very low, but sweetly, till they came within six or eight steps of the king's and white people's seats, when they stopped, and each rested his shell on a little table; but soon taking it up again, advanced, and each presented his shell, one to the king, and the other to the chief of the white people; and as soon as he raised it to his mouth, they uttered or sang two notes, each of which continued as long as he had breath, and as long as these notes continued, so long must the person drink, or at least keep the shell to his mouth. These long notes are very solemn, and at once strike the imagination with a religious awe and homage to the Supreme Being, sounding somewhat like *a-hoo-o-jah* and *a-lu-yah*. After this manner the whole assembly were treated, as long as the drink and light continued to hold out. As soon as the drink began, tobacco and pipes were brought in. The king or chief smoked, first in the great pipe, a few whiffs, blowing it off ceremoniously, first towards the sun, or as it is generally supposed, to the great spirit, for it is puffed upwards; next towards the four cardinal points; then towards the white people in the house. Then the great pipe is taken from the hand of the *king*, and presented to the chief *white man*, and then to the great *war chief*, from whence it is circulated through the ranks of head men and warriors; and then returned to the chief. After this, each one filled his pipe from his own, or his neighbour's pouch. Here all classes of citizens resort every night in the summer or moderate season. The women and children are not allowed, or very seldom, to enter the public square."

In this same year, the son of the Spanish governor of St. Augustine, in East Florida, with two of his companions, were brought in prisoners, they being then at war with that province. They were all condemned to be burned. The English traders in the town petitioned the Indians in their behalf, expressing their wishes to obtain their pardon, offering a great ransom, acquainting them at the same time with their rank. Upon this, the head men, or chiefs, of the whole nation, were convened; and after solemn and mature deliberation, returned the traders their final answer, in the following address:

"Brothers and friends—we have been considering upon this business concerning the captives, and that under the eye and fear of the great spirit. You know that these people are our cruel enemies—they save no lives of us red men, who fall in their power. You say that the youth is the son of the Spanish governor—we believe it. We are sorry that he has fallen into our hands, but he is our enemy. The two young men, his friends, are equally our enemies. We are sorry to see them here. But we know no difference in their flesh and blood. They are equally our enemies. If we save one, we must save all three. But we cannot do this. The red men require their blood to appease the spirits of their slain relatives. They have entrusted us with the guardianship of our laws and rights—we cannot betray them. However, we have a sacred prescription relative to this affair, which allows us to extend mercy to a certain degree. A third is to be saved by lot. The great spirit allows us to put it to that decision. He is no respecter of persons." The lots were cast. The governor's son and one of his friends were taken and burnt.

This must certainly appear to some as the act of barbarians, but how far is it removed from the practice of the Jews, when they so vociferously called out, crucify him, crucify him? And Pilate said ye have a custom that I should release a prisoner to you at the feast, but they cried more bitterly, not this man, but Barabbas.

A minister preaching to a congregation of christian Indians, west of the Delaware, observed a stranger Indian, listening with great attention. After the service, the minister enquired who he was? It appeared on enquiry, that he lived three hundred miles to the westward—that he had just arrived and gave this account of himself. "That his elder brother living in his house, had been many days and nights in great perplexity, wishing to learn to know the great spirit, till at length he resolved to retire into the woods, supposing that he should succeed better in a state of separation from all mankind. Having spent many weeks alone in great affliction, he thought he saw a man of majestic appearance, who informed him that there were Indians living to the south-east, who were acquainted with the great spirit and the way to everlasting life; adding that he should go home and tell his people, what he had seen and heard. For this reason, as soon as he heard his brother speak, he determined to travel in search of the people he had described, till he found them; and since he had heard what had been said that day, the words had been welcome to his heart."

A missionary made a journey to the Shawanese country, the most savage of the Indian nations. He stopped at the first village he came to, and lodged with one of the chief men. He informed the chief of his business, and opened some truths of the gospel to him by means of an interpreter who accompanied him. The chief paid great attention, and after sometime told him, that he was convinced that the missionary's doctrines were true, pointing out the right road. That the *Shawanese* had been long striving to find out the way of life; but that he must own, with regret, that all their labour and researches had been in vain. That they, therefore, had lost all courage, not knowing what they should do further, to obtain happiness. The chief accompanied the missionary to the next village and persuaded him to lodge with a heathen teacher.

The missionary then preached to him, and told him that he had brought him the words of eternal life. This the Indian said was what they wanted, and they would hear him with pleasure. After some days, the heathen teacher said, I have not been able to sleep all night, for I am continually meditating upon your words, and will now open to you my whole heart. I believe what you say is the truth. A year ago I became convinced, that we are altogether sinful creatures, and that none of our good works can save us; but I did not know what to do to get relief. I have therefore always comforted my people, that some body would come and shew us the true way to happiness, for we are not in the right way. And even but the day before you came, I desired my people to have a little patience, and that some teacher would certainly come. Now you are come, and I verily believe that the great spirit has sent you to make known his word to us."

Monsieur De Lapoterie, a French author, speaking of the Cherokees and other southern Indians, gives this account of them: "These Indians look upon the end of life, to be living happily; and for this purpose their whole customs are calculated to prevent avarice, which they think embitters life.

Nothing is a more severe reflection among them than to say, *that a man loves his own*. To prevent the use and propagation of such a vice, upon the death of an Indian, they burn all that belongs to the deceased, that there may be no temptation for the parent to hoard up a superfluity of arms or domestic conveniences for his children. They cultivate no more land than is necessary for their plentiful subsistence and hospitality to strangers. At the feast of expiation, they also burn all the fruits of the earth and grain left of the past year's crops.

Mr. Brainerd informs us, that at about one hundred and thirty miles from our settlements, he met with an Indian, who was said to be a devout and zealous reformer. He was dressed in a hideous and terrifick manner. He had a house consecrated to religious purposes. Mr. Brainerd discoursed with him about christianity, and some of the discourse he seemed to like, but some of it he wholly rejected. He said that God had taught him his religion, and that he would never turn from it; but wanted to find some who would heartily join him in it, for the Indians had grown very degenerate and corrupt. He said he had thoughts of leaving all his friends and travelling abroad in order to find some who would join with him, for he believed that the great spirit had good people some where, who felt as he did. He said that he had not always felt as he then did, but had formerly been like the rest of the Indians, until about four or five years before that time. Then he said, that his heart was very much distressed, so that he could not live among the Indians, but got away into the woods and lived for some months. At length he said the great spirit had comforted his heart and shewed him what he should do; and since that time he had known the great spirit and tried to serve him, and loved all men, be they who they may, so as he never did before. He treated Mr. Brainerd with uncommon courtesy, and seemed to be hearty in it.

2 M

The other Indians said, that he had opposed their drinking strong liquor with all his power; and if at any time he could not dissuade them from it, he would leave them and go crying into the woods. It was manifest that he had a set of religious notions of his own, that he had looked into for himself, and had not taken for granted upon bare tradition; and he relished or disrelished, whatever was spoken of a religious nature, according as it agreed or disagreed with his standard. He would sometimes say, now, *that* I like, so the great spirit has taught me, &c. Some of his sentiments seemed very just; yet he utterly denied the existence of an evil spirit, and declared there was no such a being known among the Indians of old times, whose religion he supposed he was attempting to revive. He also said that departed souls went southward, and that the difference between the good and bad was, that the former were admitted into a beautiful town with spiritual walls, or walls agreeably to the nature of souls. The latter would forever hover round those walls, and in vain attempt to get in. He seemed to be sincere, honest and conscientious in his own way, and according to his own religious notions, which was more than could be said of most other pagans Mr. Brainerd had seen. He was considered and derided by the other Indians as a precise zealot, who made an unnecessary noise about religious matters, but in Mr. Brainerd's opinion, there was something in his temper and disposition that looked more like true religion, than any thing he had observed among other heathen Indians.

Smith, in his history of New-Jersey, gives the following extract from a letter on this subject, from an Indian interpreter, the well known Conrad Wiser—145.

"I write this to give an account of what I have observed amongst the Indians, in relation to their belief and confidence in a divine being, according to the observations I have made from the year 1714, in the time of my youth to this day. If by the word *religion*, is meant an assent to certain creeds, or the observation of a set of religious duties, as appointed prayers, singing, preaching, baptism, &c. or even heathenish worship, then it may be said, the Five Nations have no religion; but if by religion we mean, an attraction of the soul to God, whence proceeds a confidence in and an hunger after the knowledge of him, then this people must be allowed to have some religion among them, notwithstanding their some times savage deportment; for we find among them some traits of a confidence in God alone, and even some times, though but seldom, a vocal calling upon him.

In the year 1737, I was sent for the first time to Onondago, at the desire of the governor of Virginia. I sat out the latter end of February, for a journey of five hundred English miles, through a wilderness where there was neither road nor path; there were with me a Dutchman and three Indians." He then gives a most fearful account of the distresses to which they were driven—particularly on the side of a mountain where the snow was so hard, that they were obliged to make holes in it with their hatchets to put their feet in, to keep them from sliding down the mountain. At length one of the Indians slipped and went down the mountain, but on his way was stopped by the string of his pack hitching fast to a stump of a small tree. They were obliged then to go down into the valley, when they looked up and saw "that if the Indian had slipped four or five paces further he would have fallen over a rock, one hundred feet perpendicular, upon craggy pieces of rock below. The Indian was astonished and turned quite pale—then with out-stretched arms, and great earnestness, spoke these words, *I thank the great Lord and Governor of this world that he has had mercy upon me, and has been willing that I should live longer;* which words I at that time sat down in my journal. This happened on the 25th March, 1737."

On the 9th April following, he was reduced so low that he gave up all hopes of ever getting to his journey's end. He stepped aside and sat down under a tree, expecting there to die. His companions soon missed him—they came back and found him sitting there. "I told them that I would go no further, but would die there." They remained silent awhile, at last the old Indian said, *my dear companion, thou hast hitherto encouraged us, wilt thou now quite give up? Remember that evil days are better than good days, for when we suffer much, we do not sin; and sin will be drove out of us by suffering; but good days cause men to sin, and God cannot extend his mercy to them, but contrarywise, when it goeth evil with us, God hath compassion on us.* These words made me ashamed; I rose up and travelled on as well as I could." "Two years ago I was sent by the governor to Shamoken, on account of the unhappy death of John Armstrong," after he had performed his errand, which was to make peace by the punishment of the murderer. The Indians made a great feast for him; and after they had done, the chief addressed his people, and exhorted them to thankfulness to God—then began to sing with an awful solemnity, but without expressing words, the others accompanied him with their voices. After they had done, the same Indian, with great earnestness said, *thanks! thanks! be to thee, thou great Lord of the world, in that thou hast again caused the sun to shine and hast dispersed the dark cloud. The Indians are thine.*"

The old king *Ockanickon,* who died in 1681, in Burlington, New-Jersey, just before his death, sent for his brother's son, whom he had appointed to be king after him; he addressed him thus, "My brother's son, this day I deliver my heart into your bosom—mind me. I would have you love what is good, and keep good company; refuse what is evil, and by all means avoid bad company." "Brother's son! I would have you cleanse your ears, that you may hear both good and evil; and then join with the good and refuse the evil; and where you see evil, do not join with it, but join to that which is good." "Brother's son! I advise you to be plain and fair, with all, both Indians and christians, as I have been. I am very weak, otherwise I would have spoken more." After he stopped, Mr. Budd, one of the proprietors of West-Jersey, said to him, "there is a great God, who created all things; that he had given man an understanding of what was good and bad; and after this life rewarded the good with blessings, and the bad according to their doings." The king answered, "*it is very true. It is so. There are two ways, a broad and a straight way; there are two paths, a broad and a straight path; the worst and the greatest number go in the broad, the best and fewest, in the straight path.*"—Smith's history New-Jersey, 149. The Indians originally shewed great integrity in their dealings, especially with one another.

Col. Smith informs us that going a hunting to a very great distance, and having got many skins and furs by the way, very inconvenient to carry, they stretched them on scaffolds and left them till their return.

When they returned some considerable time after, they found their skins and furs all safe. "Though this was a public place and Indians often passing and our skins hanging up to view, yet there were none stolen, and it is seldom that Indians do steal any thing from one another; and they say they *never* did, until the white people came among them, and learned some of them to lie, cheat and steal."—Page 42.

He further informs us that being in the woods in the month of February, there fell a snow and then came a severe frost that when they walked caused them to make a noise by breaking through the crust, and so frightened the deer that they could get nothing to eat. He hunted two days without food, and then returned fatigued, faint and weary. He related his want of success. Tontileaugo asked him if he was not hungry—he said he was—he ordered his little son to bring him something to eat. He brought him a kettle with some bones and broth, made from those of a fox and wild cat that the ravens and turkey buzzards had picked, and which lay about the camp. He speedily finished his repast and was greatly refreshed. Tontileaugo gave him a pipe and tobacco—and when he had done smoking, he said that he had something of importance to tell him—Smith said he was ready to hear. He said he had deferred his speech, because few men were in a right humor to hear good talk when they are extremely hungry, as they are then generally fretful and discomposed; but as you appear now to enjoy calmness and serenity of mind, I will now communicate the thoughts of my heart, and those things which I know to be true. Brother!—As you have lived with the white people, you have not had the same advantage of knowing that the great *being* above, feeds his people and gives them their meat in due season, as we Indians have, who are frequently out of provisions, and yet are wonderfully supplied, and that so frequently, that it is evidently the hand of the great Owaneeyo, (this in their language signifies the owner and ruler of all things) that doeth this. Whereas the white people have large stocks of tame cattle that they can kill when they please, and also their barns and cribs filled with grain, and therefore have not the same opportunity of seeing and knowing that they are supported by the ruler of heaven and earth. Brother! I know that you are now afraid that we will all perish with hunger; but you have no just reason to fear this. Brother! I have been young but am now old! I have frequently been under the like circumstances that we now are, and that, sometime or other, in almost every year of my life; yet I have hitherto been supported and my wants supplied in times of need. Brother! Owaneeyo! sometimes suffers us to be in want, in order to teach us our dependance upon him, and to let us know that we are to love and serve him; and likewise to know the worth of the favours that we receive and to make us more thankful." Was not this one of the great ends designed by a gracious God, in leading the Israelites through the wilderness for forty years—vide Lowth's Isaiah, xli. 17, &c.—vide 2 Du Pratz, 172, for account of great spirit. "Brother! be assured that you will be supplied with food and that just in the right time; but you must continue diligent in the use of means—go to sleep and rise early in the morning and go a hunting—be strong and exert yourself like a man, and the great spirit will direct your way." The next morning, Smith rose early and set off. He travelled near twelve miles and was just despairing, when he came across a herd of buffaloes and killed a large cow. He loaded himself with the beef, and returned to his camp and found his patron, late in the evening in good spirits and humor. The old Indian thanked him for his exertion and commanded his son to cook it—which he did, but eating some himself almost raw. They put some on to boil, and when Smith was hurrying to take it off his patron calmly said, let it be done enough, as if he had not wanted a meal. He prevented his son from eating but a little at a time, saying it would hurt him, but that he might sup a few spoonsful of the broth. When they were all refreshed, Tontileaugo delivered a speech upon the necessity and pleasure of receiving the necessary supports of life with thankfulness, knowing that *Owaneeyo* is the great giver. Sometime after they set off for home, Tontileaugo on the way, made himself a sweat-house and went into it, and put himself in a most violent perspiration for about fifteen minutes, singing aloud. This he did in order to purify himself before he would address the Supreme Being. He then began to burn tobacco and to pray—He began each petition with Oh! Oh! Oh! Oh!—He began his address in the following manner.

O great being! I thank thee that I have obtained the use of my legs again—(he had been ill with the rheumatism) that I am now able to walk about and kill turkeys, &c. without feeling exquisite pain and misery. I know that thou art a hearer and a helper, and therefore I will call upon thee. Oh, Oh, Oh, Oh!—grant that my knees and ankles may be right well, and that I may be able not only to walk, but to run and to jump logs, as I did last fall. Oh! Oh! Oh! Oh! grant that on this voyage we may frequently kill bears, as they may be crossing the Sciota and Sandusky. Oh! Oh! Oh! Oh! grant that rain may come to raise the Ollentangy about two or three feet, that we may cross in safety down to Sciota, without danger of our canoe being wrecked on the rocks. And now, *O great being!* thou knowest how matters stand—thou knowest that I am a great lover of tobacco, though I know not when I may get any more, I now make a present of the last I have unto thee, as a free burnt offering; therefore I expect thou wilt hear and grant these requests, and I thy servant will return thee thanks and love thee for thy gifts."

During this time Smith was greatly affected with his prayers, until he came to the burning of the tobacco, and as he knew that his patron was a great lover of it, when he saw him cast the last of it into the fire, it excited in him a kind of meriment, and he insensibly smiled. The Indian observed him laughing, which displeased him and occasioned the following address—"Brother!—I have somewhat to say to you and I hope you will not be offended, when I tell you of your faults. You know that when you were reading your books in town, I would not let the boys or any one disturb you; but now when I was praying, I saw you laughing. I do not think that you look upon praying as a foolish thing. I believe you pray yourself. But perhaps you may think my mode or manner of praying, foolish. If so you ought in a friendly manner to instruct me, and not make sport of sacred things."

Smith acknowledged his error. On this the Indian handed him his pipe to smoke in token of friendship, though he had nothing to smoke but red willow bark. Smith then told him something of the method of reconciliation with an offended God, as revealed in his bible, that he had with him. The Indian said, "that he liked that story better than that of the French priest's; but that he thought he was now too old to begin to learn a new religion; he should therefore continue to worship God in the way that he had been taught, and that if future happiness was to be had in his way of worship, he expected he would obtain it; and if it was inconsistent with the honor of the great spirit to accept of him in his own way of worship, he hoped that *Owaneeyo* would accept of him in the way Smith had mentioned, or in some other way, though he might now be ignorant of the channel through which favour or mercy might be conveyed.—Page 54, 55. He added, that he believed that *Owaneeyo* would hear and help every one who sincerely waited upon him.

Here we see, notwithstanding the just views this Indian entertained of Providence, yet though he acknowledged his guilt, he expected to appease the deity and procure his favour by burning a little tobacco. Thus the Indian agreed with revelation in this, that sacrifice is necessary, or that some kind of atonement is to be made in order to remove guilt and reconcile the sinner to God. This, accompanied with numberless other witnesses, is sufficient evidence of the truth of the scriptures."

At another time *Tontileaugo* informed him that there were a great many of the Caughnawagas and Wiandots, a kind of half Roman Catholics; but as for himself, he said, that the priest and he could not agree; as the priest held notions that contradicted both sense and reason; and had the assurance to tell him, that the book of God taught them those foolish absurdities; but he could not believe the great and good spirit ever taught them any such nonsense. And therefore he concluded that the Indian's old religion was better than this new way of worshipping God.

CHAPTER XI.

Separation of the Indian Women.

THE last remarkable fact to be mentioned is, the constant practice of the Indian nations, in the separation of their women, on certain occasions.

The southern Indians oblige their women, in their lunar retreats, to build small huts, at a considerable distance from their dwelling houses, as they imagine to be sufficient, where they are obliged to stay, at the risque of their lives. Should they be known to violate this ancient law, they must answer for every misfortune that the people should meet with.

Among the Indians on the north-west of the Ohio, the conduct of the women seems perfectly agreeable (as far as circumstances will permit) to the law of Moses.

A young woman, at the first change in her circumstances, immediately separates herself from the rest, in a hut made at some distance from the dwelling-houses, and remains there, during the whole time of her malady, or seven days. The person who brings her victuals, is very careful not to touch her, and so cautious is she herself of touching her own food with her hands, that she makes use of a sharpened stick, instead of a fork, with which to take up her venison, and a small ladle or spoon for her other food. When the seven days are ended, she bathes herself in water, washes all her clothes and cleanses the vessels she has made use of. Such as are made of wood, she scalds and cleans with lye made of wood ashes, and such as are made of earth or iron, she purifies by putting into the fire. She then returns to her father's house and is after this looked upon fit for marriage; but not before.

A Muskoghe woman, delivered of a child, is separated in like manner for three moons, or eighty-four days. Crossweeksung (the once Indian town in New-Jersey,) signifies, *the house of separation.*

By the Levitical Law, a woman was to be separated and unclean forty days for a man child, and eighty days for a female child; from which law alone it appears that the Indians could have adopted this extraordinary custom, as they must have done all their numerous laws of purity—and more especially as some of the nations observe the like distinction between male and female children.

The young women, at our people's first coming among them were very modest and shame-faced—both young and old women would be highly offended at indecent expressions, unless corrupted by drink: They were very neat and cleanly except in some instances when they neglected themselves. Smith 138.

CHAPTER XII.

The Conclusion.

HAVING thus gone through with a collection of facts, that has taken much time, great attention and strict enquiry, in order to prevent the writer from being deceived himself; or his being the innocent cause of deceiving others; he is now brought to draw some conclusions from the whole taken together. On a subject like this, where there is so much to hope, and so much to fear, he would use great modesty and diffidence. He would avoid all dogmatical assertions, or unreasonable confidence in any thing that he has collected, or any observations he has made, as he considers this a subject for the exercise of wisdom, research, enquiry and mature reflection. But nevertheless, while he uses every necessary precaution, and wishes perfect freedom of inquiry on the best evidence, yet he earnestly solicits the reader to keep in mind that his principal design, in these his labours, has been to invite and tempt the learned and the industrious, as far as they can obtain opportunities, to enquire further into this important and useful subject. What could possibly bring greater declarative glory to God, or tend more essentially to affect and rouse the nations of the earth, with a deeper sense of the certainty of the prophetic declarations of the holy scriptures, and thus call their attention to the truth of divine revelation, than a full discovery, that these wandering nations of Indians are the long lost tribes of Israel; but kept under the special protection of Almighty God, though despised by all mankind, for more than two thousand years, separated from and unknown to the civilized world? Thus wonderfully brought to the knowledge of their fellow men, they may be miraculously prepared for instruction, and stand ready, at the appointed time, when God shall raise the signal to the nations of Europe, to be restored to the land and country of their fathers, and to Mount Zion the city of David, their great king and head, and this in direct, positive and literal fulfilment of the numerous promises of the God of Abraham, Isaac and Jacob, their pious progenitors and founders, near four thousand years ago.

Would not such an event be the most ample mean of publishing the all important facts of both the Old and New Testament to all the nations of the earth, and thereby lead all men to the acknowledgment, that the God of Israel, is a God of truth and righteousness, and that whom he loves, he loves unto the end? They would be convinced that his all seeing eye had been open upon them in all their wanderings; under all their suffering, and that he had never forsaken them; but had shewn his watchful providence over them, and that in the latter day, "it shall come to pass, that the mountain of the Lord's house shall be established in the top of the mountains, and shall be exalted above the hills; and all nations shall flow unto it. And many people shall go and say, come ye, let us go up to the mountain of the Lord; to the house of the God of Jacob; and he will teach us of his ways, and we will walk in his paths: for out of Zion shall go forth the law, and the word of the Lord from Jerusalem."—Isaiah ii. chap. 1, 3.

St. Paul certainly entertained some such views of this extraordinary event, when he so pathetically sets forth this glorious issue of the providence of God.—Speaking of Israel, "I say then, have they stumbled, that they should fall? God forbid, but rather, through their fall, salvation is come unto the gentiles to provoke them to jealousy. Now if the fall of them be the riches of the world, and the diminishing of them, the riches of the gentiles, how much more their fulness. For if the casting away of them, be the reconciling of the world, *what shall the receiving of them be, but life from the dead.*"*

The writer will not determine with any degree of positiveness on the fact, that these aborigines of our country are, past all doubt, the descendants of Jacob, as he wishes to leave every man to draw the conclusion from the facts themselves. But he thinks he may without impeachment of his integrity or prudence, or any charge of over credulity, say, that were a people to be found, with demonstrative evidence that their descent was from Jacob, it could hardly be expected, at this time, that their languages, manners, customs and habits, with their religious rites, should discover greater similarity to those of the ancient Jews and of their divine law, without supernatural revelation, or some miraculous interposition, than the present nations of American Indians have done, and still do, to every industrious and intelligent enquirer.

This is not the first time, that the idea has been advanced, of the possibility of these tribes emigrating to America, over the straits of Kamschatka, and preserving the indelible marks of the children of Abraham, as has been already shewn in the

* Rom. chap. xi. 11, 15.

foregoing pages. In addition to which, many of the first European visitants, in a very early day, drew this conclusion from personal observation, of the then appearance of things and persons. Mons. De Guignes, who wrote so long ago, in one of his memoirs, speaking of the discoveries made of America, before the time of Columbus, says, "these researches, which of themselves give us great insight into the origin of the Americans, leads to the determination of the route of the colonies sent to the continent. He thinks the greater part of them passed thither by the most eastern extremities of Asia, where the two continents are only separated by a narrow strait, easy to cross. He reports instances of women, who from Canada and Florida, have travelled to Tartary without seeing the ocean." In this case they must have passed the straits on the ice.

Let the foregoing facts, collected in these pages, however imperfectly and immethodically put together by one whose means of knowledge have been very scanty, be impartially examined without prejudice, and weighed in the scale of testimony, compared with the language, customs, manners, habits, religious prejudices and special traditions of the Hebrews, especially under the impression of their being related and confirmed by so many authors, separated by birth, national manners, distance of time, strong prejudices, religious jealousies, various means of knowledge and different modes of communicating the facts, from Christopher Columbus, of glorious memory, and first discoverer of America, down to Mr. Adair, who lived with them in social intercourse and great intimacy for more than forty years, and Mr. M'Kenzie, a traveller of a late day, but the first who crossed from the Atlantic to the southern ocean—Portuguese, Spaniards, English, French, Jew and Christian, men of learning—plain, illiterate travellers and sea-faring men, all—all combining, without acquaintance or knowledge of each other, to establish the material facts, such as they are. Is it possible that the languages of so many hundred nations of apparent savages, scattered over a territory of some thousands of miles in extent, living excluded from all civilized society, without grammar, letters, arts or sciences, for two thousand years, should, by mere accident, be so remarkable for peculiarities, known in no other language, but the Hebrew—using the same words to signify the same things—having towns and places of the same name?

A gentleman of the first character of the city of New-York, well acquainted with the Indians in that state from his childhood, assured the writer of this, that when with them at a place called *Cohock* or *Owlflat*, now degenerated to *Cook-house*, yet well known, they shewed him a mountain to the west, very high, and that appeared from Cohock, much as the Neversinks do from the sea, at first approaching the American coast, and told him the Indians called it *Ararat*.

Is there no weight of evidence, in finding peculiar customs among the Indians, of the same import as those enjoined on the ancient people of God, and held sacred by both? Or in each people having three sacred feasts, religiously attended every year, with peculiar and similar rites and dress, to which the males only should be admitted, and these held at certain periods and at one special place of worship in a nation, and conforming, with astonishing precision, to each other, while the women were wholly excluded by both people, and particularly that connected with one of them, each people should have another of a very singular and extraordinary nature in the evening, being in part a sacrifice, in which not a bone of the animal, provided for the occasion, should be broken, nor a certain part of the thigh eaten—that if a family were not sufficient to eat the whole, a neighbour might be called in to partake with them; and if any should be still left it must religiously be burned in the fire before the rising of the next sun. That their houses and temple, at one of these feasts, were to be swept with the greatest care, and searched in every part, with religious scrupulosity, that no unhallowed thing should remain unconsumed by fire. And that the altars for the sacrifices were to be built of unhewn stone, or on stones on which a tool had not been suffered to come. That the entrails and fat of the sacrifice, were to be burned on the altar, and the body of the animal only to be eaten? When all these are compared with the Hebrew divine law, given by God himself from heaven, we find every article rigidly commanded and enforced by sovereign authority.

Then examine their other religious feasts of different kinds, and reflect on their conformity, in a surprising manner, in times, causes and effects, to the Hebrew rites and ceremonies, and what rational man, of sound judgment, but must, at least acknowledge, that there is great encouragement to the inquisitive mind, to proceed farther, and make these people the subject of attentive and unwearied inquiry. Add to all this, their general appearance—their customs and manners in private life—their communion with each other—their ceremonies and practices in society—their common religious and moral observations—their belief in a future state—their religious observation of and most sacred respect to an ark in going to war, and even their cruelties and barbarous customs in the treatment of their enemies, and ought they not to be included in the enumeration.

The strong bearings that many of the foregoing traditions have on their origin and descent—their manner of coming into this country and their future expectations, being so very similar to the experience of the Jews in their exodus from Egypt, should not be left out of the scale of testimony.

Can it be probable—nay, if we judge from past experience, may we not ask with propriety, can it be possible, unless a miracle is acknowledged, that so many Indian words should be purely Hebrew, and the construction of what little we know of their language, founded on the same principles, if there never had been any intercommunion between the two people?

There can be but little doubt, were their language well known to the learned in Europe and America, but that many more important discoveries might be made, convincing to every judicious mind, that now lie in utter oblivion.

Let it now be asked—

What, then, is the use that should be made of the facts that are thus brought to light, partial as they are? It is answered,

Ought not the nations of Europe and America to make a solemn pause, and consider the Jews, "now scattered and peeled, and expecting their Messiah," to use the phraseology of the bible, in a very different point of light, from that in which it has been customary to consider them? This has been dark indeed. They have been treated by the civilized nations as the offscouring of the earth—despised, contemned and persecuted—abused, reviled, and charged with the most abominable crimes, without evidence, unheard, and contrary to all probability. Nay, they have been treated like the wild beasts of the forest—have been proscribed, banished, murdered, or driven from one nation to another, but found safety in none. It is asserted by the best writers, that after the destruction of Jerusalem, in the time of Domitian, multitudes of Jews who had survived the sad catastrophe of the destruction of their city and temple, sought an asylum in various parts of the world. Many retired into Egypt, where a Jewish colony had resided from the time of Alexander—others fled to Cyrene—a large number removed to Babylon, and joined their brethren, who had remained in that country ever since the captivity—some took refuge in Persia, and other eastern countries. They became divided into eastern and western Jews. The western included Egypt, Judea, Italy, *and other parts of the Roman empire.* The eastern were settled in Babylon, Chaldea, Assyria and Persia. This was about the second century; but previous to the destruction of the temple, those Jews who resided in the eastern countries, sent presents to Jerusalem; repaired thither from time to time to pay their devotions, and acknowledge the supreme authority of the high-priest. But after the ruin of their country, having no longer any bond of unity, which had before been formed by the high-priests and the temple, they elevated chiefs to preside over them, whom they styled *princes of the captivity.*—Mod. Univ. Hist. vol. 13, page 156.

In the year 130, Adrian, the Roman emperor, having provoked the Jews almost to madness and desperation, they took arms, headed by one Coziba, who took the name of Barchochebas, which signifies the son of a star, pretending to be the one prophesied of in that declaration of Balaam, "there shall come a star out of Jacob," &c. After various and great successes, he was defeated and killed, and the town of Bither, where he had taken refuge, obliged to surrender. There were slain in battle five hundred and eighty thousand, besides a vast number, who perished by sickness, fire, famine, and other calamities. Vast numbers were exposed to sale at the fair of *Terebinth*, at the price of horses, and dispersed over the face of the earth.

In the year 1039, the sultan Gala Doullat, resolved to extirpate the Jews. For this purpose he shut up their academies, banished their professors, and slew the prince of the captivity, with his family. This persecution dispersed many into the desarts of Arabia, whilst others sought an asylum in the west. Benjamin, of Tudela, found a prince of the captivity in Persia, in the twelfth century.

In the time of the Crusaders, fifteen hundred were burnt at Strasburgh, and thirteen hundred at Mayence. According to the Jewish historians, five thousand, (but according to the christian writers, the number was three times greater) were either slaughtered or drowned.

It is also said, that upwards of twelve thousand were slain in Batavia. In the year 1238, during the reign of St. Louis, of France, two thousand five hundred were put to death by the most cruel tortures.

In 1240, the celebrated council of Lyons passed a decree, enjoining all christian princes who had Jews in their dominions, under penalty of excommunication, to compel them to refund to the crusaders all the money they had obtained by usury. This oppressed people were also prohibited from demanding any debts due to them from the crusaders till their return.

In the time of Ferdinand, of Spain, and Pope Sixtus, the fourth, two thousand were put to death by the Inquisition. In 1492, Ferdinand and Isabella banished eight hundred thousand Jews from Spain.

In 1349, a set of enthusiastic Catholics, called Flagellanti, incensed the populace against the Jews at Metz, and slew twelve thousand of them—set fire to their houses, which were destroyed, with part of the town.—Basnage, 686.

But as it may tend to greater certainty, and really so fully confirms what is suggested in holy writ, the following quotation from a Jewish author, complaining of their hard treatment, though long, will be excused. It is taken from a work entitled "An Appeal to the justice of kings and nations," cited in the transactions of the Parisian Sanhedrim, page 64, and mentioned by Mr. Faber in his work on the prophecies. —Vol. iii, 55, 58.

"Soon after the establishment of christianity, the Jewish nation, dispersed since the second destruction of its temple, had totally disappeared. By the light of the flames, which devoured the monuments of its ancient splendour, the conquerors beheld a million of victims dead, or expiring on their ruins.

"The hatred of the enemies of that unfortunate nation raged longer than the fire which had consumed its temple: active and relentless, it still pursues and oppresses them in every part of the globe, over which they are scattered. Their persecutors delight in their torments too much to seal their doom by a general decree of proscription, which at once would put an end to their burthensome and painful existence. It seems as if they were allowed to survive the destruction of their country, only to see the most odious and calumnious imputations laid to their charge, to stand as the constant object of the grossest and most shocking injustice, as a mark for the insulting finger of scorn, as a sport to the most inveterate hatred; it seems as if their doom was incessantly to suit all the dark and bloody purposes which can be suggested by human malignity, supported by ignorance and fanaticism.—Weighed down by taxes, and forced to contribute, more than christians, for the support of society, they had hardly any of the rights that it gives. If a destructive scourge happened to spread havoc among the inhabitants of a country, the Jews had poisoned the springs; or these men cursed by heaven, had, nevertheless, incensed it by their prayers against the nation, which they were supposed to hate. Did sovereigns want pecuniary assistance to carry on their wars? The Jews were compelled to give up those riches, in which they sought some consolation against the oppressing sense of their abject condition: as a reward for their sacrifices, they were expelled from the state, which they had supported; and were afterwards recalled to be stript again. Compelled to wear exteriorily the badges of their abject state, they were every where exposed to the insults of the vilest populace.

"When, from his solitary retreat, an enthusiastic hermit preached the crusades to the nations of Europe, and a part of its inhabitants left their country to moisten with their blood the plains of Palestine, the knell of promiscuous massacre tolled before the alarm-bell of war. Millions of Jews were then murdered to glut the pious rage of the crusaders. It was by tearing the entrails of their brethren that these warriors sought to deserve the protection of heaven. Skulls of men and bleeding hearts were offered as holo causts on the altars of that God, who has no pleasure even in the blood of the innocent lamb; and ministers of peace were thrown into an holy enthusiasm by these bloody sacrifices. It is thus that Basil, Treves, Coblentz and Cologn, became human shambles. It is thus that upwards of four hundred thousand victims, of all ages, and of both sexes, lost their lives at Alexandria and Cesaria. And is it, after having experienced such treatment, that they are reproached with *their* vices? Is it, after being for eighteen centuries the sport of contempt, that they are reproached with being no longer alive to it? Is it, after having so often glutted with their blood the thirst of their persecutors, that they are held out as enemies to other nations? Is it, that when they have been bereft of all means to mollify the hearts of their tyrants, that indignation is roused, if now and then they cast a mournful look towards the ruins of their temple, towards their country, where formerly happiness crowned their peaceful days, free from the cares of ambition and riches?"

"By what crimes, have we, then, deserved this furious intolerance? What is our guilt? Is it in that generous constancy which we have manifested in defending the laws of our fathers? But this constancy ought to have entitled us to the admiration of all nations, and it has only sharpened against us the daggers of persecution. Braving all kinds of torments, the pangs of death, the still more terrible pangs of life, we alone have withstood the impetuous torrent of time, sweeping indiscriminately in its course, nations, religions and countries. What is become of those celebrated empires, whose very name still excites our admiration by the ideas of splendid greatness attached to them, and whose power embraced the whole surface of the known globe? They are only remembered as monuments of the vanity of human greatness. Rome and Greece are no more; their descendants, mixed with other nations, have lost even the traces of their origin; while a population of a few millions of men, so often subjugated, stands the test of thirty revolving centuries, and the fiery ordeal of fifteen centuries of persecution! We still preserve laws, which were given to us in the first days of the world, in the infancy of nature! The last followers of a religion which had embraced the universe, have disappeared these fifteen centuries, and *our temples are still standing!* We alone have been spared by the indiscriminating hand of time, like a column left standing amidst the wreck of worlds and the ruin of nature."

While this picture gives another awful trait of the human character* and proves the degenerate state of man in his best natural state, and interests every feeling heart in the sufferings of this remarkable people. It also holds up, in a striking view, the threatnings of God's word and the literal fulfilment of them.—It further shews, in the most unanswerable manner, the Jews themselves being both witnesses and judges, the truth of the divine scriptures, and their strange blindness, until the end shall come, and the veil shall be taken from their eyes.

Christians are assured by unerring truth, that it has been the obstinacy and idolatry of the tribes of Judah and Israel, that have thus caused the anger of the Almighty to be enkind-

* Had the Indians a faithful historian to write in their behalf, when their cruelties in battle were recorded in their worst colours, might they not refer to the facts set forth in the few foregoing pages, and point to them as a contrast to their conduct, and say, behold these were your civilized nations.

led against them, added to the awful invocation of Judah, that the blood of the Messiah, might rest on them and their children. Yet in the end, God will call their oppressors to a severe account for the unchristian manner in which they have carried the divine judgments into execution. Little of it has been done for the glory of God. Moses did solemnly forewarn the Jews, that all this would be the consequence of disobedience to the laws and statutes of Jehovah, and that at the very time that he encouraged them with a certainty of his special favours, in case of their obedience. The inspired language is exceedingly strong. "And it shall come to pass, if thou shalt hearken diligently unto the voice of the Lord thy God, to observe and do all his commandments which I command thee this day, that the Lord thy God will set thee on high above all nations of the earth, and all those blessings (before enumerated) shall come upon thee." "*But it shall (also) come to pass*, if thou wilt not hearken unto the voice of the Lord thy God to observe and do all his commandments and his statutes, which I command thee this day, that all those curses shall overtake thee. Cursed shalt thou be in the city, and cursed shalt thou be in the field."—Deut. xxviii. 1, 2, 15, 16. The Lord shall bring thee and thy king into a nation, which neither thou nor thy fathers have known, and there shalt thou serve other Gods, wood and stone. And thou shalt become an astonishment, a proverb and a bye-word among all nations, whither the Lord shall lead thee."—Ibid 36, 37. "And they shall be upon thee *for a sign and a wonder and upon thy seed forever,*" (or for ages.)—Ibid 46. And thou shalt serve thine enemies, which the Lord shall send against thee, *in hunger and thirst, and in nakedness, and in want of all things.*

And he shall put a yoke of iron upon thy neck until he hath destroyed thee."—Ibid 48. "If thou wilt not observe to do all the words of this law, that are written in this book that thou mayest fear, this glorious and fearful name, *the Lord thy God.*" —Ibid 58. "And the Lord shall scatter thee among all people, from one end of the earth to the other."—Ibid 64. And among these nations thou shalt find no ease, neither shalt the sole of thy foot have rest, but the Lord shalt give thee a trembling of heart and failing of eyes and sorrow of mind."—Ibid 65. "And thy life shall hang in doubt before thee, and thou shalt fear day and night, and shalt have none assurance of thy life." "And it shalt come to pass, when all these things are come upon thee, the blessing and the curse, which I have set before thee, and thou shalt call them to mind, among all the nations whither the Lord thy God hath driven thee, and shalt return unto the Lord thy God, and shalt obey his voice according to all that I command thee this day, thou and thy children, with all thy heart and with all thy soul, that then the Lord thy God will turn thy captivity and have compassion upon thee and will return and gather thee from all the nations, whither the Lord thy God hath scattered thee. If any of thine *be driven out unto the uttermost parts of heaven,* from thence will the Lord thy God gather thee, and from thence *will he fetch thee.* And the Lord thy God will bring thee unto the land which thy fathers possessed, and thou shalt possess it, and he will do thee good, and multiply thee above thy fathers. And the Lord thy God will circumcise thine heart and the hearts of thy seed, to love the Lord thy God. with all thine heart, and with all thy soul, that thou mayest live. And the Lord thy God will put all these curses *upon thine enemies, and on them who hate thee,* who persecuted thee. And thou shalt return, and obey the voice of the Lord thy God and do all his commandments, which I command thee this day."—Ibid xxx. 1, 8. Thus the Lord in the midst of the severest judgments remembered mercy for the descendants of Abraham, Isaac and Jacob: and these great encouragements to obedience, he frequently repeated by his prophets, from time to time, as in Isaiah—"For Jehovah will have compassion on Jacob and will *yet choose Israel.* And he will give them rest upon their own land—and the stranger shall be joined to them and cleave unto the house of Jacob. And the nations shall take them and bring them in their own place; and the house of Jacob shall possess them into the land of Jehovah, as servants and as handmaids; and *they* shall take *them* captive, whose captives they were, and they shall rule over their oppressors."—Lowth xiv. 1, 2.

"Ho! land spreading wide the shadow of thy wings,* which art beyond the rivers of Cush, accustomed to send messengers by sea, even in bulrush vessels, upon the surface of the waters—Go! swift messengers unto a nation dragged away and plucked; unto a people wonderful from the beginning hitherto."—Chap. xviii. 1, 2. "At that season a present shall be led to the Lord of Hosts, a people dragged away and

* The translation of these verses, is taken from Mr. Faber, who quotes Bishop Horsley, in saying, "the shadow of wings is a very usual image in prophetic language, for the protection afforded by the stronger, to the weak. God's protection of his servants is described by their being safe under the shadow of his wings. And in this passage, the broad shadowing wings may be intended to characterise some great people, who shall be famous for the protection they shall give to those whom they received into their alliance." "It is not impossible however, and certainly not incongruous with the figurative language of prophecy, that since the messengers described in this prediction, are plainly a maritime nation, the shadowy wings here spoken of may mean the sails of their ships."

plucked, even of a people wonderful from the beginning hitherto; a nation expecting, expecting, and trampled under foot, whose land rivers have spoiled, unto the place of the name of the Lord of Hosts, Mount Zion."—Ibid 7. "For behold Jehovah shall come as a fire; and his chariot as a whirlwind; to breathe forth his anger in a burning heat, and his rebuke in flames of fire. For by fire shall Jehovah execute judgment, and by his sword upon all flesh; and many shall be the slain of Jehovah."—Ibid lxvi. 15, 16. Again in Jeremiah the subject is taken up. "For lo! the days come, saith the Lord, that I will bring again the captivity of my people Israel and Judah, and I will cause them to return to the land that I gave to their fathers and they shall possess it."—Jerem. xxx. 3. "Therefore fear thou not O my servant Jacob, saith the Lord, neither be dismayed O Israel, for lo! I will save thee *from afar*, and thy seed from the land of their captivity; and Jacob shall return and shall be in rest and be quiet and none shall make him afraid. For I am with thee saith the Lord, to save thee; though I make a full end of all the nations whither I have scattered thee; yet will I not make a full end of thee; but I will correct thee in measure, and will not leave thee altogether unpunished." "Therefore *all they who devour thee shall be devoured*, and all thine adversaries, *every one of them*, shall go into captivity; and *they who spoil thee*, shall be a spoil; and *all who prey upon thee*, will *I give for a prey*."—Verse 16.

Remember this, and shew yourselves men:
Reflect on it deeply, O ye apostates!—
I am God nor is there any thing like me.
From the beginning, making known the end;
And from early times, the things that are not yet done:

Saying my counsel shall stand,
And whatever I have willed, I will effect.
Calling from the east, the eagle,
And from a land far distant, the man of my counsel:
As I have spoken, so will I bring it to pass;
I have formed the design, and I will execute it.

[Lowth's Isaiah xlvi. 8, 11.

"And this shall be the covenant that I will make with the house of Israel, after those days saith the Lord, I will put my law in their inward parts, and write it in their hearts, and will be their God and they shall be my people."—Vide also xxxi. 1, 14. Joel also is very express on this subject. "For behold, says he, in those days, and in that time, when I shall bring again the captivity of Judah and Jerusalem, *I will also gather all nations*, and will bring them down into the valley of Jehoshaphat, and will plead with them there, for my people and for my heritage *Israel*, whom they have scattered among the nations, and parted my land.—Chap. iii. 1, 2.

From all this it appears, with the greatest certainty, that in *the latter day*, the house of Israel *shall be discovered*, and brought from the *land of their captivity a far off*, to the city of God, the new Jerusalem, that shall be restored to more than its former glory. And that all those who have oppressed and despised them, wherever they are, will become subjects of the anger and fury of Jehovah their God.

If then it is plain, that the Israelites have heretofore suffered the just indignation of the Almighty, for their sins and all his threatnings and fury have literally and most exactly been poured out upon them, according to the predictions of his servant Moses, what have not their enemies and oppressors to fear, in the great day of God's anger, when he cometh to avenge his people, who have been dear to him as the apple of his eye? Is not the honor of God as much concerned in executing his threatnings on one as the other? Will it not be wise then to consider our ways betimes, and sincerely to repent of all improper conduct of oppression and destruction to any, who may turn out to have been the continual objects of God's regard, though suffering under his just displeasure. If his word has been yea and amen, in punishing the people of his choice, because of their disobedience, what hope can those gentiles have, who are found to continue in opposition to his positive commandments.

Let all, then, carefully attend to the word of the Lord, as spoken by his prophets, and watch the signs of the times, seeking to know the will of God, and what he expects from those who are awakened to see their error. Much is to be done when the signal is set up for the nations; and these children of God's watchful providence, shall be manifestly discovered. They are to be converted to the faith of Christ, and instructed in their glorious prerogatives, and prepared and assisted to return to their own land and their ancient city, even the city of Zion, which shall become a praise in all the earth. Let not our unbelief, or other irreligious conduct, with a want of a lively, active faith in our Almighty Redeemer, become a stumbling block to these outcasts of Israel, wherever they may be. They will naturally look to the practice and example of those calling themselves christians for encouragement. Who knows but God has raised up these United States in these latter days, for the very purpose of accomplishing his will in bringing his beloved people to their own land.

We are a maritime people—a nation of seafaring men. Our trade and commerce have greatly encreased for years past, except during our late troubles. We may, under God, be called to act a great part in this wonderful and interesting drama. And if not alone, we may certainly assist in a union with other maritime powers of Europe. The people of Great-Britain are almost miraculously active in disseminating the gospel throughout the known world. The same spirit will carry them to accomplish the whole will of God. The time is hastening on, and if we have any understanding in the prophetic declarations of the Bible, it cannot be far off. "And I said, how long, O Jehovah! and he said, until cities be laid waste, so that there be no inhabitant and houses, so that there be no man; and the land be left utterly desolate, until Jehovah remove man far away, and there be many a deserted woman in the midst of the land. And though there be a tenth part remaining in it, even this shall undergo a repeated destruction. Yet as the ilex and the oak, though cut down, hath its stock remaining, a holy seed shall be the stock of the nation."

Have not these wonderful things come to pass, and therefore have we not reason to believe the time of the end is near at hand. When Tiglah Pilnezer carried away the tribes from Samaria, he left about a tenth part of the common people behind. Salmanazer, his successor, some few years after, less than twenty, came and carried the rest into captivity, except a few stragglers about the country, and those who had taken refuge in Jerusalem. Even this small remnant were afterwards taken by Esarrhaddon and Nebuchadnezzar, and carried to Babylon, and the whole land left desolate, in strict fulfilment of the divine word. And even yet a holy seed shall still appear to become the stock of the nation.

What, then, is the use that christians ought to make of a discovery of this nature, should they be convinced of the truth of the proposition? First, To adore with humble reverence, the inscrutable riches of the grace of God, and his infinite wisdom in his conduct towards his servants, Abraham, Isaac and Jacob, and their posterity. Secondly, To rejoice in the absolute certainty of the fulfilment of the promises as well as the threatnings of his holy word—"For though heaven and earth may pass away, yet not a tittle of his word shall pass away, but all shall be fulfilled." Thirdly, To enjoy the present benefit of the glorious hope set before them, even in the view of immediate death, knowing that when Christ shall come the second time, "in his own glory, and the glory of the Father, his saints shall come with him."—Coloss. iii. 4. "For if we believe that Jesus died and rose again, even so, them also who sleep in Jesus, will God bring with him; for the Lord himself shall descend from heaven with a shout, with the voice of an arch-angel, and with the trump of God; and then shall christians be forever with the Lord."—1 Thess. iv. 14—17. Fourthly, This makes the grave the christian's privilege and consolation. As the scriptures positively declare, that flesh and blood cannot inherit the kingdom of heaven; this would have greatly weakened their faith and hope, had they not been assured, that they would leave their flesh and blood in the grave, and rise immortal and incorruptible through the power of the Redeemer, who had previously sanctified the grave by his own presence.

But after all, suppose we should be wholly mistaken in all our conjectures, and should treat these aborigines of this land with great kindness and compassion, under the mistaken opinion of their descent? Would any people have reason to repent acts of humanity and mercy to these wretched outcasts of society? Have not Europeans been the original cause of their sufferings? Are we not in possession of their lands? Have we not been enriched by their labours? Have they not fought our battles, and spilt their blood for us, as well as against us? If we speak as an European nation, has not a large proportion of their numbers perished in our wars, and by our means? Ought not we, then, now, at this day of light and knowledge, to think much of hearkening to the voice of mercy and the bowels of compassion in their behalf? But if it should turn out, that our conjectures are well founded, what aggravated destruction may we not avoid, by an obedient and holy temper, and exerting ourselves to keep the commands of the statutes of the God of Israel? "Behold, at that time, I will undo all who afflict thee: and I will save her who halteth, and gather her who is driven out. And I will get them fame and praise in every land, where they have been put to shame. At that time, I will bring you again, even in the time that I gather you, for I will make you a name and a praise among all people of the earth, when I turn back your captivity before your eyes, saith the Lord."—Zeph. iii. 19—20.

We are very apt, and indeed it is a common practice, to blame the Jews, and charge them with great perverseness, and call them an obstinate and stiff-necked race, when we read of the grace and mercy of Jehovah towards them, in the multiplied blessings promised on their obedience, and the awful curses and severe threatnings in case of disobedience. We profess to be astonished at the hardness of their hearts and abominable wickedness of their conduct, committed in direct opposition to so much light and knowledge. Yet would not any impartial person, under a just view of our conduct to them since the discovery of this country, and the practices of a large majority of those who call themselves christians, draw a pretty certain conclusion that we had not much to insist on, in our favour—That most certainly we have not done to them, as we should have expected from them, under a change of circumstances. We go on, under similar threatnings of the same Almighty Being. We shew much the same hardness of heart, under the like denunciations of vengeance, that he will afflict and destroy, without mercy, those nations who join in oppressing his people, without regard to his honour and glory. He will be found no respecter of persons; but will fulfil, not only his promised blessings, but will with equal certainty inflict all his threatened curses on obstinate offenders. "Who is wise, and he shall understand these things? Prudent, and he shall know them? For all the ways of the Lord are right, and the just shall walk in them; but the transgressors shall fall therein." —Hosea xiv. 9. "And the Lord answered me and said, write the vision and make it plain upon a table, that he may run who readeth it—For the vision is yet for an appointed time, but at the end it shall speak and not lie; though it tarry, wait for it, because it will surely come—It will not tarry."—Habakkuk ii. 2—3.

APPENDIX.

Historical Sketches of Louisiana.

THE famous Ferdinand de Soto was sent by the Spaniards to succeed Narvaez, as governor of Florida. "He attacked the natives every where, and every where committed great slaughter; destroyed their towns, and subsisted his men on the provisions found in them. He crossed the Missisippi, explored the regions to the west of it, and in 1542 ended his days on Red River."—Page 8.

In 1562, the French growing jealous of the successs of the Spaniards, admiral Coligni fitted out a fleet, with a colony of French protestants, under Rebaud. They landed in Florida, and planted the settlers about thirty miles from St. Augustine, where they erected a fort for their protection, and called it Fort Charles, in honour of Charles the 4th. Astonishment seized the Spaniards at this unexpected intrusion. However, the Spanish governor Menandez, after recovering from the first shock, assembled his forces, attacked Fort Charles, and carried it by storm. Those miserable French who escaped the sword, were doomed to the halter, with this label on their breasts: "Not as Frenchmen, but as heretics."—Page 5.

Of all the Indians known to the French, the Natchez were the most serviceable, and at the same time the most terrible,

Settlers at various times planted themselves among them, so as to become a large body. They were favourably received by the Natchez, who supplied them with provisions, assisted them in their tillage, and in building their houses, and indeed saved them from famine and death. They soon began to encroach on the rights of the Indians, and excited their jealousy. The Natchez possessed the strongest disposition to oblige, and would have continued eminently useful to the French settlers, if the commandant had not treated them with indignity and injustice.

The first dispute was in 1723, when an old warrior owed a soldier a debt in corn. When payment was-demanded, the warrior alledged that the corn was not ripe, but it should be delivered as soon as possible. They quarreled, when the soldier cried murder. When the warrior left him to go to his village, a soldier of the guard fired at him and shot him. The commandant would not punish the offender. Revenge, the prominent passion of the Indians, drove them to arms. They attacked the French in all quarters—but by the influence of a noted chief, peace was restored, which prevented the utter extermination of the settlers. Peace was made and duly ratified by Mons. Branville; yet he took advantage of it to inflict a sudden and dreadful blow on these innocent people. He privately brought seven hundred men—he attacked the defenceless Indians—slaughtered them in their huts, and demanded the head of their chief; with which they were obliged to comply. This wanton slaughter lasted four days. A peace was then made, but confidence was destroyed. Shortly after, a French officer accidentally met a sachem, called the Sting-serpent, who appeared to avoid him. The officer said, why do you avoid me, we were once friends; are we so no longer? The indignant chief replied—why did the French come into our country? We did not go to seek them. They asked us for land, and we told them to take it where they pleased; there was enough for them and for us. The same sun ought to enlighten us both, and we ought to walk together as friends in the same path. We promised to give them food—assist them to build and to labour in the fields. We have done so. In 1729, the commandant of the fort had treated them so ill, that they obtained his being summoned to New-Orleans to answer for his conduct. This gave much joy to the Indians. The officer found means to be sent back reinstated in his command. He now determined to indulge his malice against the Indians. He suddenly resolved to build a town on the scite of a village belonging to one of the sachems, which covered a square of three miles extent. He sent for the sun or chief, and directed him to clear the huts and remove to some other place. The chief replied, that their ancestors had lived there for many ages, and that it was good for their descendants to occupy the same ground. This dignified language served only to exasperate the haughty commandant. He declared, that unless the village was abandoned in a few days, the inhabitants of it should repent their obstinacy! The Indians finding a bloody conflict was inevitable, they laid their plans accordingly. They tried by the best excuses in their power to delay the execution of his plan; but he treated all their proposals with disdain, and menaced immediate destruction if he was not gratified. The Indians ever fruitful in expedients, got permission to wait till their harvest was got in. During this interval, short as it was, they formed their plan. They held a council, and unanimously resolved to make one great effort to defend the tombs of their fathers. They proceeded with caution, yet one of their women betrayed them. The commandant would not hearken to it, but punished the informant.—Near the close of the last day of Nov. 1729, the Grand Sun, with some warriors, repaired to the fort with their tribute of corn and fowls agreed upon. They secured the gate and other passages, and instantly deprived the soldiers of the means of defence. So well was their plan laid, that all opposition was in vain. The massacre throughout the settlement, among the men, was general. The slaves, and some of the women, were spared. The chiefs and warriors, disdaining to stain their hands with the blood of the commander, he fell by the hands of one of the meanest of the Indians. In short, the whole settlement, consisting of about seven hundred men, were wholly destroyed. They proceeded to two neighbouring settlements, at Yazous and Wastulu, which shared the same fate; a very few escaped to carry the news to the capital.—Pages 46---52.

The governor of New-Orleans, persisting in destroying this nation, they fled over the Missisippi, and settled one hundred and eighty miles up the Red River, where they built a fort for their protection. After some time, the governor pursued them to this place with cannon, &c. besieged the fort, and they were obliged to surrender at discretion. The women and children were reduced to slavery, and scattered among the plantations. The men were sent to St. Domingo as slaves. Their villages at first consisted of twelve hundred souls. Of all the Indians, they were the most polished and civilized.—They had an established religion among them, in many particulars rational and consistent—as likewise regular orders of priesthood. They had a temple dedicated to the great spirit, in which they preserved the eternal fire. No doubt these tokens of their religion were ever obscured and perverted by tradition—but this is rather the misfortune than the crime of the Indians. This remark is applicable to all the aborigines of America. Their civil polity partook of the refinement of a people apparently in some degree learned and scientific. They had kings or chiefs—a kind of subordinate nobility—and the usual distinctions created by rank were well understood and preserved among them. They were just, generous and humane, and never failed to extend relief to the objects of distress and misery. They were well acquainted with the properties of medicinal plants, and the cures they performed, particularly among the French, were almost incredible. They were remarkable for not deeming it glorious to destroy the human species, and for this reason, seldom waged any other than defensive war.---Pages 53—4.

In short, the history of the European wars against the Indians, and particularly the Spanish, for more than two centuries, afford nothing but a series of complicated crimes, the black catalogue of which will continue to excite in every breast, the mingled emotions of pity and indignation. They made war on defenceless nations without provocation—spilt oceans of blood and involved millions of their fellow creatures in misery.—They trampled on all those laws deemed sacred by the civilized world, and their misdeeds find no other excuse than what is derived from the gratification of their avarice.—Page 58.

They not only enslaved the prisoners taken in battle, but likewise those peaceable and effeminate people who submitted themselves at discretion.—They compelled them to labour in the mines of Hispaniola and Cuba, where vast numbers perished. The natives of Hispaniola, at Columbus' first arrival, amounted to more than a million of inhabitants—fifteen years after they amounted to less than sixty thousand. In Cuba, upwards of five hundred thousand perished—a similar destruction took place on the continent.—Page 56.

The aborigines in general are extremely scrupulous in regard to the fulfilment of national compacts; though in their individual capacities they are less honest and more inclined to evade their engagements. Their want of faith in most instances, where it has been manifested may be traced either to the hard conditions imposed on them, or to the advantage taken of their ignorance. Whoever will attentively examine into the merits of the numerous quarrels between them and the whites, will be apt to find that the latter were almost uniformly the aggressors.—Page 64.

A remarkable fact with respect to Florida. While it was in the hands of the English, a plan was concerted by Sir William Duncan and Dr. Turnbull, to entice a colony of Greeks to settle in this country. It was represented to them in the most favourable light. They were promised fertile fields and lands in abundance, and also transportation and subsistence. Fifteen hundred engaged in this undertaking—but what was their surprise when they were ushered in to New-Smyrna, about seventy miles to the eastward of St. Augustine, which they found to be a desolate wilderness, without the means of support. Instead of being proprietors of land, there was none for them, but upon lease for ten years, and some could not obtain it on any terms. Hence they became labourers to the planters as slaves, and suffered hunger and nakedness. Overseers were placed over them, who goaded them with the lash—They were kept together and numbers were crouded together in one mess—The poor wretches were not allowed to procure fish for themselves, although plenty in the sea at their feet.—People were forbidden to furnish them with victuals. Severe punishments were decreed against those who gave and those who received the charitable boon. Under this treatment many died, especially the old people. At length in 1769, seized with despair, they rose on their cruel tyrants and made themselves some small vessels—But they were seized by the military, and five of the principal suffered death. This could scarcely be believed, considering the reputed humanity of the English, had it not been verified by the solemn report of a British officer who was an eye witness. —Page 121.

Fraser's Key to the Prophecies.

Speaking of the image of the beast, that it should speak, &c. &c. says, the Pope put to death in a variety of forms, such as dared to oppose him. He excluded from the privileges of civil society all such as did not submit to his claims and authority. See the decree of Alexander 3d, in the Synod of Tours—the bull of Martin against the errors of Wickliffe and Huss, annexed to the council of Constamce. There it is decreed " that men of this sort be not permitted to *have houses* to *rear families*, to make contracts, to carry on traffick or business of any kind, or to enjoy the comforts of humanity, in common with the faithful." These are almost the words which prophecy has put into the mouth of the image.

See the bull of Paul 3d, against Henry 8th, and that of Paul 5th, in the eleventh year of Queen Elizabeth.

An energetical letter, dated London 19th January, 1791, signed by three vicars apostolic of England, expressly prohibits the Catholics of that kingdom to take an oath prescribed by government, though that oath contains nothing inconsistent with Catholic principles, but a renunciation of the Pope's supremacy in temporals. They express themselves, "The apostolical vicars, in the above mentioned energetical letter, (dated October 21, 1789) declared, that none of the faithful clergy or laity, ought to take any new oath or sign any new declaration or doctrinal matters, or subscribe any new instrument wherein the interests of religion are concerned, without the previous approbation of their respective bishops, and they required submission to those determinations. The altered oath has not been approved by us, and therefore cannot be lawfully or conscientiously taken by any of the faithful of our districts." Here the lamb like beast speaks like a dragon— Ten very respectable Catholics in England, met together as a committee, and protested against this letter, as inculcating principles hostile to the government, and contrary to the faith and moral character of the Catholics.

Our adversaries account the visibility of their church as a community from the apostolic days, a demonstration of its being the true church, while they ask us with an air of triumph, where was your church before Luther? (In the wilderness where it yet is.) The prophecy furnishes a direct answer. The true church of christ ought to be invisible as a community for a period of twelve hundred and sixty years, and during all that time a harlot, pretending to be the spouse of Christ, and ought to propagate her idolatries successfully and extensively, throughout the world.

The divisions among protestants have been urged by their adversaries as an argument against them; and the ineffectual efforts of learned and pious men to unite them into one community, have proved stumbling blocks to the faith of some of their friends. But by the prophetic representation, matters ought to be as they are. Had protestants united together into one society, the church of christ would have been visible as a community, which during the currency of twelve hundred and sixty years would flatly contradict the prophecy; but the several protestant churches, having no connection with each other in government and ordinances like the ancient church, they constitute only individual members of the universal church, which as a body politic is invisible now, as it was in the tenth century. While this view should reconcile us to a certain degree of separation among protestants during the currency of the twelve hundred and sixty years, it ought to remove wholly the violence of party spirit and every degree of bitterness and rancour which they have too frequently shewed to each other. Aviolent party spirit is founded on this principle, that those who possess it are the true church of christ.—Hence they argue that those who separate from them are schismatics or heritics, and therefore ought to be treated as heathens and publicans. But the ground of their reasoning is false; according to the prophecy no particular church or party, now on earth, may claim the exclusive privileges of the universal church. Whoever does, acts the part of a daughter, usurping the place of the mother, and requiring that subjection of her sisters which the law of God does not require.—Pages 134—5—162.

FINIS.